FIRST CLASH

Kenneth Macksey

FIRST CLASH

Combat close-up in World War Three

a&ap
Arms and Armour Press

Published 1985 in Great Britain by Arms and Armour Press,
2–6 Hampstead High Street, London NW3 1QQ.

Distributed in the United States by Sterling Publishing Co. Inc.,
2 Park Avenue, New York, N.Y. 10016.

© DND Canada, 1984, 1985
All rights reserved. No part of this publication may be reproduced, stored in a retrieval system, or transmitted in any form by any means electrical, mechanical or otherwise without first seeking the written permission of the copyright owner and of the publisher.

British Library Cataloguing in Publication Data:
Macksey, Kenneth
First clash: combat close-up in World War Three
1. World War III I. Title
303.4′9 U313
ISBN 0-85368-736-6

Designed by David Gibbons. Maps by A. A. Evans. Diagrams by Canadian Forces Training Materiel Production Centre, CFB Winnipeg. Typeset by Typesetters (Birmingham) Limited. Printed and bound by R. J. Acford, Chichester, England.

Overleaf: The battlefield of Blickheim.

Below: Author (right) with advisers in a Leopard tank during the preparation of this book. Notice the low-light television camera located above the gun.

Contents

The cast, 6
List of abbreviations, 7
Maps, 9
1 In the assembly area, 17
2 In the enemy camp, 29
3 Deployment, 37
4 1st Guards Tank Division advances, 81
5 Digging in, 87
6 Contact, 100
7 The hasty attack, 113
8 Deliberate attack, flexible defence, 121
9 Blickheim – defence of a village, 135
10 Break-in, 147
11 Blocking – Papa Company Combat Team, 175
12 Sitrep – the stabilized situation, 185
13 Counter-attack plans, 190
14 Counter-attack – stabilizing the situation, 199
15 Withdrawal, 211

The cast

Friendly Forces

LCol Brian Cowdray	CO, RCD
LCol Doug Tinker	CO, 3 RCR
Maj Mycroft Brent	DCO, 3 RCR
Maj Dick Connors	OC, N Coy, 3 RCR
Maj Alan Ferrier	OC, P Coy, 3 RCR
Maj Lionel Groves	Sqn Comd, C Sqn, RCD
Maj Ian Linkman	Sqn Comd, B Sqn, RCD
Maj Tom Panton	OC, O Coy, 3 RCR
Maj Pat Vivier	BC, A Bty, 1 RCHA
Capt Andrew Barton	Ops Off, 3 RCR
Capt Peter Cummings	Battle Capt, B Sqn, RCD
Capt John Goodhart	Pl Comd, Armd Def Pl, 3 RCR
Capt Pat Kendal	FOO, A Bty, 1 RCHA (with N Coy)
Capt Angus Scott	FOO, A Bty, 1 RCHA (with O Coy)
Capt Gordon Truman	Pl Comd, Recce Pl, 3 RCR
Lt Phil Brown	Tp Ldr, No 4 Tp, B Sqn, RCD
Lt Eddie Leach	Pl Comd, No 1 Pl, N Coy, 3 RCR
Lt Dougal McGregor	Pl Comd, 3 RCR (with C Sqn RCD)
Lt Eric Olafson	Pl Comd, O Coy, 3 RCR
Lt Harry Owens	Tp Ldr, No 3 Tp, C Sqn, RCD
Lt Ron Pike	Tp Ldr, No 3 Tp, B Sqn, RCD
WO George Crane	No 3 Tp, B Sqn, RCD
Sgt Eddie Blake	Det Comd, Blowpipe Det, 1 RCHA
Sgt Pierre Claudel	1 Pl, D Coy, 1 R22eR
Sgt Al Hobbs	Sec Comd, N Coy, 3 RCR
Sgt Bud Roach	Mor FC, 3 RCR (with N Coy)
MCpl Harry Benson	N Coy, 3 RCR
MCpl Gene Petrie	Armd Def Pl, 3 RCR
MCpl Fred Terry	Carl Gustav, O Coy
Pte Paul Charrier	N Coy, 3 RCR
Pte John Grimes	O Coy, 3 RCR
Gnr Jake Martin	AD Tp, 1 RCHA
Pte Gordie Miller	O Coy, 3 RCR

Red Forces

MGen Gregor Samsonov	Commander, 1st Guards Tank Division
Col Andrei Romanov	Commander, Divisional Artillery
Col Pavel Podduyev	Commander, 301st Tank Regiment
Col Vladimir Oblensky	Commander, 290th Motor Rifle Regiment
Capt Alexei Rusalski	FOO from 164th Artillery Regiment
Lt Ivan Shulubin	Coy Comd, No 2 Coy, II Bn, 290th MRR
Lt Yuri Tursov	Pl Comd, No 3 Coy, I Bn, 301st Tank Regt
Sgt Oleg Nikolai	4th Pl, Div Recce Bn
Cpl Igor Lyubshin	Tk Comd, 290th MRR
Pte Rudi Leskho	I Bn, 290th MRR

List of abbreviations

AD	Air Defence	LAR	Light Automatic Rifle
AD Missile	Air Defence Missile	LLTV	Low Light Television
AFV	Armoured Fighting Vehicle	MAINT	Maintenance
APC	Armoured Personnel Carrier	MAW	Medium Anti-Tank Weapon
APFSDS	Armour Piercing Fin Stabilized Discarding Sabot	MP	Military Police
		MRR	Motor Rifle Regiment
ARV	Armoured Recovery Vehicle	NBC	Nuclear Biological Chemical
ASP	As Soon as Possible	NCO	Non-Commissioned Officer
AT	Anti-Tank	NDHQ	National Defence Headquarters
BC	Battery Commander	NOD	Night Observation Device
BTY	Battery	OBJ	Objective
CB	Counter Bombardment	OC	Officer Commanding
CBT SP	Combat Support	OGP	Orders Group
CER	Canadian Engineer Regiment	OP	Observation Post
CMBG	Canadian Mechanized Brigade Group	ORBAT	Order of Battle
		PAW	Personal Anti-Tank Weapon
CO	Commanding Officer	PL	Platoon
COMD & LN	Command and Liaison	POL	Petrol, Oil, Lubricant
COY	Company	R22eR	Royal 22nd Regiment
CT	Combat Team	RCD	Royal Canadian Dragoons
2IC	2nd in Command	RCHA	Royal Canadian Horse Artillery
C/S O	Call Sign Order	RCR	Royal Canadian Regiment
DCO	Deputy Commanding Officer	RGP	Reconnaissance Group
DF	Defensive Fire	RV	Rendezvous
DS	Direct Support	SECT	Section
EVAC	Evacuation	SHQ	Squadron Headquarters
EW	Electronic Warfare	SITREP	Situation Report
FARP	Forward Area Rearming/ Refuelling Point	SMG	Sub-Machine-Gun
		SOI	Staff Officer Grade 1
FC	Fire Controller	SO2	Staff Officer Grade 2
FDAMB	Field Ambulance	SOP	Standing Operating Procedure
FEBA	Forward Edge of the Battle Area	SP	Self-Propelled
FOO	Forward Observation Officer	Sqn	Squadron
FPF	Final Protective Fire	SSM	Squadron Sergeant-Major
FSCC	Fire Support Control Centre	SSO	Senior Staff Officer
FUP	Forming-Up Place	S&T	Supplies and Transport
II (GE) Corps	II (German) Corps	SVC	Service
GPMG	General Purpose Machine Gun	TAC	Tactical
GTD	Guards Tank Division	TACP	Tactical Air Control Party
HA	Holding Area (helicopters)	TC	Traffic Control
HAW	Heavy Anti-Tank Weapon	TOW	Tube launched, Optically-Tracked Wire-Guided (Missile)
HE	High Explosive		
HMG	Heavy Machine Gun	Tp	Troop
HQ GR	Headquarters Group	UMS	Unit Medical Station
ILL	Illuminating	Vandoos	See R22eR
IO	Intelligence Officer	VT	Variable Time (proximity)
IR	Infra Red	WNG	Warning
KZ	Killing Zone	WO	Warrant Officer

First Clash was first published on the authority of the Canadian Chief of the Defence Staff as B-GL-309-006/FT-001. This is the original Preface reproduced from that manual.

In helping the reader to understand the intent of this book it may be easier to start by saying what "First Clash" is not; it is not a manual of army doctrine.

This book may better be described as a training aid, the purpose of which is to create a mental image of company groups/combat teams in defensive operations. It is designed to assist in the training of officers and men who have not had the experience of operating within an all arms team.

The literary technique used is an illustrated narrative of battle scenarios dealing in chronological order with the successive phases of a Battle Group's approach to and involvement in mobile defence against a Soviet Tank Division in the European setting, the summer circa 1984. Although the activities of higher formations and units are described, the narrative focuses mainly upon the Combat Team. At that level, the story involves key individuals and tactical groups (both friend and foe) describing the parts they play and the way they interact as confrontation ensues. It is this interaction which forms the basis for the departure from the highly-stylized format which characterizes our tactical publications. While the plot line is based on fact, the characters and incidents are all fictitious.

Major (Retired) Kenneth Macksey, MC, the author of this publication is a former serving officer of the Royal Tank Regiment, who saw action in Normandy as a tank troop commander. A military historian, he is the author of The Shadow of Vimy Ridge, Guderian, Battle, The Tank Pioneers, Rommel, and various other works of military history.

The aim of the interactive scenario format is not only to stimulate interest by the realistic portrayal of possible tactical and leadership situations which combat arms officers may face in battle. It is also designed to heighten one's perception of the many factors affecting the combined arms team in the flux of operations, factors which can not be conveyed adequately by our more traditional and stereotyped approach to doctrine publications.

Thus, incidents occur in the story which may appear to contradict our doctrine. The lesson is that our doctrine is a factor tacitly considered by the commander as he estimates a given situation. Doctrine is the background against which he weighs the other factors of enemy, ground, own forces, etc. It may be necessary, under given conditions to make a considered deviation from formal teachings to accommodate factors unforeseen in the syndicate rooms of a staff course.

The incidents portrayed are also the products of complex human relationships which demand a flexibility of mind we hope our leaders have maintained.

This publication may not be quoted as an authoritative source for any detail of technique or procedure. It portrays what could happen in one situation.

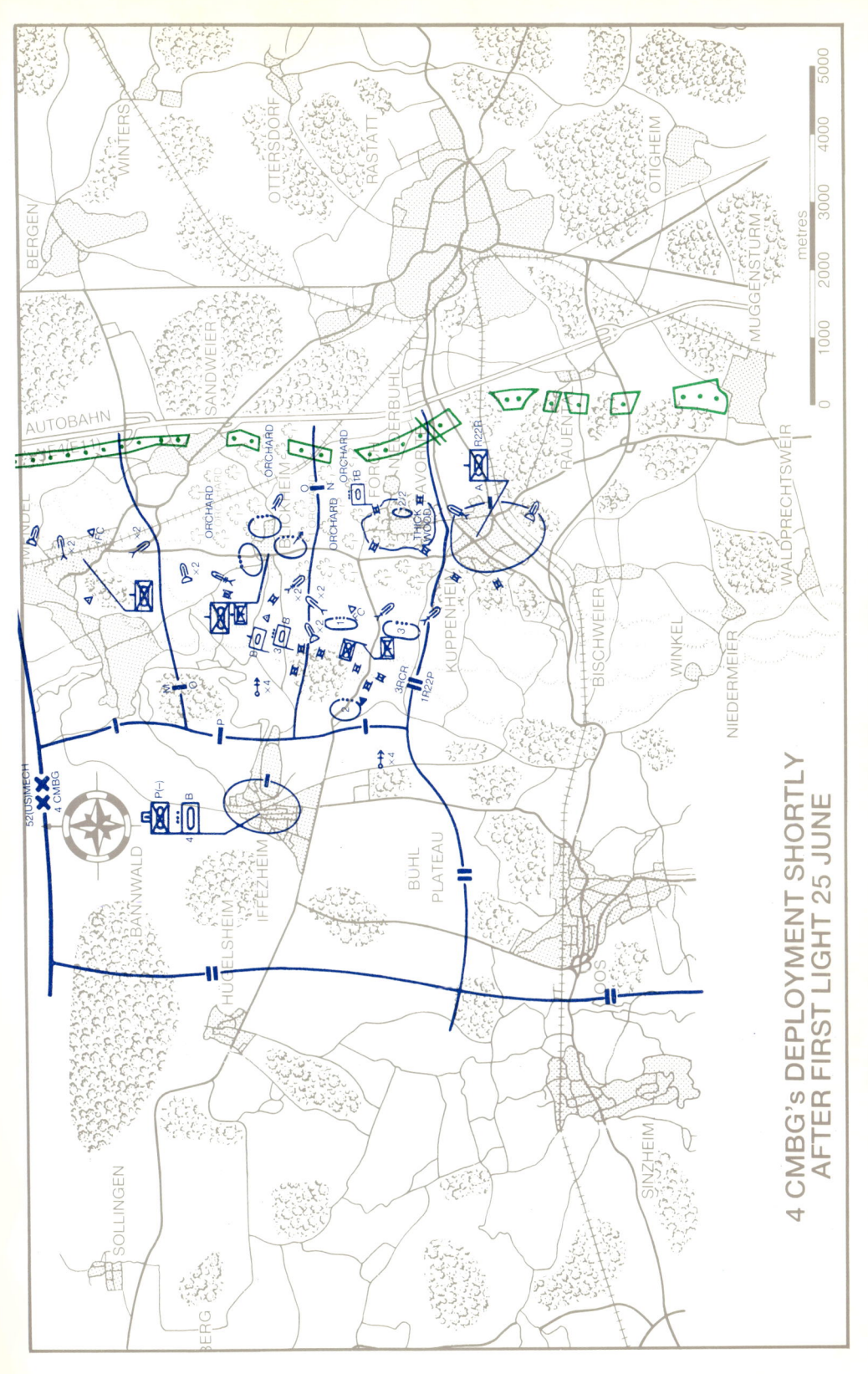

4 CMBG's DEPLOYMENT SHORTLY AFTER FIRST LIGHT 25 JUNE

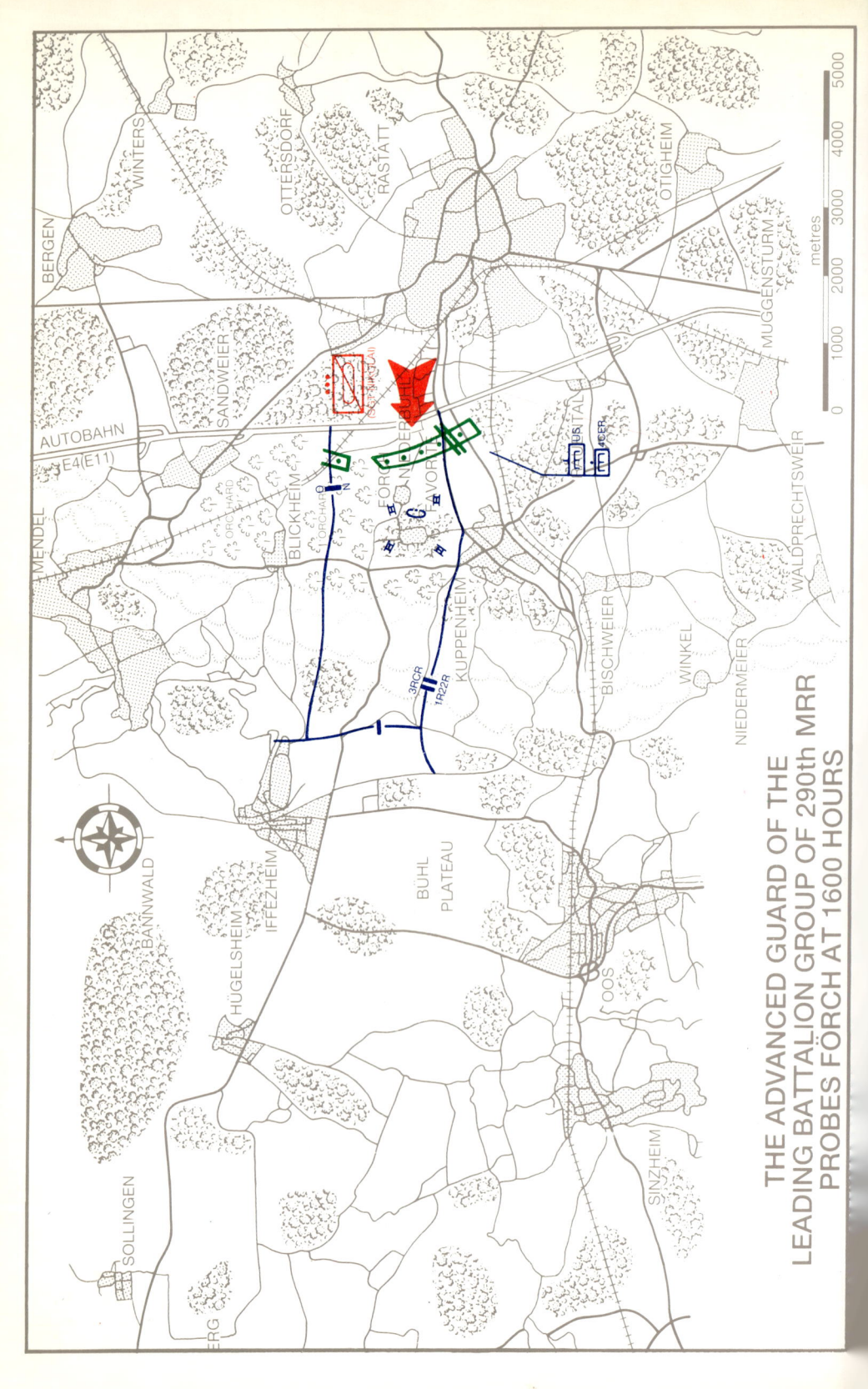

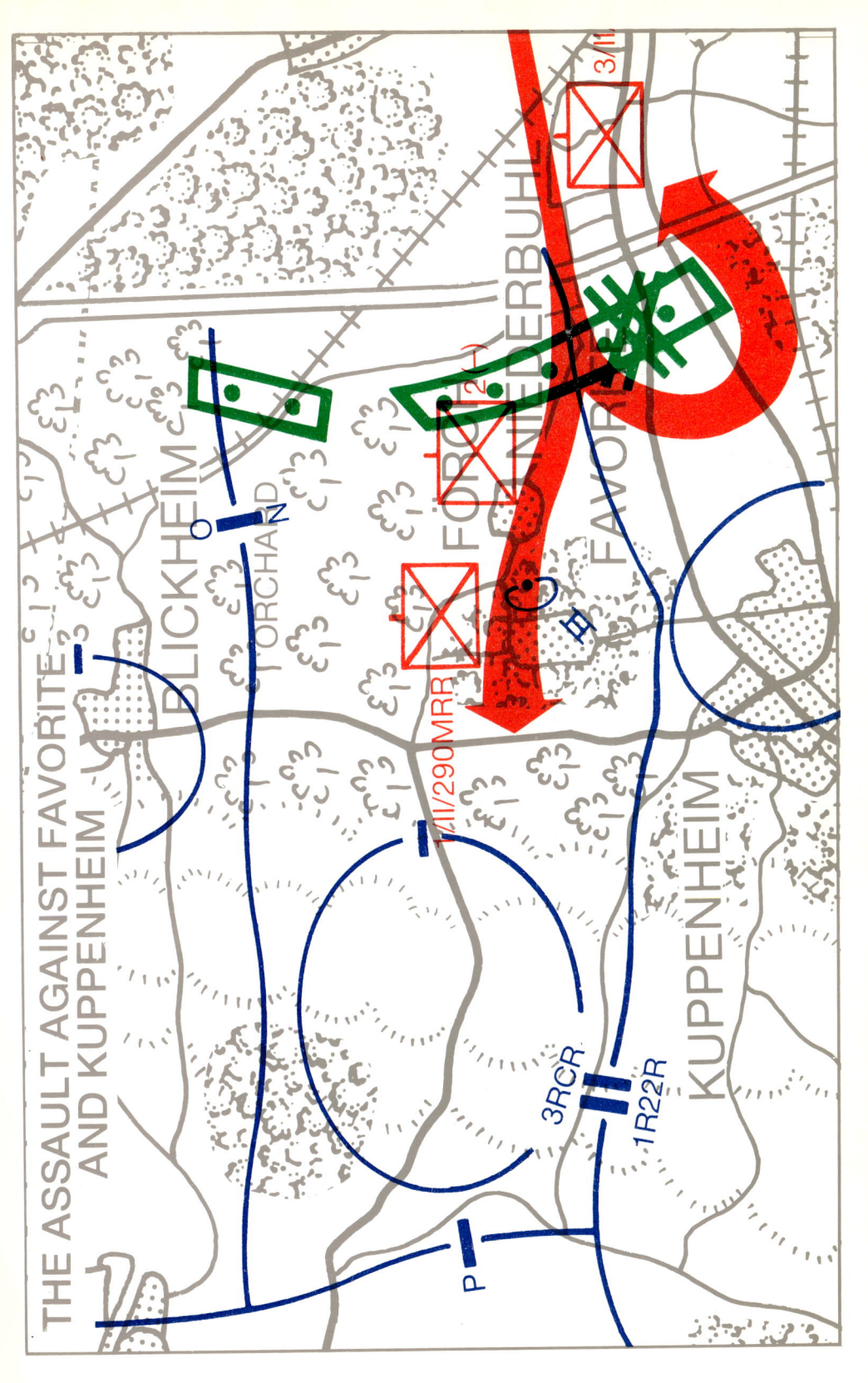

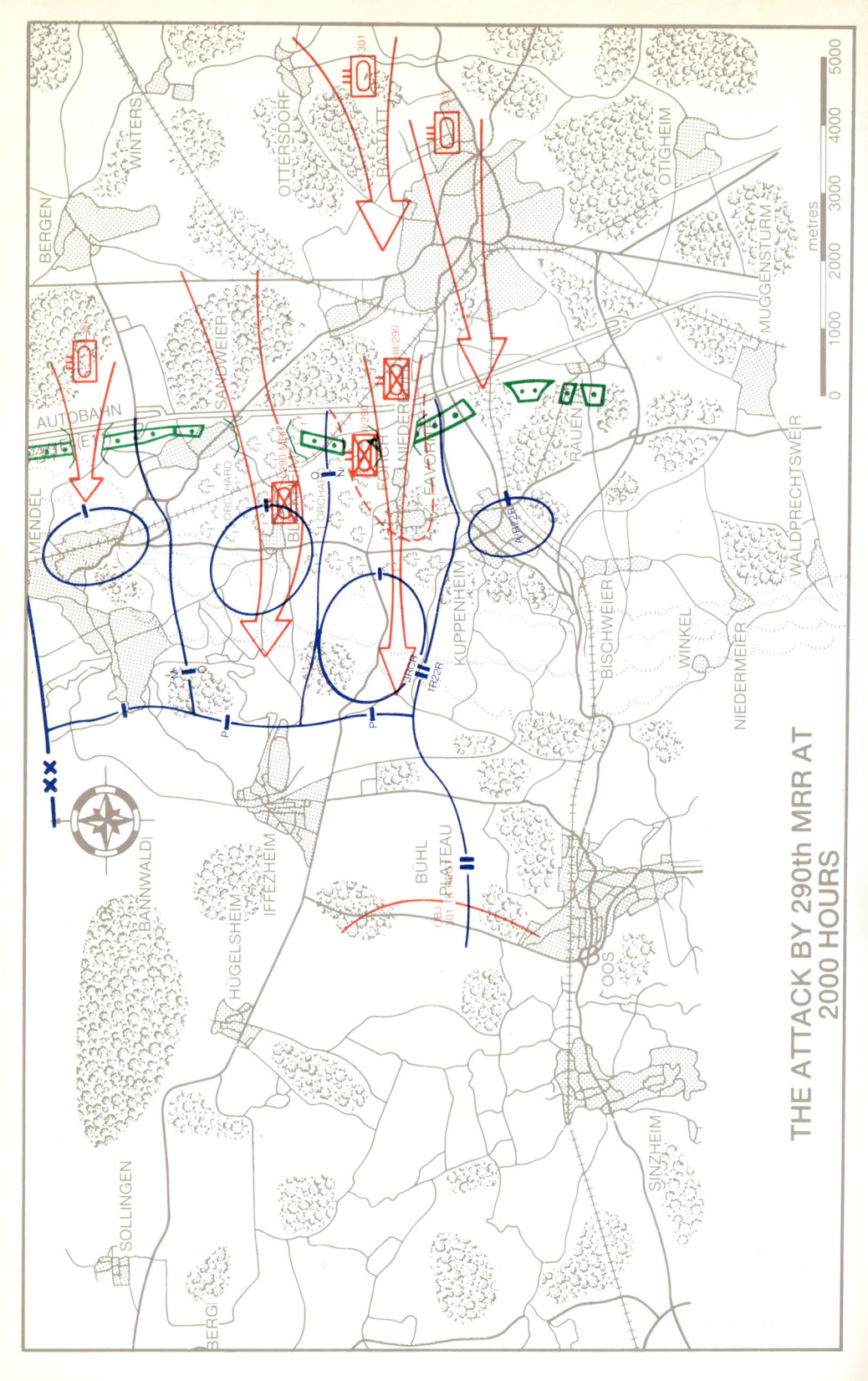

THE ATTACK BY 290th MRR AT 2000 HOURS

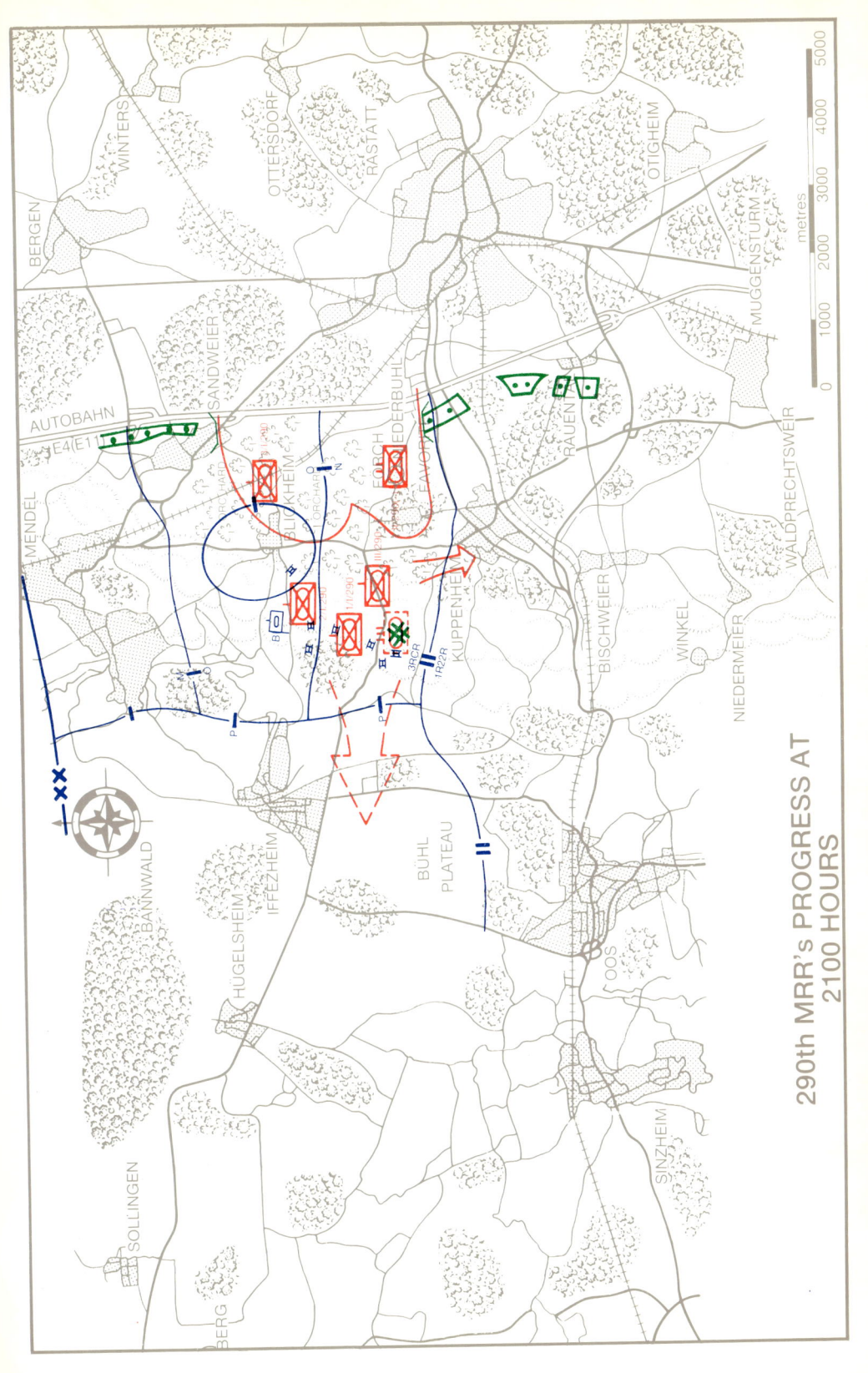

290th MRR's PROGRESS AT 2100 HOURS

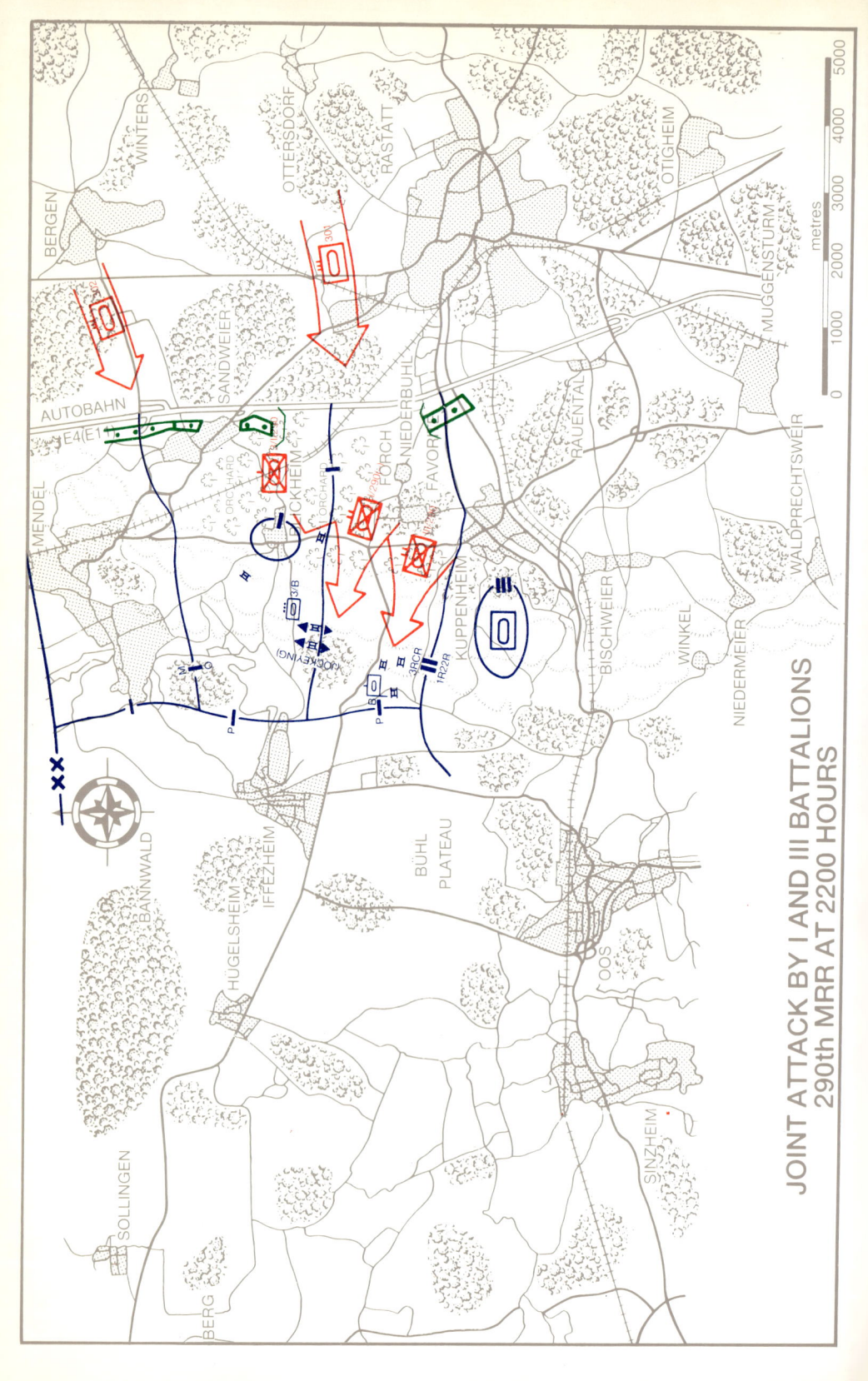

JOINT ATTACK BY I AND III BATTALIONS 290th MRR AT 2200 HOURS

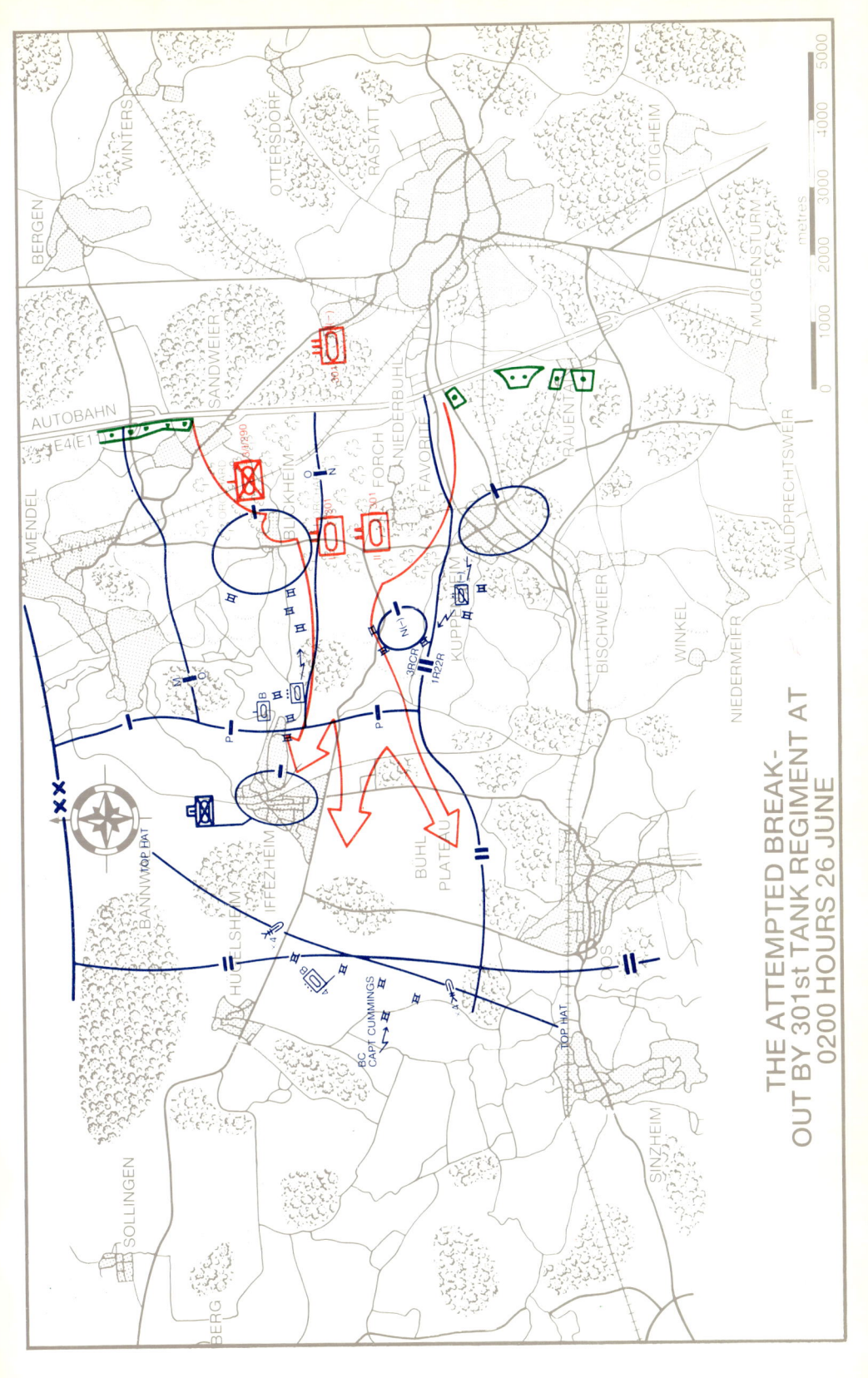

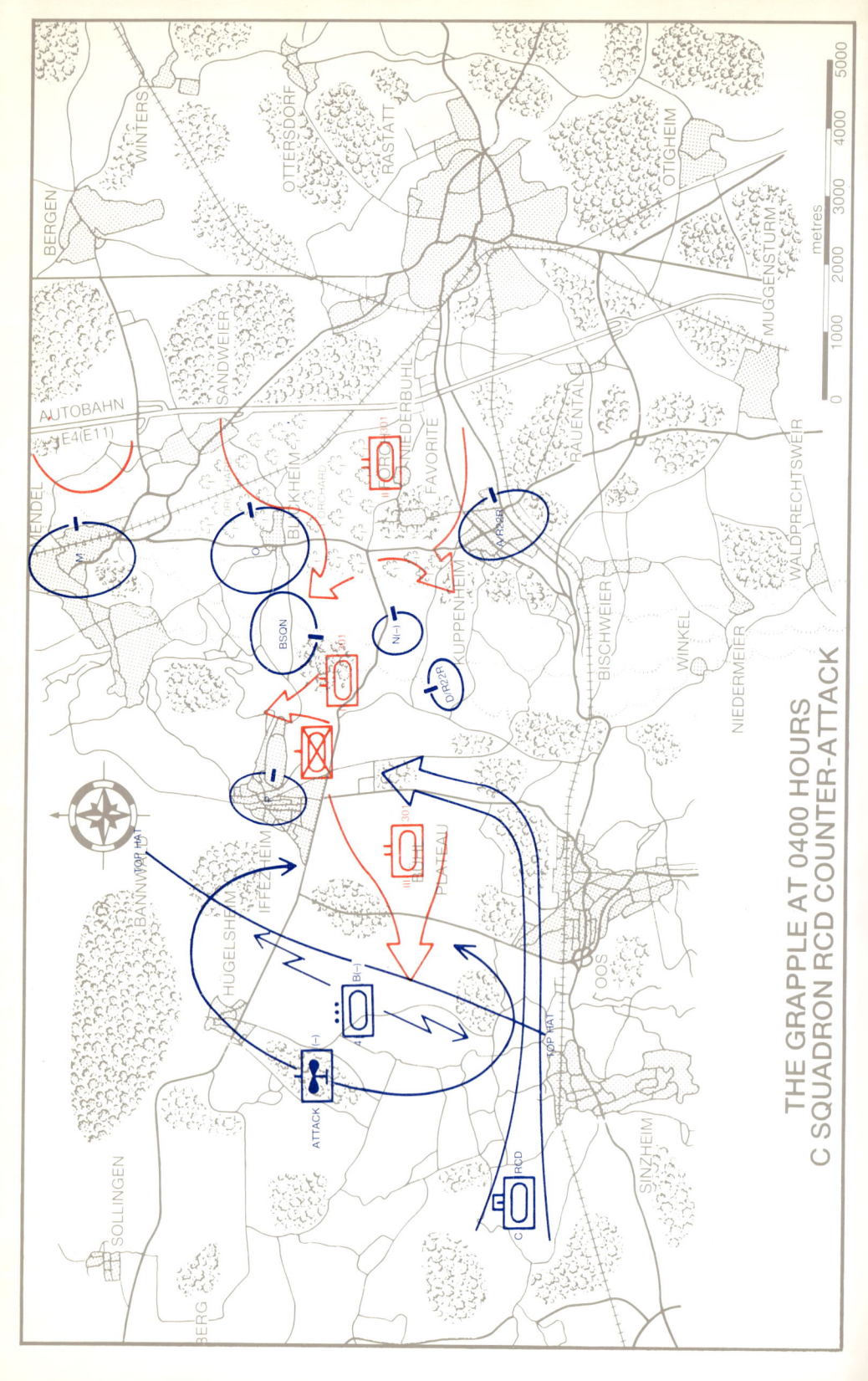

1 | In the assembly area

It scarcely seemed three weeks ago that the latest political furor had loomed over the horizon. Like so many of its predecessors, its characteristics at first had looked no different to all the other threats which, in the past, had risen to a crisis and then receded in response to diplomacy and political manoeuvre. But this time the onward march of events, of threat and counter-threat, had escalated unabated until, on the 15th of June, in response to unusually heavy and persuasive evidence of a build-up of Warsaw Pact military force in Eastern Europe (as well as increasing activity by Soviet forces almost everywhere they were to be found around the globe), the moment for NATO taking overt precautions could no longer be avoided. To the astonishment of the NATO people, successive states of readiness for war were declared, reinforcements warned to go to Europe, reserve equipment and stocks made ready for use, and transport facilities positioned in readiness to move the reserve units and begin the evacuation of civilian dependants.

Perhaps it was the departure of families, school teachers and the other dispensable categories of camp followers which most brought it home to the officers and men of 4 Canadian Mechanized Brigade Group that this time it was going to be the real thing. The prior arrival of reinforcing sub-units – the squadron of the RCD, the battery of 1 RCHA, the companies of 3 RCR and 1 R22eR, the two field troops of 4 CER, along with other minor elements – had acted as a sharp warning of what was going on; but after that, all had been in the nature of previously rehearsed exercises. Taking away the women and children cut a link with peace which placed the brigade, psychologically, on a war footing before the order to leave barracks and move to its operational assembly area was received on the 21st.

On the 24th of June, they were at war. It had begun with widespread air attacks followed by the landing of airborne troops in the rear, disruptive sabotage by guerrillas and the crossing of the

17

THE FIRST DAY

Above: Leopard crews loading 105mm ammunition prior to moving to the assembly area.

frontier on the night of the 22nd/23rd by strong Warsaw Pact forces. So far the Canadians lay relatively undisturbed despite the almost ceaseless manifestations above of air warfare, the heavy rumble of battle away to the east, and the tensions induced by anticipation, by occasional bombing and rumours of spies and saboteurs at large amid the towns, villages and woods where the brigade group lay hidden in wide dispersion for fear of nuclear attack. To a minority of hot-heads, for whom the prospect of action was a lure, the 36 hours' inactivity was galling. To the majority, the leaders above all who needed all the time possible to improve the combat readiness of their commands, the extended period in waiting was welcome, a heaven-sent opportunity to smooth out the rough edges among troops who were conditioned to barrack life. It also gave a chance to absorb reservists and others who, until a few days before, had been enjoying the soft delights of life at home in Canada.

Major Dick Connors, OC N Company 3 RCR, in the manner of three fellow rifle company commanders of 3 RCR, and four more in the Vandoos, felt that his command was ready for war and, moreover, the best in the brigade. A small percentage of his men were militia, the bulk had trained together for at least 12 months and some for much longer. War, coming when it did, had pre-empted the summer posting season, so officers and men were at their peak. Of course there were deficiencies. Standards of marksmanship with all weapons left something to be desired, and Connors had taken the

THE FIRST DAY

Above: M113s entering the assembly area.

opportunity within 24 hours of entering the assembly area to take over a suitable nearby quarry for use as a range. Here he watched Lieutenant Eddie Leach putting No. 1 Platoon through intensive practice against man-size targets. Still higher on his list of priorities for improvement was the standard of field defences construction. Although the company was situated within a village, with its M113s parked at hand between buildings, he had insisted upon the men digging in instead of sheltering in rooms and cellars. That way they could practise and have emphasized to them the vital matter of always being responsible for their own protection. But the initial spadework had been slow. It had taken an aggressive MiG, of unrecognized nomenclature, with a roar of gunfire and the resultant loss of a comrade severely wounded, to bring it home to his men that this was a dangerous business which affected them personally. At that, the company accelerated its rate of earth shifting remarkably!

After stand-to on the morning of the 24th, Connors had walked the rounds, watching his men at work after breakfast, sensing their mood, giving a word of encouragement here, a reproof there. Bracing them for the oncoming test. With gratification he watched his sergeant-major and senior NCOs supervising the soldiers. In a barn, close by soundly constructed trenches with stout overhead cover which toned in well with the farmyard, Sergeant Al Hobbs was checking his section's equipment. Each man had his NBCW kit laid out and his weapon stripped for inspection, the working parts of

19

THE FIRST DAY

SMGs, FNs, 7.62 GPMGs and the .50 HMG exposed for his meticulous scrutiny. Inside the section's 113, Private Paul Charrier was looking to the stowage of M72 PAWs to see they were readily at hand and not liable, as sometimes had been the case on exercises, to be buried under personal kits. In peacetime, weapons tend to take second place to comfort; in war priorities change. At a corner of the village, Connors came across Gunner Jake Martin scanning the sky away to the east. Ready at hand was his Blowpipe AD missile in case another MiG decided to disturb their repose. Last time, the sheer

Right: Attention to cleanliness, the vital act of weapon maintenance. Left: .5in HMG; foreground, Carl Gustav MAW; on tripod, .30 MMG.

THE FIRST DAY

unexpectedness of the attack had taken the entire detachment by surprise; next time, he vowed, it would be different, providing, that was, he received enough warning and could raise and launch the missile in time. They talked about the problem of target acquisition and were joined by Captain Pat Kendal, the FOO from A Battery 1 RCHA who was attached to N Company. Together, the officers walked towards company HQ, discussing their future collaboration.

A similar procedure of inspection allied to man management was being employed half a mile distant in the midst of the evergreen

wood occupied by Major Ian Linkman's B Squadron RCD. Deep among forest paths, his four troops of Leopards and their associated command and administrative vehicles lay hidden, the drivers and signallers engaged upon maintenance, commanders and gunners checking sights and the low-light-level TV, and practising fire orders and gunnery techniques. The training programme was being supervised by the battle captain, Captain Peter Cummings, a gunnery instructor who had long held the uneasy belief that the complex array of controls, sights and instruments which festooned the commander's and gunner's side of the turret might, in combat, overload the ability of both men to cope and actually degrade instead of improving the accuracy of shooting. At this very moment, Cummings was criticizing errors in the orders just given by No. 3 Troop Leader, Lieutenant Ron Pike, which had led to utter confusion for his gunner. "For God's sake remember," he pleaded, "if you find that sort of difficulty on the day, get back to 'steam' gunnery, using the Mark One Eyeball for range-finding and set aside all the gadgetry. But as of now, start all over again and get your drills right while there's time."

Linkman was talking to Warrant Officer George Crane of 3 Troop, a discontented warrant officer whose Leopard was off the road until the mechanics had changed its transmission. Watching the ARV crew winching in the replacement unit, Crane bitterly commented: "Just another hangover from going left handed round the airfield track, I suppose, but why must it happen to me?" And Linkman commiserated, but pointed out to one of his most experienced troop warrant officers that it might have been worse – it could have happened in battle. As usual, a road run had revealed hidden faults.

O Company of the RCR was engaged in very much the same activity as the others, although a remark by the CO, Lieutenant-Colonel Doug Tinker, had led its OC, Major Tom Panton, to guess that he might well be called upon to hold a village in any defensive scheme the battle group might be called upon to take part in. He talked it over with his second-in-command and platoon commanders while, from different parts of the company locality could be heard NCOs putting men through their paces – Master Corporal Fred Terry practising with his Number 2 on the Carl Gustav MAW; Private John Grimes undergoing a local refresher course in stoppage drill on the 113's 50-cal gun.

THE FIRST DAY

In the Reconnaissance Platoon of 3 RCR, that 'élite group' as its commander, Captain Gordon Truman, chose to call it, they were checking the surveillance kit supplied to their Lynx and M113 vehicles. Truman harboured no illusions about the inferior combat ability of his vehicles, but he was a convinced advocate of the vital role they could play, particularly at night, in locating enemy movement between widespread company localities and round open, exposed flanks. This was his reason for ensuring that all were in working order and that his men, once more, fully understood the vital role of the AN/PPS-15 short-range radar; the AN/TVS-501 medium-range NOD; and the shorter-range passive-viewing devices with which his troops were lavishly equipped. Truman had a feeling that the other infantry elements in 3 RCR battle group might not accord quite the same importance to these instruments of darkness as he did – the one exception being, perhaps, the TOW platoon which, uniquely, had the benefit of the long-range crew-served weapon sight (to enable it to make better use out to 2000 metres of their guided HAW's full 3750 metres range). Truman was pleased to observe a TOW operator, parked nearby in his M113, paying similar close attention to his night sighting devices – but Master Corporal Gene Petrie, like Truman, was also somewhat of a perfectionist. At every spare moment, he sought to practise weapon drills with his crew and, if possible, obtain the use of the simulator to maintain his own skill in target tracking. Like everybody else, he realized the vital importance of the Leopards with their 105 mm guns, but he also liked to think that TOW, with its long-range capability, would have an important part to play in the anti-armour battle.

Only in P Company was the atmosphere noticeably different from the others, but this was hardly surprising. It had been living in Canada less than a week ago and the OC, Major Alan Ferrier, felt somewhat more anxious about the future than his fellow company commanders. It was not that his men were untrained; many indeed had served in Europe before, as he had himself. It was simply that the sudden disruption of life was unsettling, and he had to be sure that his techniques fell in line with the others. With this in mind, he had driven over to B Squadron for a chat with Lieutenant Phil Brown, 4 Troop Leader, to make his acquaintance in the knowledge that they might find themselves teamed for combat in the future. Their meeting had been fruitful, but it took him away just before the CO called in to look over the company in an endeavour to search out any weaknesses

THE FIRST DAY

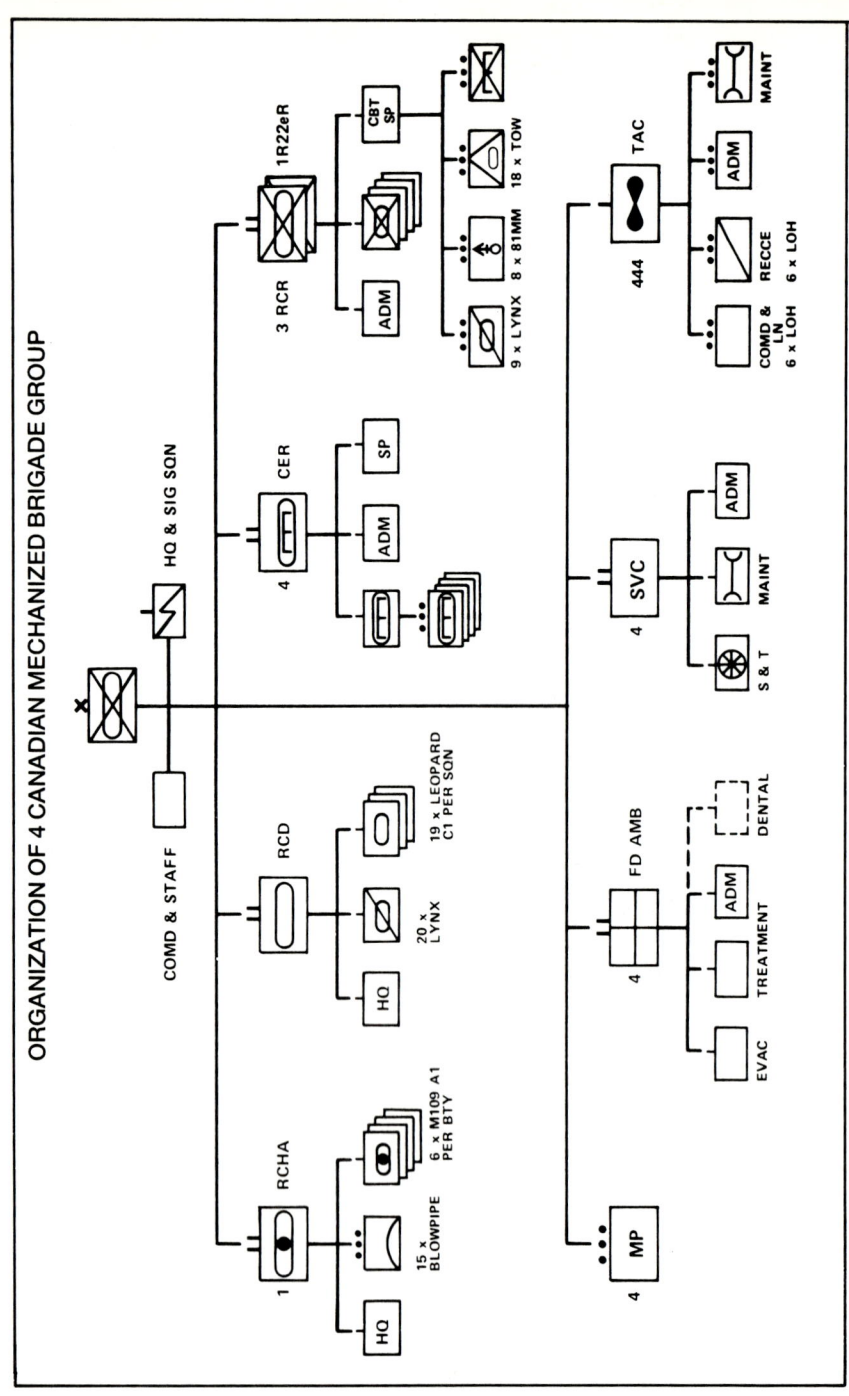

which might so easily be found in the least-well-known part of his command. Inspecting, along with the company second-in-command, Tinker was able to spot and correct a few defects. He recognized several NCOs and men with whom he had served before, and that gave a sense of continuity and made him feel better. At the same time, he welcomed men from other regiments who now found themselves posted to a strange unit. Also he warned the 2IC to nominate one platoon for detachment to C Squadron RCD if, as seemed likely, that squadron became the Brigade Reserve, and had to be strengthened with an infantry platoon from the RCR.

This was indeed the task C Squadron would have to perform and it, like P Company, had but recently flown in from Canada, and was still not fully master of its Leopards. The permanent caretaker party, as Major Lionel Groves was prepared to concede, had kept the tanks in fine condition – but no self-respecting crewman would ever admit that another could prepare a tank as well as he could himself. Feverish activity engulfed each tank, and Lieutenant Harry Owens of 3 Troop was heard defending the caretaker party's efforts (for which he had been responsible) against a moan of discontent from a brother officer, and in return was crisply criticizing the state of training of the new arrivals. "That", remarked Lieutenant-Colonel Brian Cowdray, CO of the RCD, with a smile, "is the sort of thing I would expect in the circumstances. They'll forget it all in a day or two, but, Lionel, you must take every opportunity to divert them from housekeeping to training. Above all, concentrate on the gunnery side. We live or die by that – and so does the brigade."

In all honesty, Lieutenant-Colonel Doug Tinker would have agreed with that assessment by his armoured opposite number. Convinced infantryman that he was, he harboured few illusions over the threat posed by massed enemy armour and the probable inability of his companies with their TOWs, Carl Gustavs and M72s to withstand a concentrated artillery and tank threat without the close support of Leopards and his own artillery. Back in his M577 command post alongside a gasthaus, he contemplated the roles 3 RCR battle group might have to perform. Before they had left barracks, the Brigade Group Commander had held a conference with his senior officers to update them about the current situation and to verify the task 4 CMBG might be called upon to play and the manner in which he proposed to tackle it. In fact it was the same plot that they had so often studied in the past. The brigade would be held back

THE FIRST DAY

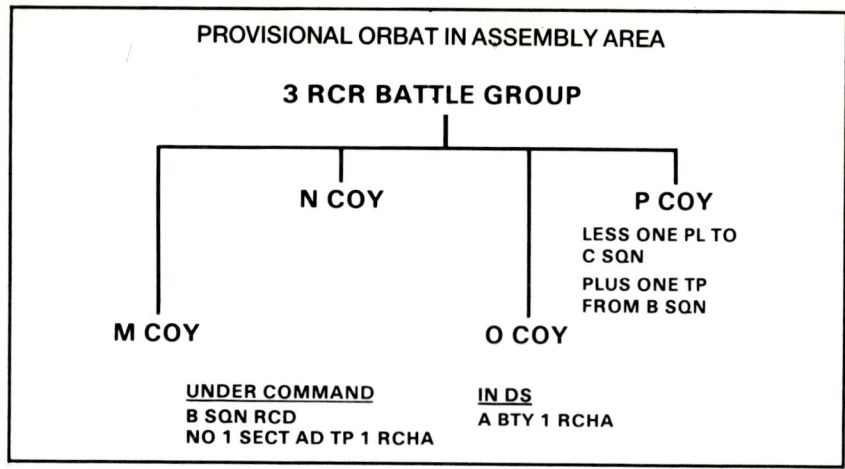

in reserve, designated to block enemy forces which had penetrated either II (GE) Corps or VII (US) Corps. They would most likely come under operational command of the latter. Bearing in mind that his was a predominantly infantry formation, the Commander was aware – and devoutly hoped – that in all probability he would be called upon to hold inherently defensible ground – the sort in which infantry could be deployed on reverse slopes overlooking a natural or artificial obstacle, and where tanks could manoeuvre and fire from a variety of hull-down positions covering the infantry locations and obstacle. On these assumptions, the commander had decided, prior to entering the field, to carry out preliminary grouping within the assembly area. That is 4 CER and D Squadron RCD would be positioned ready to lead the way, while the other combat units were split up into battle groups. So far as Tinker was concerned, this meant that he would take under command in his location, B Squadron RCD and No. 1 Section of five Blowpipe detachments from the AD Troop 1 RCHA; along with A Battery 1 RCHA in direct support, the BC and three FOOs of the latter to live from the outset with 3 RCR while the six 155 mm M109A1 Howitzers remained concentrated elsewhere with the rest of 1 RCHA. He anticipated, however, being ordered to relinquish to the RCD at least one platoon (along with a platoon from the Vandoos) to give them an infantry element commensurate with its role as Brigade Reserve.

As for his future deployment – well that, as Tinker knew, would depend on the situation, the ground and, perhaps to some extent, the weather, which was holding fine and clear. Ideally, he hoped for either a two-company or three-company frontage, held by M, N and O Companies, leaving the newly arrived P Company to lie back in the blocking role. This he had in mind when he arranged with Ian Linkman to attach 4 Troop to P Company, and earmarked a platoon from that same company to go to C Squadron if called for. It was orthodox, but to orthodoxy he pinned his hopes. For this was the sort of allocation of forces to which his men were accustomed by training, and nothing seemed more desirable to Tinker, at that moment, than that his command should be committed to its first action with the minimum of disconcerting innovations which might throw it off balance. Grimly he realized that the enemy would be doing his utmost to achieve surprise and there was no need to make his task any easier.

With these somewhat uncompromising thoughts in mind, he had returned to his command post, there to be joined by A Battery commander, Major Pat Vivier, with advanced news of impending battle from gunner sources, called on a civilian telephone.

CONTROLLING FACTORS

★ The need to bear in mind the psychological effects of separation from families.

★ The need to make use of every possible opportunity to improve preparedness for combat and to care for the morale and training of all ranks, with particular emphasis on marksmanship and drills.

★ The special problem of integrating fly-over units and individuals.

★ The problems of security, of impressing on everybody the need to dig in and to be constantly on the alert for their own protection.

★ The necessity to avoid unorthodox improvisations if they tend to throw sub-units and individuals off balance; allied to the vital necessity to seek to surprise the enemy and to avoid being surprised in turn.

THE FIRST DAY

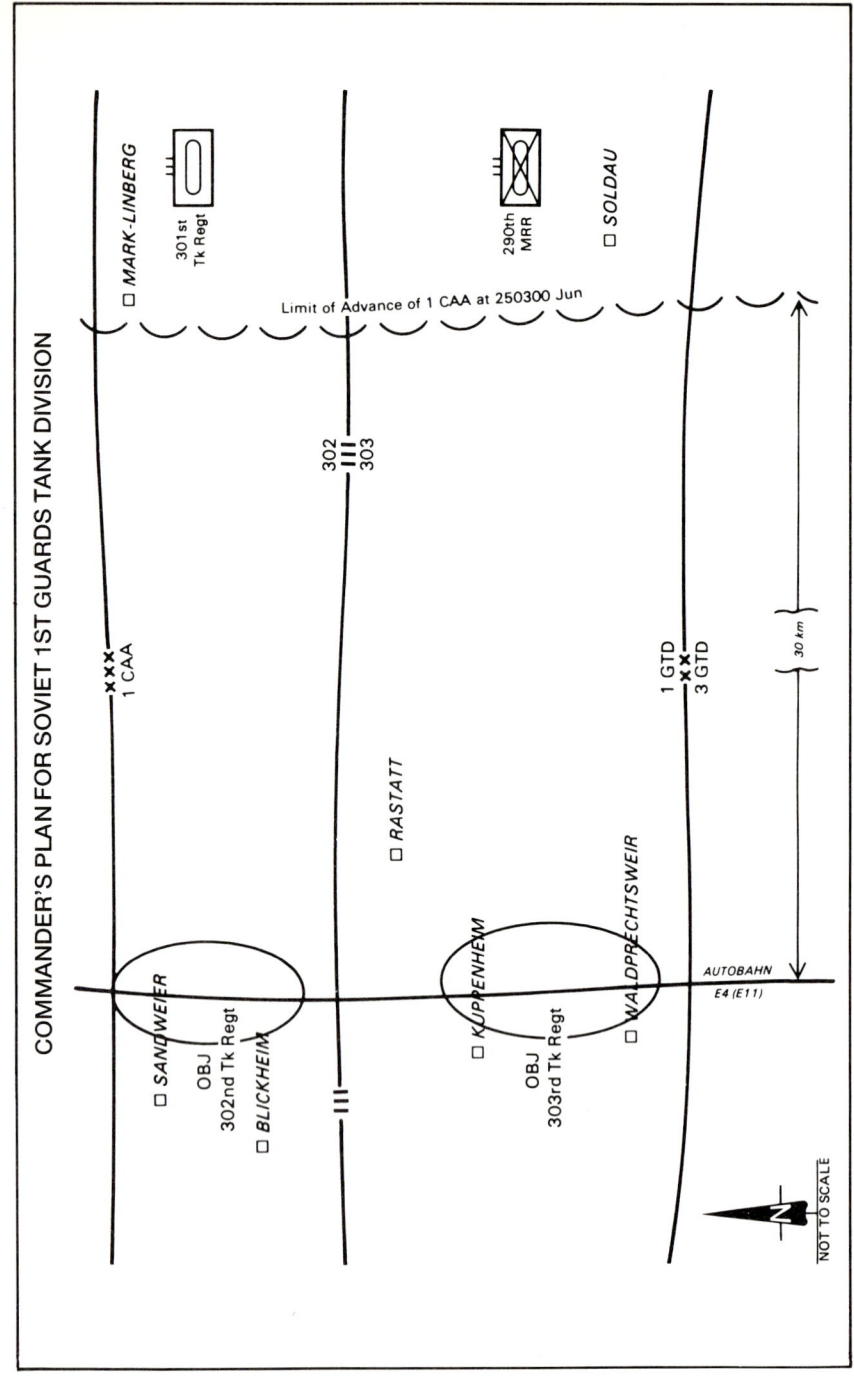

2 | In the enemy camp

Major-General Gregor Samsonov was awaiting orders – and with them the pursuit of his destiny as a well-thought-of senior tank leader in the Red Army. Only potential commanders-in-chief were appointed to 1st Guards Tank Division, just as only élite formations found themselves part of First Combined Arms Army (1 CAA) committed to the task of leading the long-awaited assault upon the NATO forces in the West. And yet, when the final provocation by the Western Powers had at last driven the Supreme Council to open hostilities, Samsonov's determination to succeed was as much the product of dread as of single-minded ambition; the commander of 1 CAA was even more renowned for his ruthlessness than Samsonov. And already, at midday on the 24th of June, it was apparent that his superior's patience was being tried. Progress was not as rapid as intended. Both the Americans and the Germans opposing the initial assault by Motor Rifle Divisions and massed artillery had put up a far better fight than anticipated. Already it was plain that the offensive capabilities of NATO fire-power were denying 1 CAA the swift victory it had banked upon.

Nevertheless, progress was being made. A few minutes ago, reports had been monitored indicating a significant penetration of VII (US) Corps front. It did not require a crystal ball to foresee the advent of a desperate American counter-stroke and to expect its defeat followed by the pre-planned lunge deep into the enemy rear, in which 1 GTD would play its dramatic part. Samsonov already had a pretty clear notion of where, when and how he would launch his division. Once the front had broken open, his principal objective would be the spaces of the Bühl Plateau, that broad expanse of open ground stretching beyond Rastatt where his three tank regiments would find most room in which to advance in mass. With luck, his leading elements would be entering that profitable hunting ground in the enemy rear some 48 to 72 hours after the Motor Rifle Divisions

THE FIRST DAY

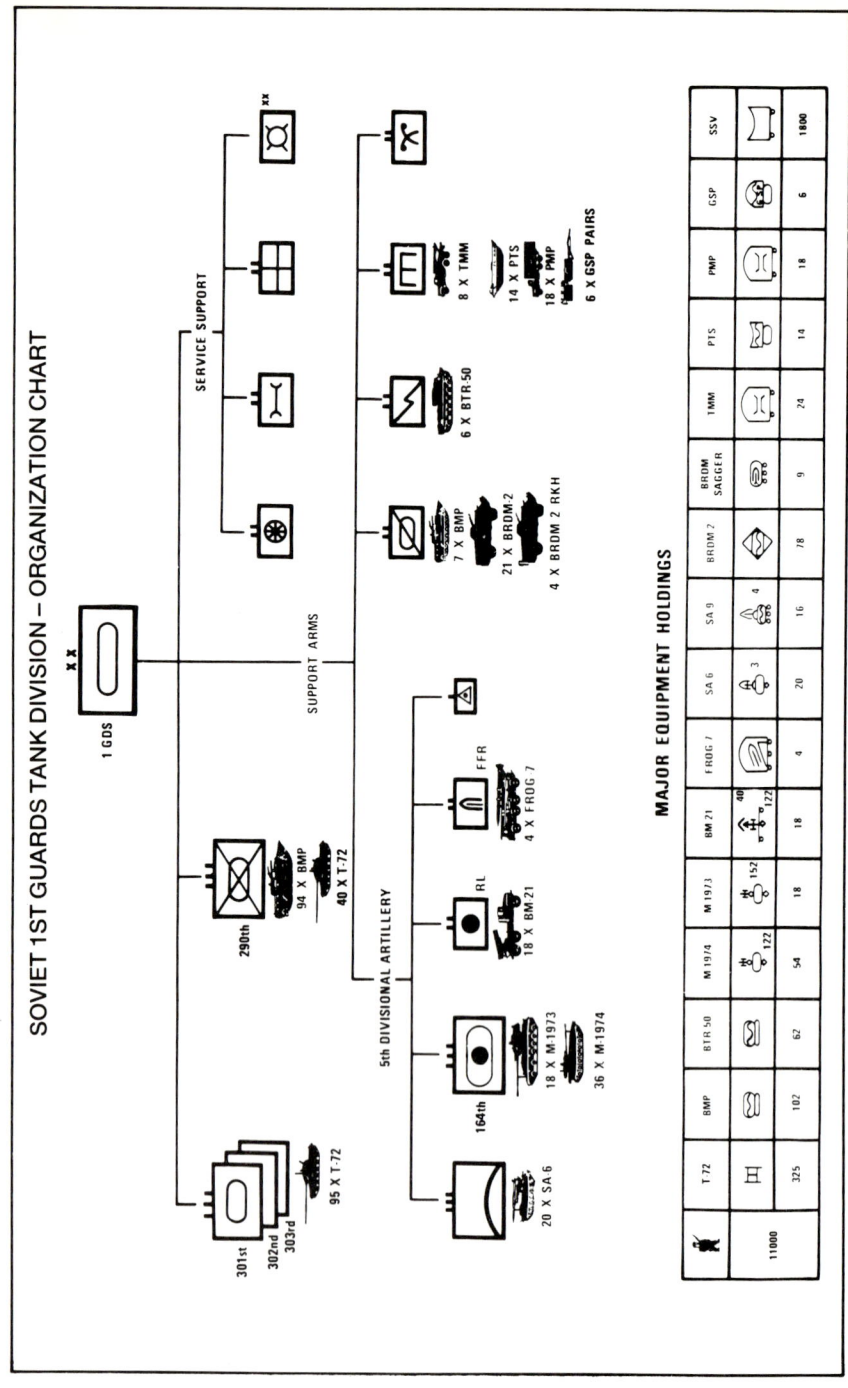

had crossed the frontier. Yet already that possibility looked remote. Indeed, the success achieved by the enemy in defence was beginning to give Samsonov reason to vary his plan. On the assumption that the enemy would collapse, he had intended to advance with two tank regiments up, meaning to burst through the built-up zone in the vicinity of Rastatt by sheer weight of armour. Since, however, the enemy's resistance was prolonged and might even be extended in its effectiveness throughout the built-up area, he now contemplated leading with his MRR, using its preponderance of infantry to smother defenders among the houses.

He mentioned this thought almost in passing to Colonel Andrei Romanov, Commander of the Divisional Artillery. Romanov, in accordance with a private understanding with the commanders of 301st (Colonel Pavel Podduyev), 302nd and 303rd Tank Regiments and 290th Motor Rifle Regiment (Colonel Vladimir Oblensky), passed it on to them. A year's experience of Samsonov had taught them all to stick together when confronted by their meteoric divisional commander, and their fear of him was transmitted throughout the division. By stages in quick succession, news of a change in the wind reached out-stations in the divisions, each recipient being affected in accordance with its personal impact.

To Lieutenant Ivan Shulubin, the commander of No. 2 Company II Battalion 290th MRR, a sudden call to visit his battalion commander acted as the first stage in a process which indicated to him that, quite soon, he and his men in their ten BMPs might be to the fore rather than following up, as at first seemed likely, in the drive westward. For Sergeant Oleg Nikolai, although he did not yet know it, the honour of actually leading one of the point recce patrols of 1st Guards Tank Division in his BRDM 2 scout car was a foregone conclusion. As a skilled member of the 4th Platoon of the division's Recce Battalion, he was chosen as a matter of course, and for prudence, due to his skill, for the most difficult tasks; that way, the divisional commander was least likely to be provoked into fury by any failure.

Lieutenant Yuri Tursov, on the other hand, was not too disappointed to hear on the grapevine that No. 3 Company I Battalion 301st Tank Regiment, was not necessarily going to be among the division's main body, let alone with the leading battalion group. Perhaps, he ruminated, with half his mind fixed on his newly-wed wife Nina, the war will be almost over before we are committed

31

– but he did not really have much hope of that. Anyway, it gave him more time to look over his ten T72 tanks once again, and attempt to raise the most recently joined conscripts (whose prowess left much to be desired), to the same level of proficiency as the older crewmen. He knew there were other officers with the same complaint. And he accepted, too, that the only way to solve it was remorselessly to obey the unspoken rule of the division: "Do as you are told and don't argue."

Intent upon special techniques, Corporal Igor Lyubshin, a T72 tank commander in the tank battalion of 290th MRR gave attention to the mounting of the KMT 5 mine-plough fitted to the front of his tank. Clumsy piece of equipment that it was, he was convinced it must soon be used if only because there was no better way of quickly clearing mines. On exercises when he had been sent to work with MR Battalions of 290th MRR, he had invariably found himself called upon to perform this task. As for Private Rudi Leskho, a humble member of I Battalion 290th MRR, the past few weeks had been bewildering. He was in no doubt that if his country had not gone to war it stood in peril of being invaded by the predatory Western Powers. That had been obvious for as long as he could remember. Yet the rapidity of his transfer from a comparatively comfortable billet in Poland to an uncomfortably cramped seat in the back of a BMP had come as an unpleasant shock. The intensification of training, with its emphasis on chemical warfare measures and dismounted action, was all in the day's work. Simply, the inexplicable haste of it all had shaken him. Somehow his slow mind had grown to a belief in a gradual transition from peace to war . . .

By tradition, it was the Soviet artillerymen who assumed for themselves the role of decisive arm – no matter how confidently the tankmen boasted their claim. Captain Alexei Rusalski, a FOO serving in 1st GTD 164th Artillery Battalion, was both extremely competent and fully alive to the historical part played by massed guns in all the great Soviet victories in the Great Patriotic War of 1941–1945. He also knew that, in theory, he had the power to bring down the concentrated fire of a stupendous weight of artillery – not only from his own battery's six 122 mm Howitzers but, also, from the other 12 guns belonging to the battalion, or those integral to the tank and rifle regiments, or possibly, any additional 122 mm or 152 mm guns attached from the 5th Artillery Division. And this was not all. The 120 mm mortars from the 290th MRR were also

THE FIRST DAY

Above: Feeling his way – a leading patrol of 1st GTD consisting of a motorcycle and a BRDM.

available to add their high rates of fire to what could amount, under ideal conditions, to concentrations of an intensity and ferocity rivalling anything mounted in previous wars. A convinced advocate of fire-power above all, that he was, Rusalski also knew that in practice the Soviet system and communications were likely to allow him to control only his own battalion's guns. He knew, too, that enemy fire-power was also likely to be fearsome, and might even be sufficient to stop Soviet armour if, as a preliminary, the enemy artillery and anti-tank weapons were not swept aside, or at least neutralized by Soviet air-power and artillery.

It was a philosophy to which Samsonov was not by any means unreceptive. His plans, like those laid by most Soviet commanders, took full account of the use of sustained artillery fire at every stage of an advance. But as the moment drew closer for a final decision on the plan he would adopt, it increasingly looked to him as if a straightforward charge by massed armour, the tactics which the inflexibility

THE FIRST DAY

of Soviet doctrine and training historically tended to dictate, might suffice. As the day wore on, information began to accumulate; the impending American counterattack at its beginning in the morning had, happily, been defeated by about 1600 hours. Two hours later, it was not only clear that the Americans had shot their bolt, but were on the verge of giving ground. Again the Motor Rifle Divisions were beginning to make headway, this time against slackening resistance.

At 2000 hours, the Army Commander came on the phone. "Samsonov, you'll be pleased to hear we are winning. Both 8th and 10th Rifle Divisions are advancing again. There are many prisoners and quantities of equipment beginning to fall into our hands. Indications are that the enemy will attempt to retire and break contact during the night." "That is good news," remarked Samsonov in expectation. "I congratulate you." "It is good news for you too Samsonov, your chance will come tomorrow," responded the Army Commander. "Be ready to pass through 8th Division at first light, at 0330 hours. By then, they should have got as far as the line Soldau-Marklinberg and the way will be clear for you to advance, as planned, on Rastatt. Your objectives will be the same as those we originally discussed. You must bypass all resistance and seize the crossings over the autobahn beyond Rastatt; establish yourself on the Bühl Plateau and advance without pause as far to the west as you can. The rest of the army will follow. The 3rd Guards Tank Division will keep pace on your left. I take it you have no questions – no reservations since last we spoke?"

"No, sir," replied Samsonov. "I did wonder if it might not be advisable, in view of the stiffer-than-expected American resistance, to lead from the start with the 290th MRR in order to deal with all those towns and villages dotting the plain between here and the autobahn. But because you say the enemy will be in full retreat, I see no reason now to change the original plan. 303rd Tank Regiment will move along the left axis, 302nd the right. The 290th MRR will be held back for use in seizing the approaches to the plateau, particularly if, as seems likely, it is seriously defended. 301st Tank Regiment will exploit once I have a foothold on the plateau."

"That is good," acknowledged the Army Commander. "You will still be provided with at least two extra 152 mm regiments and also all the artillery that can be made available by 8th Division. Transport helicopters wil be on call if you require them, along with ample gunships, but I must warn you that their losses already have

THE FIRST DAY

> **CONTROLLING FACTORS**
>
> ★ The Soviet doctrine of rapid exploitation by ruthlessly led and driven armoured forces strongly supported by overwhelming artillery fire.
> ★ The built-in lack of flexibility in command and control of Soviet land forces.

been heavier than we expected. It is deemed advisable only to use them if the enemy shows signs of being in some disarray. His missiles are not without effect upon the determination of the crews."

"What information have we about enemy defences beyond the autobahn?" asked Samonov, his mind reverting as previously to the possibility of seizing the ground between Blickheim and Kuppenheim by helicopter *coup de main*, using elements of 290th MRR. "Much as before," came the reply. "Intelligence sources confirm that it might be held by the Canadians, and indeed I have just been told that there overlay and an embryo Obstacle Task Table. The development of a barrier of mines to reinforce the terrain and blunt the first onslaught of Warsaw Pact massed-armour was, the sappers knew, a vital task

Below: Massed artillery. The backbone of the Red Army's firepower, the M1973-152mm SP.

THE FIRST DAY

are signs of activity in that area. You must assume it will be held and held strongly by troops we cannot despise. Your best hope, as I've said before, is to get there before they are ready. The slightest delay in reaching Blickheim will be to your detriment. Roll over them!"

The conversation ended. Samsonov looked pensively at the silent instrument and then at his chief operations officer who had been monitoring the conversation. As usual, he reflected, it was to be a race against time and the enemy – but on this occasion, the stakes were far higher than ever before in his experience.

WARNING ORDERS

Contents of a Warning Order
The amount of detail that can be included in a warning order depends upon the time and means of communications available, and the information it is considered necessary to send to subordinates. Where applicable, as many as possible of the following points should be included:
- Enemy situation, events, probable mission, task.
- Earliest time of move or degree of notice to be given to the main body.
- Rendezvous and time for orders groups, stating whether commanders or representatives are to attend and maps required, and/or the time at which written orders may be expected.
- Orders for preliminary action – reconnaissance, surveillance, observation.
- Administration instructions – special equipment required, regrouping of transport, preliminary moves to assembly areas, if necessary. (Extract from B-OL-303-002/FP-001)

Warning order sent by Commander 4 CMBG at 241635 Jun
"WNG O, 4 CMBG TO DENY ACCESS TO BÜHL PLATEAU FOR AT LEAST 48 HRS COMMENCING FIRST LIGHT 25 JUN. NO MOVE BEFORE 2000 HRS. OGP GR922073 241900 JUN. ACK."

3 | Deployment

Orders to deploy
"Apparently", remarked Lieutenant-Colonel Tinker to his assembled principal subordinates, "the Commander of VII (US) Corps has told our Brigade Commander to emulate Nathan Forrest, 'to get there fustest with the mostest!' That means we've a busy night ahead."

The warning order had reached 4 CMBG at 1600 hours, having left HQ VII Corps the moment it was plain to their commander that his counter-attack had irretrievably failed. Under the conditions of radio silence which had applied to the brigade since it had left barracks, the message had been sent by telephone, in the same manner as within the brigade where most messages were also being sent that way or by messenger or through liaison officers. It was only 45 minutes later that battle groups and the other units within 4 CMBG, spread as they were over a ten-mile radius, had received their own warning order, telling them briefly all that was necessary to know at that moment; saying they must soon move to a new specified location where the brigade would take up a blocking position; no move to take place before 2000 hours – that is, shortly after last light. It stated, too, that the Brigade Commander's Orders Group would be held in the village of Blickheim at 1900 hours without saying who would attend. (The latter was unnecessary since, in accordance with SOPs, all battle group and other unit commanders knew they must be there.) The warning order went on to confirm that a standard overlay order, along with a movement order, would be issued as soon as possible and that, in the meantime, only the essential reconnaissance groups and advanced parties would be allowed to go forward.

At 1700 hours, the Corps' Commander had visited 4 CMBG in his helicopter and issued verbal orders, along with the famous quote from Nat Forrest. With them came his repeated insistence upon the importance that 4 CMBG "must, within its boundaries, deny access

THE FIRST DAY

BATTLE PROCEDURE – INFANTRY BATTLE GP

Bn RGP	Coy RGPs	Pl RGPs	Main Body
Bn WngO prep and issued. RGP joins CO			
	Coy WngO issued		
RGP movs fwd to bde OGP	Assemble and prep to mov	Pls warned and start prep for op	Prep for op under DCO and coy 2ICs
			Routine adm prep conts, incl issue of eqpt, ammo, rat, POL, final check of vehs and wpns
CO and supporting arm comds attend bde OGP			
Remainder of RGP wait nearby			
			Tps rest
CO briefs RGP, completes time appreciation, map appreciation, recce plan and issues supplementary wng info. RGP movs to bn area, completes recce and plan and completes prep for bn OGP	Supplementary wng issued to pls		
	Leave for bn OGP in fwd aea	Brief pl WOs and leave for fwd RV	Spec adm prep, if reqr
			Recce party movs fwd
	Briefed by IO. Assemble for OGP		

THE FIRST DAY

Bn RGP	Coy RGPs	Pl RGPs	Main Body
Bn OGP starts	Attend bn OGP		
			Feeding of tps
Bn OGP ends	Time appreciation map appreciation, recce plan		
	Coy comds recce and plan		
	Prep for coy OGP		Hd of colm passes SP
CO meets coy comds in coy areas for coord		Arrive at fwd RV	Colm movs fwd
		Mov fwd for orders	
	Coy OGP starts	Attend coy OGP	
			Colm arrives in fwd area
	Coy OGP ends	Pl comds detailed recce	Coys mov to coy RV
	Coy comds meet pl comds to coord layout of posn	Send guide to coy RV for pls	Pls arrive at coy RV, meet guides who take them fwd to pl locs for orders
		Pl comds give orders to pls	
			Start prep posn

39

THE FIRST DAY

to the Bühl plateau for at least 48 hours commencing first light on 25 June." The SSO Operations of 4 CMBG had been present and immediately afterwards had listened to his commander give an outline of the brigade's mission to his SO 2 Operations and principal arms advisers. No sooner was that over, and the SSO was turning his attention to the preparation of the operations overlay order and the movement order, the Brigadier accompanied by the CO 1 RCHA, the CO RCD, the SO 2 Operations and CO 4 CER were taking off in Kiowa helicopters to examine the ground upon which they were to fight. The commander, as his profession demanded, was thinking two levels down. Time was short. It would be dark by 2000 hours and it was desirable that, if possible, not only battle groups but also combat team commanders should examine the ground before nightfall. Hence he had calculated that, if he could cover the 30 miles to Blickheim in 15 minutes and carry out his recce in 45 minutes prior to having a discussion with his advisers before 1830 hours, it should be possible to hold his O Group at Blickheim at 1900 hours, allowing his subordinates about 30 minutes to formulate their own ideas and another 20 to point out the ground to the OCs of the companies and the combat team in daylight. It mattered less that the units should arrive in daylight; indeed it was highly desirable, on grounds of security, that it should complete its deployment in darkness. In the glimmer provided by a moon in its second quarter, some sort of reconnaissance could be carried out and planning would not be seriously impeded.

Tinker read his commander's mind acutely, recalling past study periods and relating their conclusions to the implementations of the warning order. His own warning order, carried by messenger throughout the battle group, had reflected Brigade's and fixed an RV with his subordinates on the outskirts of Blickheim at 1830 hours. A telephone call to Brigade had elucidated (what might have been included in the warning order) that it was this sector that his group would occupy, and that the Vandoos would be on the right – news which extracted a mild protest (overruled) that the Royal Canadian Regiment was accustomed, by tradition, to stand right of the line! Tinker and his R Group (his IO and the BC along with Commanders' Armoured Defence and Mortar Platoons) travelled in one-quarter ton trucks. There were no helicopters for them since 444 Tactical Helicopter Squadron had too few machines for every task and, in any case, was already fully engaged in work laid down by higher priority.

The CO himself was, in fact, already flying over the operational area, plotting the likely tasks to be undertaken by TOW-armed Cobras of the US Army if they were assigned under operational conditions. Rapidly, he was assembling on his map the chinagraph lines denoting likely killing zones (KZ) and their associated fire positions (FPs), blocking position (BPs), RVs and forward area re-arming and refuelling point (FARP).

To a well-known drill, the leaders of 4 CMBG congregated for the greatest test of their professional lives. As combat team commanders, along with their platoon commanders and fire controllers, moved to battle, riding in M113s, those who flew and those who travelled by road were able to form an impression of the scene. In the distance, smoke rose from fires lit by air attack. Overhead, aircraft tangled in combat. On the ground, signs of a scared population on the move could be detected – not the wholesale panic evacuation of refugees such as history taught them was once prevalent in 1940, but of large-enough dimensions to strain the efforts of the German police to control, and to pose a threat to the smooth and punctual implementation of the movement order then on the verge of being issued by 4 CMBG. Tinker knew how critical timing must be and sensed (as had Samsonov) that they were engaged in a race. He watched the Polizei dealing firmly with a nose-to-tail convoy of cars and trucks. This overflow of traffic from routes reserved for refugees caused him to diverge from map planning. "I hope to God they get that lot out of the way before tonight," he remarked anxiously to his travelling companion, Pat Vivier. But the BC merely nodded and went on studying the map and making an initial allocation of fire tasks he might require to cover the front they would soon occupy. He hardly expected everything to go smoothly; if it didn't in training, why should it in war?

Nor, for that matter, did the overlay order and attached movement order imply precise implementation. The latter certainly embodied allowances (within strict staff criteria) for things going wrong. But the delivery of these documents at HQ 3 RCR at 1830 hours provided the operations officer with just enough time to brief combat team liaison officers with sufficient detail to enable them to launch their approach to battle on schedule.

Sub-units were in the throes of packing up. In November Company, Connors was engrossed preparing his maps and studying the ground they disclosed. His second-in-command was supervising the move itself, making sure nothing was forgotten. For Connors it was important that at this stage, when the previous training of his men was being really put to the test, he should remind them of lessons which had not invariably seemed vital during exercises: "Never forget, you're always responsible for your own protection," he said to his O Group. "Stay alert! Keep hidden, too, as much as possible. Don't strip off nets until it's dark, the enemy will find us soon enough. Let's have it as a surprise for him when we are ready.

THE FIRST DAY

Left: The essentials of high combat morale – plentiful food, as required. This crew has cooked privately prepared food inside its M113. The official rations are reserved for emergencies!

Finally, eat well and sleep when you can. 28 Bravo (kitchen truck) will turn out a hot meal before you move. It might be a long time before you eat well again. Make the most of it and get all the sleep you can. It'll be a long night and tomorrow you'll all be digging or fighting."

Eat they would. Sleep was more difficult to come by, for the tension was high, and the coming and going of officers, giving and receiving orders in haste, did nothing to reduce it.

43

Below: The approach to the Bühl plateau, looking east. Rastatt in the distance; the autobahn runs from left to right in the middle distance in front of the woods; Favorite is in the woods to the right; Blickheim is off picture to the left.

ARMOURED DEFENCE WEAPONS COMPARISON DATA

Weapon	Missile arming range	Effective range	Rounds per minute
TOW	65	300-3,500	2
CARL GUSTAV	—	700	3
M72	—	200	5–6
LEOPARD	—	0-2,000	4–6
T72	—	2,000	7
SAGGER	300	3,000	1/2
RPG7	—	500	4–6

THE FIRST DAY

Commander's. He heard that the Commander expected the enemy to attempt a breakthrough between Blickheim and Kuppenheim – in other words, in full force against 3 RCR with only a lesser incursion against the Vandoos on the right. Cowdray had told him the sappers were going to construct an obstacle, mostly of mines, across their front from Sandweier on the left to the wood beyond Kuppenheim on the right, and that it was likely that he, Cowdray, would be in overall command of an inadequately small counter-attack force which would be located behind, in the Bannwald.

This, as it turned out, was the plan actually decided upon by the Brigade Commander. It was therefore the essence of what Tinker was to tell his own O Group half an hour later when it gathered round him in the setting sun under the shelter of fruit trees which grew profusely on the forward slopes falling away before them. A quick chat with Linkman settled the anti-armour plan in outline. M Company commander was the last to arrive from the left flank where he had found himself regarding, with some relief, a complex bit of terrain he knew was ideal for defence. It would soon be dark, Tinker had not quite completed his notes and time was running short. As usual, the IO put them in the picture about the current situation. "The enemy", he reported, "are advancing again on a wide front, although so far, only Motor Rifle Divisions have been positively identified. Both air and other sources have reported, though, that one, perhaps two tank divisions are lying up close behind the enemy front; their commitment can be expected at any moment, maybe during the night; more likely early tomorrow. Enemy air attack continues to be very active, and although his losses have been heavy, it would be unwise to count out the likelihood of attacks on our own troops in the open."

Tinker took up the thread. As for friendly forces, he said, VII (US) Corps was attempting to disengage with a view to realigning its front on the strong defensive feature of which the slopes forward of the Bühl Plateau were a part. It intended to hold here for at least 48 hours as of tomorrow mid-day, by which time it was hoped the realignment would be complete with 52nd US Mechanized Division secure on the Canadian left and 10th US Infantry Division on the right. The good news, he concluded, was to be noted in a couple of fresh attachments – the allocation of a US Army Engineer Battalion to help 4 CER construct the obstacle, and the arrival of 1-40th Battalion US Army Artillery, equipped with M110A2, 203 mm self-

49

THE FIRST DAY

> **CHOICE OF DEFENSIVE POSITIONS**
>
> The following factors influence the choice of positions:
> - Enemy approaches and associated obstacles.
> - The need to deny to the enemy ground of tactical importance.
> - The need for concealment.
> - The need to cover any obstacles with fire.
> - The availability of reverse-slope positions.
> - The availability of defiladed positions.
> - In mobile defence, the existence of ground which facilitates disengagement.
> - The need for all-round observation and interlocking fields of fire by day.
> - The need for suitable fire and surveillance positions by night.
> - The likely effects of the terrain on chemical cloud behaviour.

cannon shells raked a line of vehicles, setting several on fire and slashing through people crouched in a ditch. At about the same time, however, they were encouraged by the sight of an enemy air attack being dealt with by the US Army's air defence – a Chaparral missile bringing down a MiG 21 Fishbed from about 2000 feet and a Vulcan battery making short work, with a rasping burst of fire, of an unwary low-flying MiG 23 Flogger. Distractions such as these delayed their arrival at Blickheim, and so they had been able to spend only half an hour looking over the ground. Sensible forethought on the part of their CO, Tinker, had been beneficial. He had obtained from the SO 2 Operations an outline of the Brigade Commander's planned layout of the defensive position and the area 3 RCR would cover. The intelligence officer had met them and told each combat team commander his sector and passed on a rough allocation of supporting weapons the CO hoped to make to sub-units.

In the village, the Brigade Commander's O Group was in full swing; a meeting of officers grappling with shortage of time, endeavouring to compress and telescope the standard deployment drills. Tinker had fallen behind schedule as the result of delays along the route from the assembly area. For him there was scant time to formulate a quick appreciation of the ground, make an overall plan in consultation with Linkman, (the OC B Squadron RCD) and settle a preliminary allocation of supporting forces to combat teams. Yet he had been able to short-circuit some of the procedures. At one stage, for example, he had held a brief consultation with Brian Cowdray, CO of the RCD, and gathered from him the brigade anti-armour plan and, with it, confirmation that his own assessment of the Blickheim ridge as vital ground coincided with that of the Brigade

AD measures included in our SOPs will augment the umbrella of coverage provided by the AD systems deployed by corps and higher formations. Some additional protection will be provided by the AD detachments interspaced in the column. Speed, 30 kilometres per hour. Density, 20 metres apart. Lights, blackout drive. TC, our own MPs will man the SP and release point, there'll also be the American MPs here and there and, above all, the German civil police who have their hands full, but who, I'm told are going to give us all the help they can. They're not giving us a traffic ticket today! They also know it's in their interests to help. Service Support, unit first-line recovery as usual, but 4 Service Battalion is bringing a recovery detachment up the route after everyone has gone through. Medical, normal. POL, you're all topped up now – I take it – eh?" Was there a slight hint of sarcasm in the question as he looked keenly at past offenders who had forgotten before – just once? "Top up in the assembly area once you get there. Command and signal, the strictest of radio silence of course, as of now. And I do mean that! Impress it again on your signallers: no press-switch pushing, but monitor your sets continuously. We'd like to surprise the Russians; no need to tell them we're coming. Questions?"

They were few, and short. All wanted to return quickly to their vehicles to pass on the orders and make the final arrangements. This was the moment when, in the absence of officers on reconnaissance, company and squadron sergeant-majors along with the warrant officers and sergeants, came into their own, setting the example of meticulous preparation once the orders were known. Passing on as much information as possible to all the men, supervising the careful stowage of kit, the readiness of weapons, the briefing of signallers, the feeding and, as of habit, the cleaning up of the area before they left it – each act the inculcated product of ingrained routine spread over generations of older soldiers. Trying above all to make it look all in a day's work.

Laying out the defence
Crouched in a huddle beneath a fruit tree, Dick Connors and Nick Panton compared notes. Already they had experienced a few of the realities of war. They had been witnesses to the bewilderment on the faces of refugees and, at a couple of villages through which they had forced their way in a heavy traffic jam, they had seen that bewilderment turn to terror when jet aircraft flew low overhead and

THE FIRST DAY

Orders for the move of 3 RCR battle group were issued verbally at 1900 hours by the operations officer to company squadron 2ICs. They reflected in the briefest terms those which had been received from Brigade in the operation overlay order and the movement order. To save time, everybody had marked up his map from the trace which had been transferred onto a map displayed in the operations room – the inn's dining-room. Captain Andrew Barton, the operations officer, and a stickler for the formalities of staff duties, tried his best (and succeeded) in keeping briskly to the laid down sequence of orders, but failed somewhat in holding his excitement entirely under control. Sometimes, even he permitted an aside to betray the seriousness of the occasion. That way he kept everybody steady by avoiding any suggestion of surprise innovation; at the same time, he managed to transmit confidence by raising a few laughs.

"OK," he began, glancing round the assembly of officers with their maps and note pads poised, "orders – and they're not to say the exercise is off because it'll all cost too much. This time its for real!" and he launched into the familiar sequence, which now both thrilled and chilled them by its meaning.

Some of the things Barton mentioned were already known and these he kept to a minimum. Under situation, enemy forces, he merely repeated what had seeped down from above about the enemy progress and that which they had already looked at on the Intelligence Officer's map. Friendly forces and attached and detached units remained unchanged. 4 CMBG would use two routes – Diamond and Club. Barton felt no need to underline the mission, which was largely as expected.

"3 RCR will move to an assembly area in the Bannwald prior to occupying a defensive position in the area of Blickheim."

"OK? Execution," he went on. "Deployment will be effected by simultaneous movement and, on our route Diamond, we'll have 4 CER, D Squadron RCD, Recce Platoon, Mike Company, the Mortar Platoon, Armoured Defence Platoon and the Pioneers, Oscar Company, Battalion HQ, November, B Squadron, Papa, and Echelon. Form up with head of the column at Karlsbad crossroads and move off at 2100 hours so as to arrive at the brigade start point at 2115 hours. There are no specific critical points; could be the whole thing'll be that way since there's a hell-of-a-lot of civilian stuff starting to join the roads. So there'll be no deliberate halts – just keep going best you can. Air defence, enemy still has air superiority. The

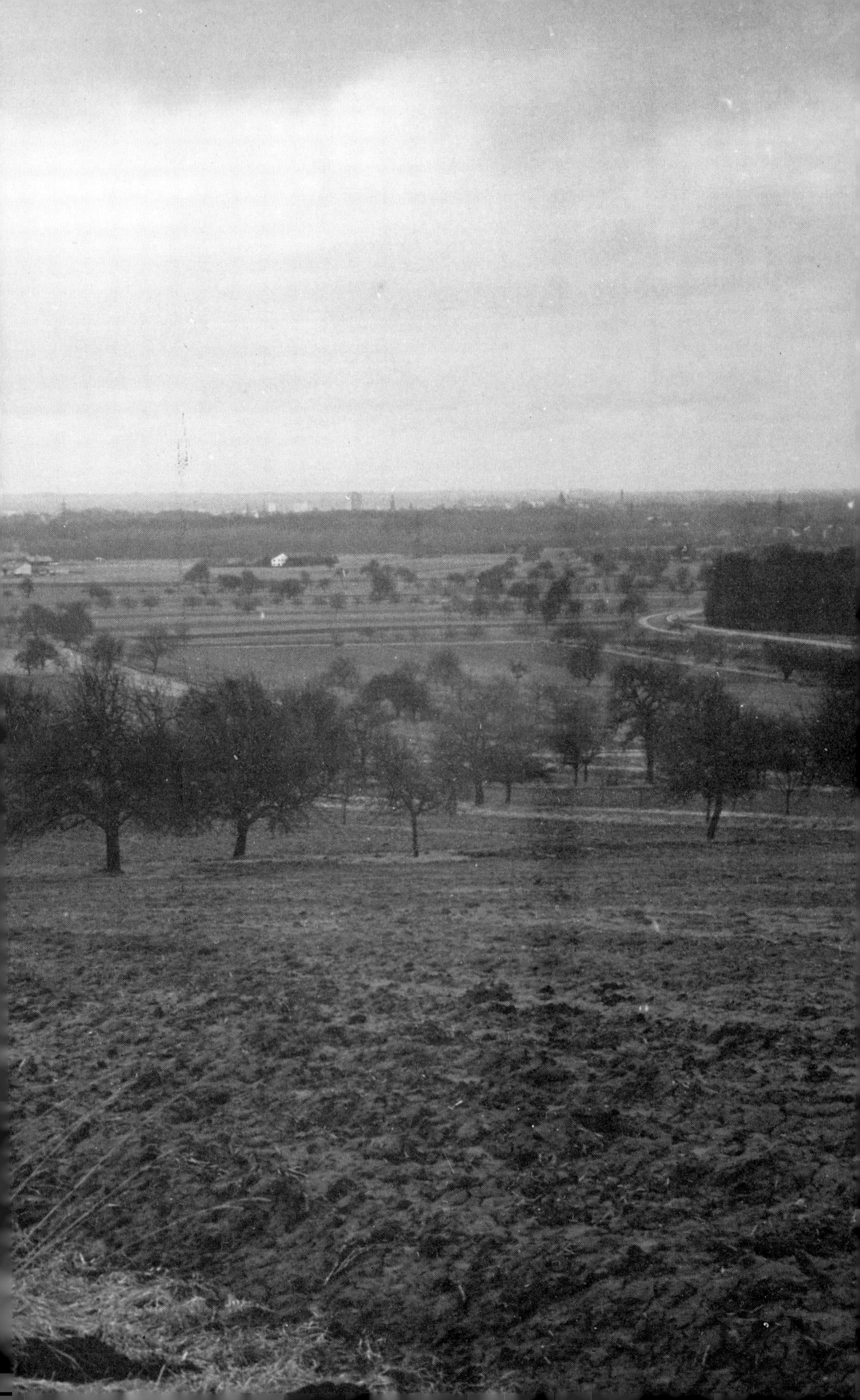

THE FIRST DAY

Left: Coordination – Battle Group, Combat Team and armoured squadron commanders in conference. The picture was taken by the FOO.

INITIAL DEPLOYMENT ORBAT

M Company	Left
Under Command	Two sections, Armoured Defence Platoon
With	FOO
	FC
In Location	Detachment, AD Troop
O Company	Centre
Under Command	Section, Assault Pioneer Platoon
	Two sections, Armoured Defence Platoon
With	FOO
In Location	Two detachments, AD Troop
	Troop, B Squadron RCD
N Company	Right
Under Command	Section, Assault Pioneer Platoon
	Two sections, Armoured Defence Platoon
With	FOO
	FC
In Location	Two detachments, AD Troop
	Two troops, B Squadron RCD
P Company	In reserve
Under Command	Troop, B Squadron RCD

propelled Howitzers in direct support of 4 CMBG, the latter making a powerful addition to fire-power. Direct air support was considered unlikely except for an on-call company of TOW Cobras with the reservation, that due to its casualties, effective strength would be close to a platoon. Area air defence would continue to be provided by US Army Chaparral and Vulcan, and that would be extended as close to the FEBA as possible. Nuclear weapons were at the alert but, so far and hopefully, there was no immediate prospect of either side wishing to employ them.

"Well, there it is," said Tinker, "much as we've always expected, and never as bad as it may sound. The Americans have done well and it's bad luck they've had to give way for the moment. Now it's our turn. They want a breather. But time's short and you've got a lot to do before the troops start arriving later tonight. So, gentlemen, 'Mission'!"

"3 RCR battle group will defend within boundaries from 0300 hours 25 June," and Tinker employed the normal orders sequence, telling each subordinate commander his grouping and task within the meaning of that express mission. Mike Company on the left would consist only of its three platoons plus, under command, two sections

51

THE FIRST DAY

of TOW; in location, a detachment of Blowpipe. Deployed as it was in readily defensible ground dominated in its tank approaches by flanking positions, it would not have tanks in location; with the company, a FOO and FC. Oscar Company, the designated defenders of the Group's centre based on Blickheim, would retain all its platoons and be allocated, under command, a section of Assault Pioneer Platoon and two sections of TOW; with the company, a FOO. In addition, it would have in location, a troop of Leopard and two detachments of Blowpipe. On the right, November Company would acquire the largest support of all. In addition, to its three platoons, they would have, under command, a section of Assault Pioneer Platoon and two sections of TOW; with the company, an

Right: The combat team O Group. Right, the Commander flanked by the armoured commander and the FOO; left, the platoon commanders and FC.

THE FIRST DAY

FOO and an FC. In location would be two detachments of Blowpipe, two troops of B Squadron RCD and, probably, the OC of the squadron and his Leopard. OC B Squadron did indeed intend to begin proceedings with his headquarters on the higher ground to the west of Blickheim where he could best control the three troops remaining in his squadron, and their activities shared between Oscar and November Companies. He would have one other squadron HQ tank with him (with the bulldozer blade), making 14 tanks in all. The rest of his squadron, (the battle captain in his Leopard and the fourth troop) were held back in the blocking role under command Papa Company in Iffezheim. From here, along roads and tracks radiating outwards, the company (less one platoon detached to C Squadron

THE FIRST DAY

RCD in Brigade Reserve) could rapidly re-deploy to any threatened point within 3 RCR sector, or even fight close by the village.

There were no queries for Tinker when he came to the end. The arrangement made sense and each sub-unit commander would have his chance later to ask for changes or adjustments. As of that moment, each was impatient to go back to his sector and make a firm plan before it was too dark. First, however, Ian Linkman explained the way in which he intended to shape the anti-armour plan as it fell within the brigade's intentions.

"The minefield must be covered by fire," he pointed out, "and, as you can see, the amount of cover given by fruit trees down there – particularly around Favorite – means we don't have much of a field of fire over 1000 metres. So I'd like to keep the TOWs on the high ground and site them so as to shoot across the front using their maximum range. I took a look behind Blickheim just now and that's quite promising. The tanks will, as you already know, be in location and a quick glance tells me there's all sorts of little hollows where they'll tuck in. Just remember, I don't want to expose them to view too early. That applies particularly to you, Dick. I suspect you'll be tempted to put something forward of Favorite to buy time on the obstacle, eh? Well, OK! But although time must be bought, as Colonel Tinker said, we can't afford to lose tanks in the first skirmish. So watch it and then we'll talk it over. Other than that, I'm staking a lot on A Squadron, with the Vandoos, covering the obstacle in front of Favorite. So bear that in mind. There's not a hell-of-a-lot of depth in the position here from my point of view, so please don't expect me to push everything in the shop window. Mostly we'll lie back. The higher we are up the slope, the farther we can see and shoot – and the better the hull-down positions, too!"

Nobody was very surprised, and Tom Panton was perfectly content to have the troop of tanks and the TOWs put behind his location. Connors, on the other hand, was already inclined to ask for tanks nearer to the forward edge of his area, and so Linkman's plea sounded a warning. So limited in range were his own anti-tank resources (he did not reckon to open fire with Carl Gustav in excess of 200 metres – less if possible) that he felt compelled to dig-in on a reverse slope while attempting to persuade the tanks to occupy the forward slope – the intention again being to buy time. As so often on exercises, and also in the preceding hours, he cast his mind over the alternatives confronting him. He needed no check list to spell out the

THE FIRST DAY

DEFILADE

- Protection from hostile observation and fire provided by an obstacle such as a hill, ridge, or bank.
- A vertical distance by which a position is concealed from enemy observation.
- To shield from enemy fire or observation by using natural or artificial obstacles.

ENFILADE FIRE

- Weapon fire originating from a flank and directed across the front of an attacking or defending force.

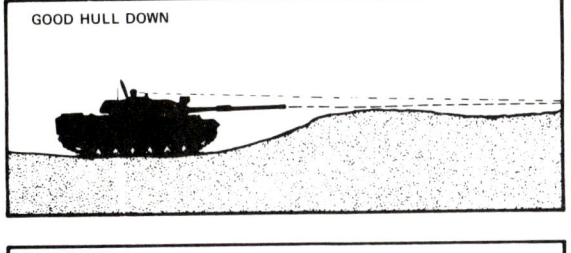

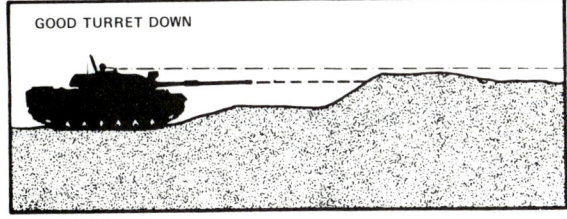

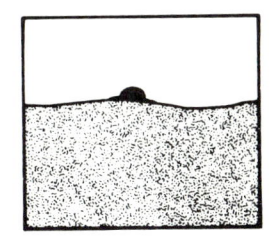

GOOD HULL DOWN

GOOD TURRET DOWN

THE FIRST DAY

desirability of destroying enemy tanks at long range; maintaining the obstacle intact as long as possible; compelling the enemy infantry to dismount from their vehicles as soon as possible; and reserving his own fire to short range from defiladed positions. And he was perfectly aware of the incompatibility of those conflicting ideals. Compromise there would have to be, but he was not too sure, under the present circumstances (in which the enemy and not, as in the past, the exercise umpires would be the final arbiters), of the extent to which Ian Linkman would be accommodating.

CONTROLLING FACTORS

★ The need for commanders at all levels to attempt to obtain advance information of their superiors' intentions to enable them to save time by contingency planning themselves.

★ The merits of engendering an atmosphere of aggressive confidence while in the process of disseminating defensive orders.

★ The importance of obstacles and the need to cover them with observation and fire.

★ The vital importance of co-operation between all arms from the initial stages of developing a plan.

★ The desirability of obtaining the advantages of maximum range for all heavy-armoured defence.

★ The problem of balancing the protective qualities of a reverse-slope position with the need to strike the enemy at long range.

★ The necessity of providing local protection for OPs and heavy weapons such as tanks and TOWs.

★ The special problems of defending built-up areas and the need for engineer assistance in this task.

★ The problems of dealing firmly with the civil populace and the need for close co-operation and understanding with the local authorities.

★ The need to strike the enemy in depth with artillery fire.

★ The necessity to site light-armoured defence weapons in defiladed positions.

★ The importance of providing well-concealed dug-in positions, in order to enhance surprise as well as protection.

★ The desirability of allowing each weapon to function to its best advantage without being circumscribed by the demands of other arms but, at the same time, without seriously undermining the principle of all arms co-operation.

★ The merit of surprising the enemy by the adoption of ambushes.

Oscar Company

Major Tom Panton's way of putting Blickheim into a state of defence was both simple and easy. At a glance, it was easy to see that he must maintain a hold between the forward edge of the village and its centre if he was to maintain observation over the obstacle as well as keep control of the main crossroads. It was plain, too, that, by so doing, he would give protection in depth to the TOW and Blowpipe missile launchers which were to be tucked in behind the village on the higher ground. And he knew already that the nearby tank troop would prefer to manoeuvre into fire positions on the flanks and the rear of the village, without exposing itself to the front or getting involved among buildings. Therefore, Panton concentrated his efforts upon selecting three platoon positions which provided fields of fire out to some two to four hundred metres without becoming overlooked from front and flank. He chose a tightish perimeter which allowed each platoon commander to place two sections covering open ground to his front, and held back the third section in depth. There were many good 'slots' where M113s could be parked close alongside buildings adjacent to their infantrymen, but each man would be required to dig in or shelter in cellars with immediate access to fire positions. Panton, like any other commander, was thinking 'two down' and paying close attention to the overriding needs of firepower and protection – insisting, that is, upon the need to shield his men from the heavy shell fire he knew the enemy would employ, while giving every opportunity to use their weapons to full effect.

Militarily speaking that seemed splendid, but there was a snag! The local German population had to be taken into consideration and the Mayor of Blickheim was none too happy about the impending desolation of his village. Panton spent a frigid 15 minutes with that worried leader and his distraught chief officer, debating what had to be done. Old enough to recall the devastation of Germany in 1945, the mayor was conditioned in some part to the exigencies of the situation and sufficiently realistic to conclude that he had no choice other than to acquiesce in the soldier's irresistible demands. Blickheim was doomed.

"But what of the people?" asked the mayor plaintively. "The Government tells me they must stay where they are. How can I make them do that and expose them to a full-blooded battle?"

Panton was diplomatic but firm. "I have my orders, Mr. Mayor," he said, "and I sympathize deeply. These are terrible days. It

THE FIRST DAY

Above: Blickheim from the east. Note the crest line and, on the forward slope, the fruit trees obstructing fields of view.

would be wrong to insist upon your people staying in their homes and we will do all we can to facilitate their evacuation. But there is not much time. They must go now – within the next two hours – and cannot take much with them."

They were joined by the village policeman and quickly reached agreement over what had to be done. The people would move in a convoy of cars at midnight, led by the mayor and conducted through side roads by the police, under arrangments made by the civil and military authorities. It would be a heart-rending business and one from which the soldiers could not wholly insulate themselves, especially since Panton was carrying out his reconnaissance at the same time as the officials were trying to persuade the populace to leave. In fact, there would be stolid German people, notably the older ones, who would obdurately refuse to go, preferring to stay and face the consequences. So when Panton met his platoon commanders in the village centre, it was as witnesses to a community in distraught turmoil, a scene to distract them from the hard task confronting them and a human factor that could never be thrust from his mind.

Grimly, Panton pointed out the town hall where his headquarters would be located. They walked round the perimeter of what would be the inner defended zone, each officer shown his area and its associated interlocking fields of fire; each noting the civilians who stayed. Primarily, Panton founded each position upon the platoon's

THE FIRST DAY

Above: The obstacle sappers minelaying – speed essential, concealment of lesser importance.

main anti-armour capability; that is, upon the Carl Gustavs and dismounted 50-cal HMGs but ensuring too, that the small arms from each section provided maximum cover for the heavier weapons. In effect, the machine-gunners and riflemen provided escorts for the major weapon systems (including the Leopards and TOWs), reserving their M72 PAWs only for emergencies close-in – at anything between 100 metres and point-blank range. This, as they all knew, must turn into a slugging match – and the man inside the village had the edge over the one outside.

The Sappers start work

The officers and reconnaissance NCOs of 4 CER were the first to enter 4 CMBG's assigned area. Closely followed by the brigade recce squadron, their job was to confirm the brigade obstacle plan which existed for the moment as only a series of green markings on an

MINEFIELD STORES

Nomenclature	Approximate weight (kg)	Number per 5-ton vehicle
MINE, AT, DM 21, (GERMAN)	8.8	374
MINE, AT, M 15, (US)	14.3	320
MINE, Anti-Personnel (ELSIE)	0.114	8,600
MINE, Anti-Personnel (CLAYMORE)	1.6	3,000

> **MINEFIELD LAYING TIMES**
>
> Typical average rates of uninterrupted operations – includes recording and marking.
>
> **By hand, buried** – Engineer Troop or 40 x infantrymen can lay:
>
> - 125 x AT mines per hour in daylight.
> - 75 x AT mines per hour by night.
> - 75 x AT mines plus 225 x anti-personnel mines per hour in daylight.
> - 45 x AT mines plus 135 x anti-personnel mines per hour by night.
> - 600 x anti-personnel mines per hour in daylight.
> - 360 x anti-personnel mines per hour by night.
>
> **By hand, unburied** – Engineer Troop or 40 x infantrymen can lay three times as many unburied mines as buried mines in the same time.
>
> **By mechanical means** – Minelayers should be planned to operate 24 hours a day. One Engineer Field Troop required to supply each minelayer, which includes fencing and recording. Planning estimates for laying by night should be 25 per cent greater than figures for day operations.

in giving the brigade a means of slowing the enemy and providing more lucrative targets for the guns and missiles of the armour, artillery and infantry.

Reconnaissance parties visited every part of the brigade front. Often they needed to stop only long enough to confirm that the obstacle planned from the map and air photos would do the job efficiently. At other spots, adjustments were made and obstacles were added, modified or deleted from the plan. This work produced a steady stream of data back through to regimental headquarters, where the planning for the forward delivery of mines and explosives, and the allocation of field troops and equipment were completed in fine detail.

Each field troop was subsequently assigned a sector of the front in which to complete all obstacles. In addition, on completion of the brigade obstacle, they were to support their affiliated battle group in the preparation of their defences. Given the short time available, even if the promised US Engineer Battalion could offer its services, the assistance to the battalions was not likely to amount to much more than the excavation equipment not employed on the principal barrier, and the professional advice of the troop commander. This latter would also be closely co-ordinating the near edge of the obstacles with the combat team commanders to ensure a mutual siting which would best permit fire to be brought down on the obstacle without immediately giving away the defenders' firing positions.

THE FIRST DAY

Though the complexity of the task was made no easier by the gathering darkness, the regiment, to a man, pushed themselves to the limit. Although tired, they were inspired by the certainty that dead men have ample time to rest but that a well-sited obstacle, constructed with depth and strength to sap the enemy's momentum, would save lives in the hours ahead.

The Artillery team
With the confident air of a man who knew to perfection the indispensability of his role, Captain Angus Scott, the FOO with Oscar Company, was busy selecting concealed OPs in Blickheim, endeavouring to fit in among the infantry while gaining complete observation by day and night, over the most likely avenues of enemy approach and, above all, the obstacle. Of course, Scott's responsibilities would range farther afield than the boundaries of Oscar Company, encompassing as they would everything visible on both flanks, particularly those parts which might lie in dead ground to his fellow FOOs with Mike and November Companies and the 3 RCR FCs with those companies. Already at his disposal was the BC's

Below: A 155mm howitzer M109A1 prepares for action. Note the gunner at the ready with the HMG. Not even gun positions are exempt from attack by enemy infantry and tanks.

61

THE FIRST DAY

CANADIAN FORCES — FORCES CANADIENNES TARGET LIST NO. N° DE LISTE DE CIBLE 1				SECRET SECURITY CLASSIFICATION CLASSIFICATION DE SÉCURITÉ	COPY NO. - COPIE N° 8	SHEET OF FEUILLE 1 DE 1		
REFERENCES — RÉFÉRENCES								
MAPS — CARTES DEUTSCHLAND 1:50 000				PLACE OF ISSUE (MAY BE IN CODE) LIEU D'ORIGINE (PEUT ÊTRE CODE)				
				ISSUING HEADQUARTERS — QG D'ORIGINE				
CO-ORDINATE SYSTEM — SYSTÈME DE COORDONNÉES UTM				DATE/TIME OF SIGNATURE DATE/HEURE DE LA SIGNATURE 242330Z JUN				
ATTITUDE (IF NOT GRID NORTH) — ORIENTATION (S'IL NE S'AGIT PAS DU NORD DU QUADRILLAGE)				MESSAGE REFERENCE NO. N° DE RÉFÉRENCE DU MESSAGE				

LINE NO Ligne n°	TARGET NO Cible n°	DESCRIPTION	LOCATION Emplacement	ALTITUDE	SIZE Dimensions		ATTITUDE Orientation	SOURCE/ ACCURACY Source/précision	REMARKS Remarques
					Lg Longueur	Wd Largeur			
1	ZU1201	Coy Area	2548 3637	110	400	300	1400		
2	ZU1202	Woods	2541 3810	105	200	200	1800		FPF
3	ZU1206	Hide	2610 3709	140	150	300	3600		
4	ZU1209	Cross roads	2612 3610	100					
5	ZU1213	Houses	2512 3414	105	50	50			
6	ZU1214	Woods	2516 3612	106	175	200	1800		
7	ZU1215	Hide	2408 3918	108	300	300	2100		
8	ZU1222	Road	2316 4023	112					
		MORTARS							
24	ZM1000	Woods	2512 3515		200	200			FPF
25	ZM1001	Bridge	2500 3020						
26	ZM1002	Hide	2650 3550		150	300			
27	ZM1003	Crossroads	2536 3415						
28	ZM1004	Barn	2416 3212						
29	ZM1005	Houses	2320 3010						
30	ZM1006	Woods	2160 2925		200	200			FPF

DISTRIBUTION — DIFFUSION (*WHEN REQUIRED - AU BESOIN)
AUTHENTICATION — AUTHENTIFICATION
SECURITY CLASSIFICATION
CLASSIFICATION DE SÉCURITÉ
SECRET
SIGNATURE OF COMMANDER
SIGNATURE DU COMMANDANT

CF 643 (10-80) 7530-21-883-4186

Above: Example of a target list (not related to this action) as prepared by CO 1 RCHA and his staff.

suggested defensive fire list likely to be agreed for this sector between the battle group commander, the CO 1 RCHA and his own BC. The process of allocation had begun almost at the moment of the first warning order being received and had now reached that stage at which it only needed the Brigade Commander to make final amendments, at the same time giving authority for the issue of the definitive protective fire (FPF) targets on the DF list. In effect, everybody in authority among the gunners, plus FCs, combat team commanders and their immediate subordinates, would be informed of the precise grid references of three close-in artillery defensive fire tasks per combat team, plus the integrated mortar fire tasks. Transferred to the consolidated trace which, in due course, would be issued by the gunners, these tasks appeared as numbered crosses spread across the front, selected to coincide with defiles, possible forming-up places, axes of advance, likely infantry dismount areas and so on. Additionally, targets in depth were selected by the Brigade Commander: major assembly areas, vital crossroads and possible communication centres – several of them likely to be undertaken by the attached US Army's 203 mm Howitzers which would also have the job of undertaking counterbattery and interdiction tasks besides joining in the general scheme of defence under their own forward observers (FOs) as well as 4 CMBG's. Based on the framework of designated tasks, controlled by CO 1 RCHA and directed by his BCs, FOOs and the infantry FCs (with assistance in emergencies from tank or infantry officers) a network founded on radio and telephone links, spreading out from the Fire Support Co-ordination Centre (FSCC) in the 3 RCR Mortar Platoon's M577 at Battle Group HQ, was being assembled in order to afford a full and flexible programme of devastating concentrations of fire, the centres of which could be adjusted and switched from place to place at will and, above all, quickly from target to target in the designated killing zones. And to these concentrations, too, might be added support from ground attack aircraft and armed helicopters whose activities could also be directed by the FOOs who were trained as forward air controllers, or called upon by anybody else within the battle group.

November Company
Connors had surveyed his rather complex sector while being driven with his platoon commanders and FC in a carrier across the re-entrants or orchard slopes on the left and right, and through the

THE FIRST DAY

closely enclosed woods of the Favorite Castle to the front, and the beechwood paths to the rear, split in two by the second-class road leading back from Favorite. Not for him a formal session with his subordinates huddled round a map. Instead, Connors allowed the planning (which had begun when he had been first told his task and which had been consolidated at first glance over the ground) to evolve as he moved from place to place. The initial subdivision of territory to platoons had hardened amid discussion into a positive scheme sketched in chinagraph on the talc of his map-board as they toured from left to right. Fundamentally, it was based on the anti-armour plan and, hence, where Carl Gustavs and 50 cals were sited to cover the most likely tank approaches. Underlying the debate was the desire of all concerned to make the best of ground and weapons

---

NOVEMBER COMPANY ORAL ORDERS
Delivered by Maj Dick Connors, OC N Coy 3 RCR, 242205

1. Situation
  a. *En Forces:* 1 GTD is advancing steadily EAST to WEST hard on the heels of a withdrawing U.S. Force.
  b. *Friendly Forces:* 4 CMBG is deployed to stop the enemy advance; 3 RCR left, 1 R22eR right.
  c. *Atts and Dets:* In loc G11 (FOO from A Bty 1 RCHA)
                      5B (FC from Mor Pl)
                      2 sect, Aslt Pnr Pl
                      4 and 5 sect, Armd Def Pl
                      1 and 2 Tp, B Sqn RCD
                      72 C, 72 D, AD Tp, 1 RCHA

2. Mission
Coy will def assigned sector from 250300 Jun.

3. Execution
  a. *General Outline:* Two pls up, left 1 Pl, right 3 Pl, in depth 2 Pl. Coy def posn centred on BLICKHEIM RIDGE WEST of FÖRCH facing east. B Sqn will superimpose its fire on our layout. We will provide intimate support to a B Sqn ambush in FAVORITE.
  b. *1 Pl*
      (1) *Grouping:* In loc 4 sect, Armd Def Pl
                    72 C, 72 D, AD Tp
                    FC
      (2) *Task:* Left forward pl, sector and arcs as laid out on our recce.
  c. *2 Pl*
      (1) *Grouping:* Det one sect to under comd 1 Tp, B Sqn in FAVORITE initially.
      (2) *Task:* Depth pl, sector and arcs as laid out on our recce. Be prepared to conduct local counter-attacks into 4 or 6 Pl sector on order.
  d. *3 Pl*
      (1) *Grouping:* In loc 5 sect, Armd Def Pl.
      (2) *Task:* Right forward pl, sector and arcs as laid out on our recce.

available, always remembering that other arms were nearby in support. At a personal level, each platoon commander cared for his command, even haggling with a colleague to avoid becoming overstretched, always remembering their men would not forgive them for overlooking their best interests.

"You're stretching me a bit thin down there, sir," the newest joined subaltern felt bound to complain, to be countered by Lieutenant Leach with the standard retort of an older hand: "Welcome to Europe!"

It was nearly dark when they started, and progress was retarded despite a moon in its second quarter. But by the time he was done, each of his subordinates had a fair idea of the terrain he must defend and the overriding overlap of arcs of fire demanded of the Carl

---

- e. *Coy HQ:* Dig in at assigned location.
- f. *2 Sect, Aslt Pnr Pl:* Assist dig-in of Coy HQ. Assist pls in prep of obs and fd defences.
- g. *Arty:* FOO, c/s C11, will be with me.
- h. *Coord Instrs*
    - (1) *Timings:* Main body arr def posn from 2315 hours.
    - (2) *Moves:* Under comd 2ICs at each level, the move forward has already commenced.
    - (3) *Fire Plan:* FOO will brief pl comds in their location. FPFs on my command only.
    - (4) *Pris Of Work:*
        - (a) Fire trench for every man to stage II.
        - (b) Protective minefields.
        - (c) Clearing arcs of fire.
        - (d) Dig to stage III.
    - (5) *Deception/Concealment:* Posn will be occupied at ni. No use of white li.

4. Service Support
- a. *Ammo:* 2 x maintenance ld of HMG and 84 mm HEAT to be delivered to pl posns ASP.
- b. *Feeding:* Commence hard rations on arrival on site. No fires. Tactical feeding when possible.
- c. *Med:* Ambulance w/Coy HQ; Med A to recce routes to UMS.
- d. *Def Stores:* Start w/basic ld; additional revetting materials will fol as time and tac sit permit. Make max use of locally aval materials.

5. Command and Signal
- a. Coy HQ GR
- b. Radio silence broken on contact only. Lift on order c/s 0.
- c. Each pl to maintain a runner at Coy HQ until line is laid.
- d. *Passwords:* Issued with SOI.
- e. *Nicknames:* Ambush position around old castle FAVORITE is OLD KNIGHT.

Gustavs and the HMGCs, besides the hides for M113s and where the heavy supporting weapons would move in. That done, he paused for reflection before the next move, checking each subordinate's plan and making adjustments; also searching out Captain Pat Kendal, his FOO, who was studying a patch of shrubbery within No. 1 Platoon's proposed position on the left flank, and reaching agreement with the platoon commander as to the sort of protection it might be given if he chose it as a hide for his OP party.

Together, Connors and Kendal walked down to the road where, at any moment, they expected to meet Tinker as he, too, toured his battle group sector, interrogating each subordinate commander in turn and tightening up the co-ordination of effort between flanking sub-units. Connors still had to liaise with the OC of the neighbouring Vandoos combat team on his right, but had to abandon the idea in the realization that he might well fail to find him in the dark and could thus waste precious time. In any case, he was not averse to sitting by the roadside mulling over matters with Kendal, smoking a cigarette and drinking coffee brewed by the gunner's driver. So absorbed had they become in the formulation of plans, they scarcely noticed the changing scene and heightening of tension around them. Suddenly, the distant flash of battle contrasted more sharply with the gloom of the night. At the same time, the noise of gunfire became subordinate to the rumble of traffic on nearby roads. All at once they became aware that the narrow secondary road running through their sector was alive with traffic – some of it, the civilian kind, bearing lights; the rest, US military traffic, blacked out; all of it pressing away from the battle. This was a population and an army in doubt and retreat, one that threatened to choke the roads. With foreboding, they asked themselves what might be the result of this westward moving traffic heading into the main stream of 4 CMBG which, at that moment, was starting to drive in the opposite direction?

What adjustments to plan might be necessary, Connors asked himself, if his company arrived late or if some never got through at all before the enemy presented himself at Favorite? Pursuing that gloomy, but not invalid, train of thought, he began to assemble in his mind the order of priorities appropriate to specific tasks within his position – assessing which sector must be occupied by the first arrivals and which could be left until the appearance of late-comers; adjusting his thoughts to what might be necessary or subject to re-adjustment if less time than planned was left available for digging-in.

THE FIRST DAY

Would he, under those circumstances, for instance, dare let the infanteers fight from their M113s, hoping against hope that the carrier's thin armour would provide adequate protection against a storm of artillery fire? Probably not, but they'll have to dig mighty fast.

The sounds of trucks approaching and the sight of Tinker's tall silhouette stepping out of a Jeep put an end to his reverie. He was back with the present, explaining his intended deployment and entering into a debate, in which Linkman was intimately involved, concerning the method of defending the obstacle in front of Favorite.

"It'd be easy and a lot less risky to leave the wood unoccupied and no short-range fire into Förch where the obstacle crosses the road," admitted Connors, "but I don't reckon that meets the aim to slow them down, eh? OK, Pat Kendal can pound hell out of the place, but they'll clear the mines and soon fill in any crater the sappers blow there, easy as pie. So I want to make 'em pay for it – buy perhaps an hour by hitting whatever turns up first. See?"

"So what d'you propose, Dick?" asked his CO.

Connors directed the answer more at Linkman than Tinker. "I want to put a troop and a section in Favorite to shoot into Förch for as long as they can stay. I've looked at it, Ian, and there's some fine wide paths and tracks through which the tanks can get back, without being seen, into the main position."

"I've looked, too," said Linkman. "Matter of fact I think you're right. So smile! I'll do as you want and, of course, one of your sections is essential to act as escort there until we abandon the position. I think, Colonel," he went on, addressing Tinker, "that the contribution the Vandoos company in Kuppenheim makes becomes all the more important. I know they have only a limited view through the orchard across the front towards Förch, but I do hope you'll try to impress on them how important their role is, particularly since the Reserve Demolition lies within their boundaries."

"Well that's where I'm going next," said Tinker. "It cuts both ways, of course. They'll expect you two to back them up from the higher ground here. Right. Dick, I've nothing more to say about your layout, except I want you to have two, not one, TOWs pointing out towards Kuppenheim. You'll get a useful long-range shot there and the Vandoos will expect it of you."

They went on to check the gunner plan and minor details, and then drove off towards the boundary with the Vandoos, travelling

THE FIRST DAY

via the track junction which had been designated as a junction point and which, if all was in order, would be held by a section of D Squadron RCD's Lynx command and reconnaissance vehicles.

B Squadron Combat Team

Ian Linkman had been engaged in a juggling act from the outset, endeavouring to keep his squadron of Leopard tanks intact in a balanced posture commensurate with the conflicting demands of the anticipated tactical situation (as he and his CO, Brian Cowdray, envisaged it), without appearing to deny the infantry the direct help they so fervently requested for survival. Nothing would be easier than to abdicate control of his troops by giving one to each company. Nothing, in his opinion, would contribute more surely to the collapse of the anti-armour plan through a failure to use the main anti-armour weapons – the Leopards and the TOWs – concentrated. His resistance to suggestions by Connors that tank troops should be tied to infantry localities had, he guessed, sown seeds of mistrust that he might leave them in the lurch. It was partly as a concession to erase that impression that he had permitted a troop to be deployed initially in the exposed Favorite position.

As a matter of priority, Linkman was determined to dominate the ground, the enemy and, if necessary and possible, the activities of 3 RCR Battle Group. For a start, he intended to dictate to the enemy by engaging him at long range – a task which, paradoxically, must fall mainly to the Leopards (with their maximum effective range with 105 mm APFSDS out to 2400 metres). The TOWs (with a maximum 3750 metre range) would be sited to fire across the front but were unlikely, in any event, in the close country to the front to be able to track a moving target for sufficient time, in order to complete their engagement with a time of flight in excess of ten seconds. It was Linkman's intention, therefore, to encourage the Favorite troop to spring an ambush which would force the enemy to halt and deploy prematurely. Thereupon, he would pull the troop back to the crest and snipe at enemy armour closing in, taking on tanks rather than infantry carriers and leaving the latter to the artillery whose 95-pound projectiles would be effective on the more lightly-armoured BMPs. The Leopards would always fire from hull-down positions – either from behind the crest or from hollows and scrapes (improved where necessary by the bulldozer tank) on the forward slope – and always sited to enable each tank to move by a concealed route to a new location with a background of terrain or trees to make it more difficult for the enemy to spot them. On principle, Linkman aimed to baffle the enemy by presenting him with what appeared to be a plethora of assailants firing at a deadly and rapid rate. Realizing that the majority of engagements across this terrain would take place at less than 1000 metres, he reckoned to decimate the advancing host before the fighting had come close and simulate, too, greater strengths than he possessed. That way, there was a good chance that the enemy tanks would become separated from their BMPs before reaching the Canadian infantry, thus making it easier for the dug-in infantry to cope with the BMPs and their occupants. He nevertheless decided to detach his battle captain and one troop to Papa Company in the blocking role, anticipating an enhanced role for him in the future, and wishing to relieve the troop leader of distractions such as the need to dismount to attend O Groups and the like. Indeed, it was his intention to repossess that troop at the earliest opportunity, or, at least, ensure that when it was brought into action it would be alongside the rest of the squadron, operating under his control in support. The very thought of tanks coming into action in dribs and drabs was anathema to Linkman.

The framework of 3 RCR battle group's plan had taken shape. Only the strands of loose ends remained to be woven into the fabric of an interlocking pattern. Throughout the night, the Brigade Commander, the battle group and combat team commanders would circulate within their areas of responsibility improving schemes here, checking co-ordination there and, with the handful of subordinates present, putting on the final touches. The process of thought, reconnaissance, discussion, instruction and more thought would never stop, but would be valueless until the men arrived and commenced work. And had the planners but known it, there was every reason to be unsure, as the night progressed, when or in what order the troops would reach their release points at the end of the line of march. For in the dim moonlight on congested roads, occasionally lit by flares from searching, strafing aircraft, and filled by people on the move and under stress, not everything was going to plan.

Approach march

Throughout the 3 RCR assembly area a throb of engines disturbed the evening air as starters whirred, engines came to life and vehicles began to emerge from their hiding-places. Where previously the

Above: Approach march – a B Squadron Leopard passes 3 RCR M113s at the start point.

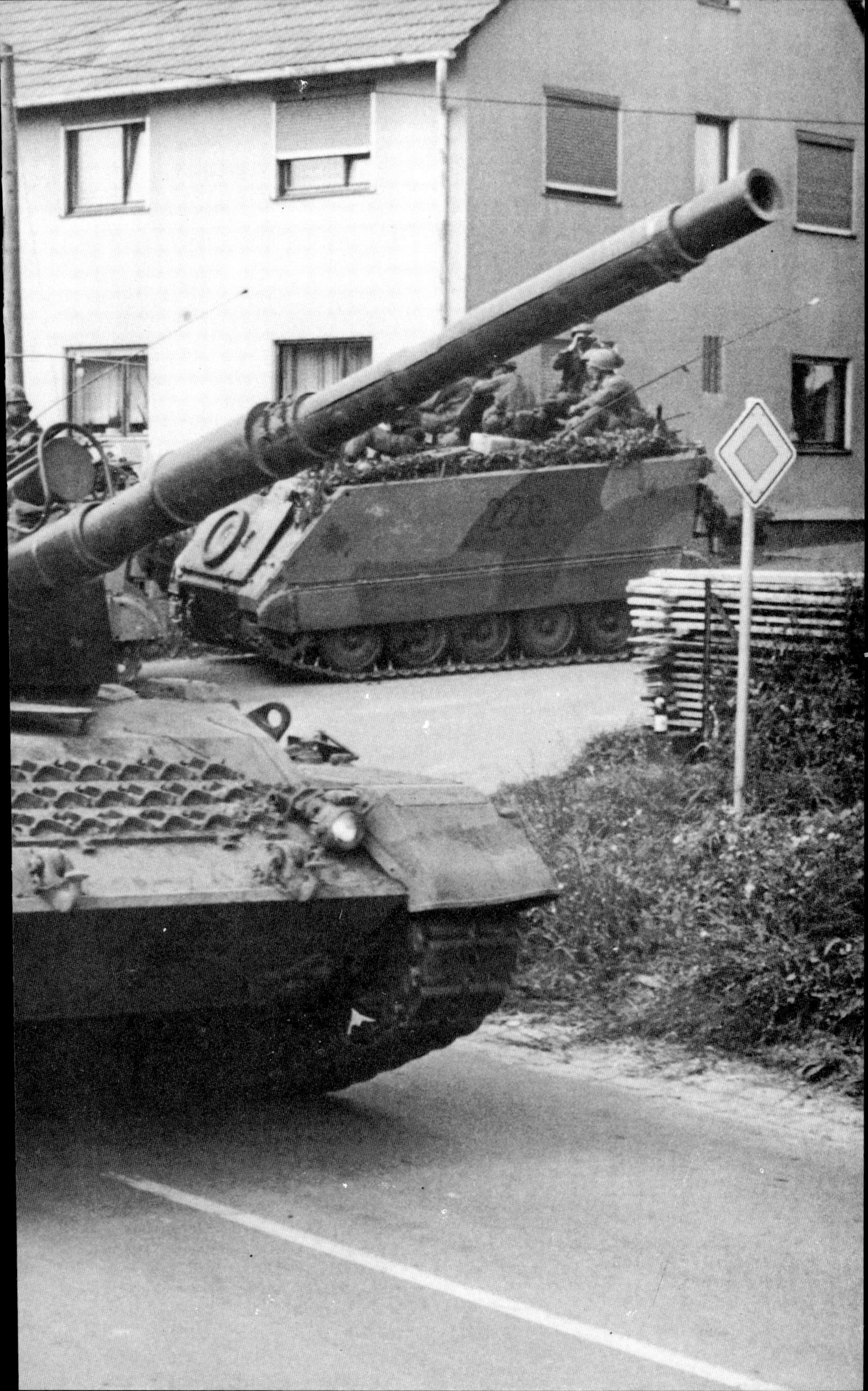

dispersed fighting machines had lain under camouflage, there now stood exposed a battle group in the open, cloaked only in darkness since, as the last shreds of light faded (and not a moment before) the crews had taken down and packed away the nets. Already, too, every item of kit had been stowed and, in many instances, men had entered their machines to settle down and grab what sleep they could. But in the majority of cases they stood around in groups, savouring the night air and delaying to the last their incarceration behind steel. Tension was rising quickly as the moment for approach to battle drew closer, and could be detected in some by a reflecting silence; in others by voices raised louder than usual and a tendency to quip or talk quickly.

B Squadron RCD's Battle Captain, Peter Cummings, sensed it as he lolled in the cupola at the head of the squadron, waiting to make for the battle group start point. He attempted to break the silence of 3 Troop leader, Lieutenant Ron Pike, with a question, ending in a chuckle.

"Nervous, Ron?" and got his reward.

"No worse than when they posted me to NDHQ!"

In the distance, the mutter of engines rose loudly, 4 CER were off and, away to the right, the Vandoos also were starting. Systematically, according to plan, companies, squadrons, batteries and platoons converged from their scattered hiding-places to assume the correct order of march at unit SPs before flowing, without halt, to the critical brigade SP where military police checked off each arrival against the movement order and, with shielded lights, waved it on its way. That was the easiest part of their task. Up ahead, the MPs knew, chaos beckoned. The reports coming back, even before the leading vehicle of 4 CER crossed the line, spoke eloquently of trouble caused by enemy-harassed, intermingled civilian and military traffic entangled at numerous points. But at first all went well. 4 CER, with attached trucks from 4 Service Battalion carrying mines, pressed steadily on, followed by the fighting vehicles of D Squadron RCD and Z Battery RCHA, the latter's long guns pointing threateningly ahead. Recce Platoons of 3 RCR and half of Mike Company had gone through the brigade SP before the first hesitations shunted their way backwards through the long column of evenly-spaced vehicles. And then the concertina effect took over.

Friction between a panicky German civilian and the other better-behaved members in a clutch of refugees trying to force their way through, had led to an attempt on his part to pass where no room existed. As the tail vehicles of 4 CER were clearing the outlying building of the village, a collision blocked the street. A fracas between the local police and the refugees delayed operations by a Canadian recovery vehicle to drag the wreckage aside. D Squadron RCD was forced to a halt, its battle captain stomping through the village to find out what the trouble was and to seek a way round. Twenty minutes elapsed before this impediment was removed and by then the traffic stream from both directions had throttled movement over a considerably wider area. As a result, the removal of the initial stoppage did not at once permit the original speed of advance by D Squadron and those behind. Within the first hour, the timetable of the original brigade movement order was 30 minutes in arrears. Nor was this the final stoppage. Frequently there were repetitions; inexorably 4 CMBG's Diamond Route was clogged while Club Route was only marginally affected. Anxiety at the higher levels of command was reflected by worry, irritation, and a downright sense of angry frustration among even the lowliest soldiers. Drivers' discipline was tried to the limit by the need to stop and start repeatedly, and by their endeavours to maintain distance so as to reduce the chances of harm from enemy aircraft which dropped flares and diligently sought to attack them at the roadside.

Here and there vehicles were damaged by air attacks. Occasionally they broke down, to be pulled off the road and repaired as soon as possible by first-line mechanics, as they arrived at the tail of each serial. Under radio silence, every communication had to be through personal contact. Often it was battalion or US MPs, driving up and down the shunting convoy, which located and unravelled local problems – chased off offenders who held up progress, reported trouble to unit vehicle mechanics, directed recovery teams and sought ways to bypass major blockages. It was due to one of their patrols that a diversion round one village was reconnoitred and found, and the German police persuaded to put a total stop to other traffic to allow the Canadians to use this important way round. Inevitably, the column began to break up into smaller packets, with the result that some vehicle commanders, who had not expected to lead the way, all at once found themselves presented with the task of map-reading through a detour for which they were not prepared. It did not worry Sergeant Al Hobbs of November Company when, suddenly, a US MP signalled him off the main road, telling him to

THE FIRST DAY

Approach march. **Right**, M113s of 3 RCR meet the vanguard of the refugees.
Bottom right, emergency repair to an M113.
Below, a Lynx of 3 RCR's recce platoon checking off arrivals at the release point.

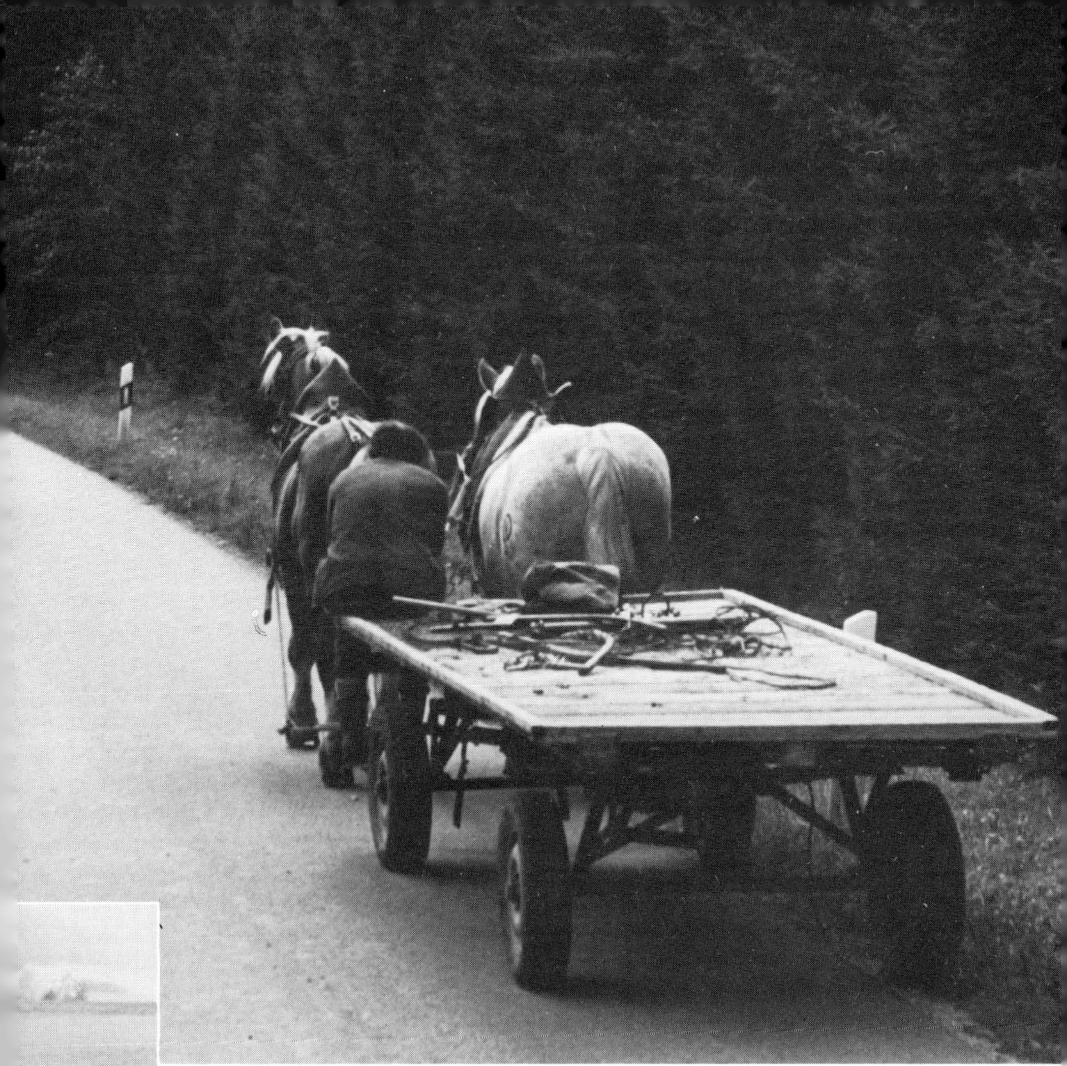
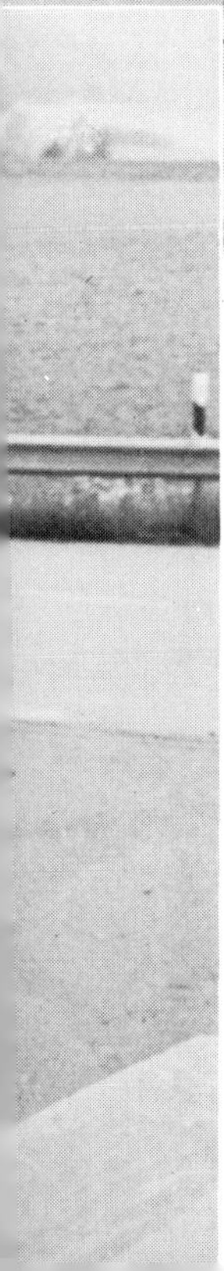
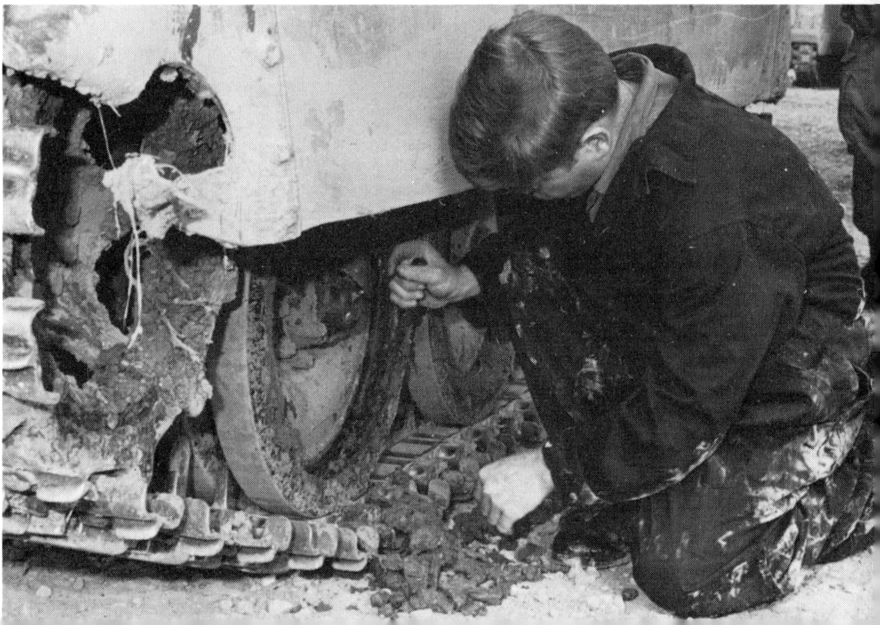

THE FIRST DAY

make his way through side tracks round the village. He merely nodded and studied the map. But a less well-trained Master Corporal Harry Benson, faced three minutes later with the same diversion, managed to get off course and end up at a dead end with six M113s behind him, they having followed him, sheep-like, without bothering to check the route on their own maps. The company sergeant-major, catching up with the wayward, had short, sharp and rude words to say to the unhappy Benson before guiding him back on course.

Improvisations regulated the night, as indeed they regulate nearly every operation of war once the planning is done. Travelling back to the battalion release point in order to watch the first of his men arrive, Tinker was met with the news (brought ahead by a messenger from the Recce Platoon) that delays and fragmentation to the combat teams must be expected. Platoons which should have put in an appearance at 2315, would be lucky if they showed by 0030 hours the next day. It was small comfort to be told that the sappers were about on schedule and that the RCD Reconnaissance Squadron would soon be taking up its screening positions on the far side of the autobahn. Tinker contemplated driving to the release point in search of fresh information, but rejected the notion for the same reason that he rejected the idea of sending a message warning his subordinates about the impending trouble. Both rejections were for the same reason; there was nothing to be gained by either act and, in any case, he knew his subordinates well enough to guess that they would pull out every stop to overcome their difficulties – present or future. So Tinker sat down to sweat it out and was later joined in his meditations by combat team commanders who had come to meet their men.

Hours passed slowly. The noise of aircraft superimposed on the rumble of traffic coming from the east symbolized two of the main threats to 3 RCR's carefully laid plans. Whenever something was heard approaching from the west, their expectations rose. But it was not until 0100 hours that the first Lynxes of the Reconnaissance Platoon roared up, dust flying from their tracks as drivers endeavoured to catch up on lost time. Captain Gordon Truman offered a brief explanation of the state of the battle group, as reported to him when he passed through the brigade release point. As rapidly, the CO presented him with details of his next task, which was to man the release point and assist with the battle group's dispersal off the line of march, prior to assuming the Reconnaissance Platoon main task of

THE SECOND DAY

manning junction points on the flanks of the Group. Bit by bit the rest of the Group began to arrive – Mike Company intact, but some 15 minutes behind the Reconnaissance Platoon, the Mortar and Armoured Defence Platoons somewhat jumbled up due to the need, at one point on the line of march, to go cross-country around a traffic jam; the Pioneers and Oscar Company in a well-ordered block, but with a couple of TOW 113s somehow intermingled with them.

Then November Company's Command M113 and nearly a platoon's worth of carriers which had stuck together before the rest lost their way, and a long gap before the roar of Leopards could be heard coming up the road.

Dick Connor's heart sank. He had sympathized with the other company commanders faced with the task of sorting out fragmented columns, but at least they were now nearly all complete and smugly leading their vehicles from the vicinity of the release point to the staging assembly area each had settled upon, adjacent to their operational sector. Apparently two-thirds of his lot were missing and nobody was too sure where they were. He had in mind several choice words to greet the platoon WOs concerned, but, as of then, elected to make the best of it – taking forward the first arrivals (fortunately, 2 Platoon which he had nominated for the depth position and as the provider of a section to initially hold Favorite). He left his unhappy and blasphemous 2IC to send on the rest as and when they arrived. It was at least heartening to see Ian Linkman welcoming a squadron that was complete except for one tank broken down; to have the Dragoons' assurance (perhaps pompously) that he would hold the front while Connors sorted himself out; and watch the Leopards moving purposefully to their preliminary assembly area for topping-up with fuel.

Time was pressing. When Papa Company rolled in, there was but 30 minutes to first light and still only stragglers of November Company had turned up, each vehicle having to be extracted from the sub-unit it had become intermingled with and sent its separate way towards its destination on the right flank. Connors cursed his luck and blessed the Reconnaissance Platoon for the assistance it gave in shepherding individual carriers forward.

Ian Linkman, meanwhile, was regretting having not brought his troop officers with him at the outset. His predilection for keeping troops intact now meant that the orders he gave would have to be hurried. Each troop leader must be despatched to his battle station

THE SECOND DAY

without the opportunity for careful joint study of the ground. In fact, it transpired better than he hoped. He had completed his orders before 0245 hours and was personally able to lead the entire squadron (less 4 Troop which was to remain behind with Papa Company), to cover the crest overlooking Favorite, shortly before 0315. This gave him the opportunity to describe the ground as first light began to reveal their future battle ground. Inevitably, now, the position would have to be occupied in daylight, thus exposing much to the enemy. But really that had always been likely and, in any case, the intensive activity of the sappers burying mines along the obstacle would leave the enemy in no doubt concerning their opponents' intention to stand and fight between Blickheim and Kuppenheim. Furthermore, early morning mist cloaked the valley and fingered the slope. The best any of the combat team commanders could hope to achieve in the way of surprise rested on the ability of their men to

---

CONTROLLING FACTORS

★ The need for all commanders to think 'two down' while formulating plans.

★ The desirability of deploying under cover of darkness if possible.

★ The need to take account of attempted disruption by enemy action behind the lines, and by refugee traffic jams, when planning troop movements.

★ The necessity of maintaining security precautions until the last moment before moving off.

★ The advantages of following the standard drill, as much as is practical, in order to simplify execution of orders and to reduce the chances of misunderstanding.

★ The need for forethought in administrative matters. The importance of such matters as traffic control, protection on the line of march and recovery drills.

★ The need to maintain radio silence as a contribution to security.

★ The need for all vehicle commanders to follow the route on the map and not fall into the error of merely following the next vehicle ahead.

★ The likelihood that the initial plan will break down under pressure, and therefore, a readiness to improvise.

★ The obligation to refuel once the march is complete.

★ The vital necessity to feed well, keep dry and warm and to rest as much as possible. Failure to observe these requirements tends to undermine morale which will lower resistance to fear in the face of an enemy who will do all he can to induce that effect.

THE SECOND DAY

enter their positions with the minimum fuss, to hide themselves and their vehicles carefully and to distract enemy attention with dummy positions. But before creating dummies, every effort had to be spent constructing the real thing. As it grew lighter, with first light at 0330 hours, the fields overlooking the plain of Rastatt were the scenes of toil — men and machines digging for their very lives in the dedicated endeavour to get below ground level and hidden from view in a fighting posture, before the enemy put in an appearance.

Meanwhile post-march maintenance took precedence in temporary assembly areas where vehicles were concealed as soon as they arrived. Trucks of the Echelons moved jerkily from vehicle to vehicle, filling each up from pods or containers. Commanders reported their arrival to HQs and made requests for such BLUEBELL assistance as was needed to rectify mechanical troubles. Those who got in early had time to have a meal of bacon, eggs and coffee; the late arrivals were lucky to get a snack from a can. Fitness for battle overrode all other considerations, and now even the most careless soldier required only a hint of supervision to make him give his best. For the dawn chorus this day was the spur to action; there was intense air activity right overhead, as the Russians began to accelerate an advance (which had made distinct headway during the night) and advertised their intentions by a searching reconnaissance of the way ahead.

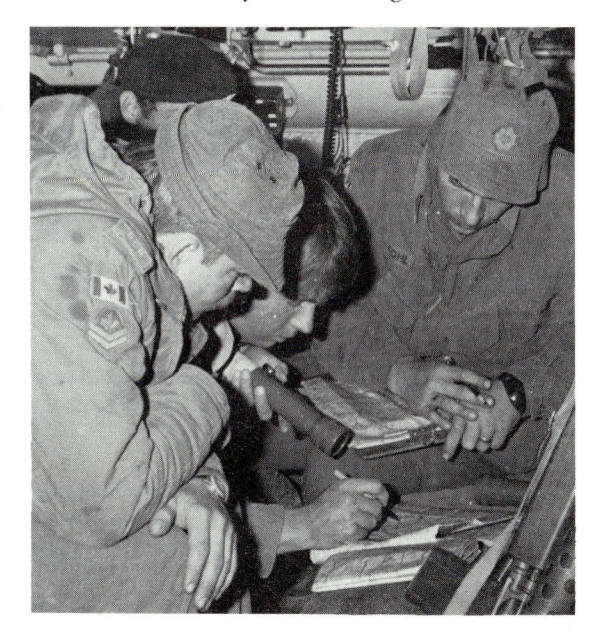

Left: Night planning: a platoon commander briefs his section commanders inside an M113.

THE SECOND DAY

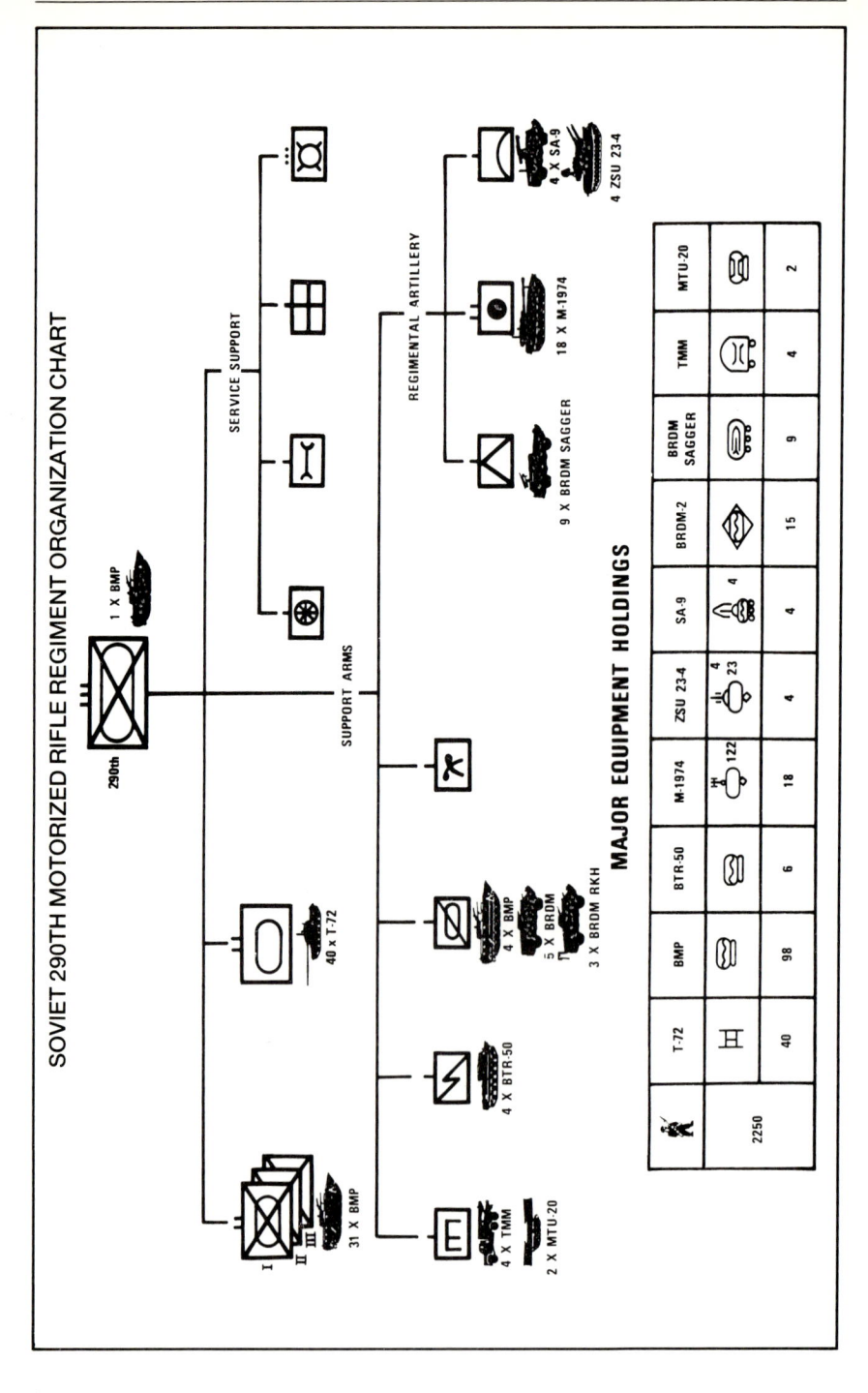

SOVIET 290TH MOTORIZED RIFLE REGIMENT ORGANIZATION CHART

- 290th
- 1 X BMP
- 40 X T-72
- 4 X BTR-50
- 31 X BMP
- I, II, III
- 4 X BMP
- 5 X BRDM
- 3 X BRDM RKH
- 4 X TMM
- 2 X MTU-20
- 9 X BRDM SAGGER
- 18 X M-1974
- 4 X SA-9
- 4 ZSU 23-4

SERVICE SUPPORT
REGIMENTAL ARTILLERY
SUPPORT ARMS

MAJOR EQUIPMENT HOLDINGS

T-72	BMP	BTR-50	M-1974	ZSU 23-4	SA-9	BRDM-2	BRDM SAGGER	TMM	MTU-20
40	98	6	18	4	4	15	9	4	2

2250

80

4 | 1st Guards Tank Division advances

Vladimir Oblensky had grabbed as much sleep as he could that night, in the certain knowledge that it would be a scarce commodity in the days to come and in the hope that his 290th MRR would not suddenly be called upon to vacate its hide. But being held in reserve had its advantages, the Colonel reflected when he entered the command post to hear reports of the night's events. That way he might acquire a useful feel of the battle which had developed when the leading tank regiments of 1st GTD attacked, and save himself mistakes when his turn came. It could even be that those tank regiments would do so well they would actually seize the outer defences of the Bühl Plateau and save him the trouble. What his operations officer reported, however, made him reject that notion and even regret he had not spent another half hour in bed. For the news was not brilliant. The Motor Rifle Divisions in the line had failed to make the progress expected of them. Enemy resistance had been more tenacious; a belt of demolitions had caused traffic delays in the dark, and cross-country movement at night had not proceeded smoothly (officers and men seemed to have lost the panache exhibited in peace-time exercises). So the tank division was compelled to fight its way out instead of entering an undefended void. As a result, the start time for 302nd and 303rd Tank Regiments had been delayed until 0400 hours to enable them to make fresh arrangements – and the Army Commander sounded as if he were displeased.

Throughout the morning, Oblensky and, some two miles distant, his colleague commanding 301st Tank Regiment, Colonel Pavel Podduyev, listened on the command radio link to remarks of comrades at the front. Gradually, as they studied the stream of reports, a pattern of events began to emerge, one which soon would be recognizable on the ground when, later that morning, Samsonov came on the air in person, ordering 290th MRR to leave its hiding place and advance according to plan. Oblensky was glad to go, if only because of the rooted belief shared by many Soviet commanders that, with the ever-present threat of nuclear attack by the enemy, the farther one was separated from the front the greater the chance of becoming a target. Therefore, the closer one hugged the enemy, the better.

Oblensky led the way, seeking to make contact at the earliest moment with the commander of 302nd Tank Regiment through whose sector he was to attack. The journey towards Rastatt was of absorbing interest, carrying him through territory so recently hard fought for by the Motor Rifle Divisions and into the wake of the tank regiments where, but a few hours before, they had begun to roll over the Americans. Except the term "roll over" had now to be qualified. By the carnage to be seen on the ground, where the Americans had

Below: O Group – Red Army style.

THE SECOND DAY

fought so hard, it was plain that the attackers had far from had it all their own way. Although there was ample evidence of enemy casualties in the shape of wrecked vehicles, destroyed guns and unburied dead, strewn all about among shattered towns and villages, splintered copses and beaten down crops, there lay in view far more numerous examples of Soviet losses. Almost everywhere he looked, Oblensky saw crippled or burnt-out Red Army vehicles and guns in considerable quantities. At a modest estimate he put the exchange rate at five to one against his own side. Here and there it was not just a few of the leading tanks or infantry carriers knocked out, but what looked like entire companies caught in the open and annihilated. In places, it was encouraging to see the devastation caused by his own side's intense concentrations of artillery fire and observe the dejected demeanour of American prisoners being marched back, but it was all too clear that the price paid by the Red Army was higher than expected. Furthermore, the closer he came to the front (in terrain which had not been defended with the same determination as that to the east), the more it became obvious that, in withdrawal, the Americans were offering a defiance which could easily impact upon his own immediate plans.

Traffic was not flowing smoothly due to numerous diversions imposed along the route. Bypassing was frequent where the enemy still resisted, or to get around cratered roads, blown bridges or uncleared minefields. Oblensky worried about the movement of his regiment and its attendant echelon when they came to negotiate the zone of demolition the enemy had left behind. He also began to ask himself to what sort of shape 302nd Tank Regiment was now reduced. For as he progressed, he could not help but count the number of tanks out of action by the wayside and register signs of continuing battle for fortified villages on either flank from which hostile fire was still being directed. The tank spearhead might be several miles further on, but its base was insecure. The commander of the 302nd, whom he found at Seltz engaged in speaking in strong terms over the radio to his leading battalion commander, was brief in explaining what had happened. The Americans, he said, had removed their main forces but left behind a rearguard which fought sporadically from within the many villages dotting the countryside. Since these villages controlled the network of roads (which, itself, had been blocked in many places by demolitions and mines), and harboured long-range anti-tank weapons which harassed – some-

THE SECOND DAY

The punch of a Soviet Motorised Rifle regiment. **Top**, self-propelled armoured artillery. **Bottom**, a T72 tank with 125mm gun.

times dominated – the ground in between, it was impossible to ignore them totally. Many could be bypassed by moving cross-country, and left to the follow-up forces, but some had to be captured. That, as Oblensky appreciated, meant committing infantry, and since a tank regiment possessed but a single battalion, the infantry element was soon used up in these circumstances. Fire-power had done much to help him blast a way through, but, with heavy expenditure, the supply of ammunition would not last forever if roads were blocked. "We will be at the autobahn by 1500 hours if we are lucky," the tank regiment commander stated, "and then it is all yours! And then too, I suppose, your stuff coming through will prevent my supply platoon moving and I will be grounded even longer."

"And then too," added Oblensky, "Podduyev and his 301st Tank Regiment will be coming along – so do not complain. You can take a rest and your artillery can do a little shooting on our behalf. Now let us get down to basics. Tell me what you know about the ground beyond the autobahn and how the enemy seem to be working things. Tell me about the enemy helicopters. I think I saw several of your tanks looking as if they had been hit by guided missiles and I saw one or two of their helicopters as well as ours crashed."

They got down to integrating their plans as the noise of battle spread around them. Meanwhile, the 302nd's staff listened to reports coming in by radio from a reconnaissance BRDM catching its first sight of the autobahn; and an excited tank battalion commander endeavouring to cajole and bully one of his companies to move across open ground despite the attention of a couple of TOW Cobras which had just hit one of his T72s. This in no way distracted Oblensky from the task confronting him. And even if it had, the dramatic arrival of the divisional commander would have dispelled it. Samsonov was all retribution and fire, and the first to feel his wrath was the tank commander whose progress, it seemed, had not matched the desires of Samsonov, the Army Commander or the Supreme Council in the Kremlin – or wherever they happened to be just then. Having delivered himself of a cutting reproof, he swung on Oblensky. He had watched the 290th MRR "wending its way", as he put it. In fact, he had come upon it halted in a traffic jam caused by an American tank which had emerged unexpectedly from behind a barn, deep in the Red Army's rear, and which had shot up several vehicles before escaping into a nearby village which apparently still harboured an aggressive resistance.

THE SECOND DAY

"Go on like this", said Samsonov, "and you will not reach Bühl in a week, let alone this afternoon. Let me tell you, Oblensky, either you are there on time or I fear for you. Whether or not the 302nd Tank Regiment reaches the autobahn by the time your leading battalion at last arrives, you will attack at once and you will be in Iffezheim by midnight. Is that clear?"

CONTROLLING FACTORS

★ The enemy will also have his problems such as:
- traffic delays;
- upsets to plan due to unexpected fierce resistance and lay-back patrols;
- breakdowns in communication;
- fears of nuclear retribution as a counter to success by conventional operations;
- hampering of armoured operations due to lack of infantry support;
- paucity of information if our security is good.

★ He can be expected to attempt to roll over opposition regardless of loss.

Below: Infantry supplementing the sappers' task by minelaying in the dark.

5 | *Digging in*

The arbiters of indirect fire had been in consultation on the outskirts of Blickheim, staking out their claims and rehearsing their reactions to the situations which might arise when the enemy appeared. Confident that the weapons whose fire they would direct were already in readiness (although in the case of the Howitzers, some 6 kilometres to the rear, not yet completely dug-in up to their track tops), they had no difficulty settling their personal arrangements. It boiled down to this. The BC insisted upon overall surveillance across the entire sector to make full use of his guns' performance, with emphasis upon long range with a good view in the direction of Förch and Favorite. Therefore, he had Captain Angus Scott dig in his OP atop the slope at the rearward end of the village, with remote cable laid to his M113 in rear. This satisfied his main requirements even though it forfeited observation closer-in and would not grant full benefit at night to his NOD, with its limited 1500-metre range, which could be easily cut to less than 500 by smoke, dust or mist.

Sergeant Bud Roach enjoyed a measure of priority over his fellow FC located on the left flank, for whereas the FC with Mike Company would have to spread the fire of four 81 mm mortars to cover the frontage of Blickheim, Roach had virtually the exclusive use of the other four to support November Company. Dug-in on the right of 1 Platoon, he was able to see across the front towards Blickheim besides having a good view of the obstacle to his front and even a sight of Förch. Move across the road to his right and he could cover the approaches to Kuppenheim. Roach would fill a gap in surveillance, close in, and engage local targets close to the forward edge of battle – infantry dismounting from carriers and patrols trying to infiltrate. Scott, on the other hand, would range across a wider panorama, seeking primarily to engage the enemy in his assembly areas and FUPs. But while the guns Scott controlled lay back in depth, the mortars were tucked in close behind the crest and more

THE SECOND DAY

vulnerable to counter-battery fire than their bigger sisters. So each baseplate position, as laid out by the 2IC of Mortar Platoon, comprised four alternative locations – three in the open from which fire would be opened only once, and one that was to be as near permanent as possible, dug-in with ammunition dumped nearby. Both Roach and Scott, however, were responsible to a central agency, the FSCC, where Major Pat Vivier, the BC, presided in consultation with Tinker.

And Pat Vivier, at that moment, was a slightly worried man since an ammunition shortage was threatened – information he passed in strict confidence to his FOOs. The ammunition dumping programme had slipped behind schedule. Traffic congestion which had hindered troop deployment had also held up the truck convoy, and the first loads would not begin to arrive at the gun pits until 1500 hours. It would be touch-and-go. Some sort of restriction on ammunition expenditure might be imposed, but Scott decided not to pass the news at once to Panton when he got back to Blickheim, because he guessed the infantryman had problems enough of his own.

This was not entirely true, since Panton, at midday, was reasonably content with his lot. The men had worked well. All the M113s had been parked in the shelter of houses, but placed with the intention of letting them shift quickly if the need arose. 50-cal guns were dismounted and dug in, defiladed from the front so as to engage enemy at short range in the flank. Carl Gustavs and M72s were distributed among the weapon pits which, on the perimeter, were dug-in beyond the buildings. Defence stores, which he had requisitioned earlier, had been delivered and were being incorporated in the defences. Anti-personnel and anti-tank mines were now being laid in limited quantities a hundred metres out to the flank where they might best hinder a debussing enemy. Wire was used to block approaches to the eastern apex of the village while, inside, weapon pits were dug in gardens. Some cellars and buildings were linked by tunnelling and those cellars strengthened to withstand bombardment were converted to shelter stores, ammunition and communications equipment. The specialist sappers had let their imaginations and training rip in showing how best to collapse walls in a way to form barriers blocking off access to the enemy. They also supervised measures to reduce fire risk and shut off water to minimize the flooding of cellars. Main electrical power had already failed, but the local telephones

THE SECOND DAY

were still in operation and being used by Panton to speak to platoon commanders. 3 RCR's pioneers had worked strenuously, leaving the preparation of their own shelters in the village centre to last (where they would act as a reserve), and even now were industriously helping the riflemen lay mines. If the time had been available, Panton would have liked to drop some of the fruit trees to improve the field of fire to the flanks. As it was, the chain saws were mainly in use among the houses and cutting down trees close by.

Panton had been everywhere directing his officers, setting an enthusiastic example to everybody and encouraging them to use ingenuity. Frequently he spoke to his men, endeavouring to stiffen their resolve at the same time as checking that work was being carried out sensibly.

"How are you getting along with the civilians?" he asked Master Corporal Fred Terry, who was building an alternative trench for use if he decided to change position with his Carl Gustav to the right flank section in 1 Platoon.

"OK, sir. In fact, mighty helpful. Couple of 'em helped build

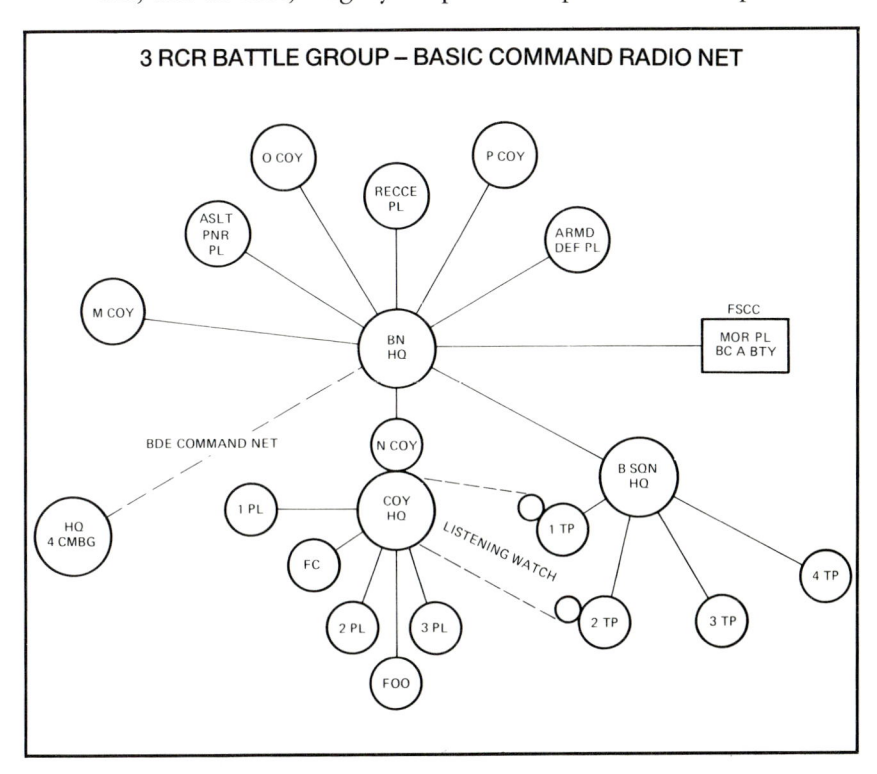

3 RCR BATTLE GROUP – BASIC COMMAND RADIO NET

THE SECOND DAY

that trench over there. Dragged in timber from all over the place. They're back in the 113 now giving a hand with the grub."

"Well, fine," said Panton, without giving away his doubts. "Though remember, they're in dead trouble breaking the rules of war, y'know if they're caught by the Russians helping you. Matter of fact, you've got a spy living with them. They say somebody was flashing a light just before dawn and thought it might be signalling. Don't overdo that sort of latrine rumour stuff, Terry, but keep your

Right: Digging in stony ground can be tough going; but when your life depends on it you work like fury. Sometimes, if the infantry is lucky, mechanical diggers are provided.

THE SECOND DAY

eyes open!"

"Will do sir," replied Terry. "Maybe it's 2 Platoon who are best off, though. Have you heard they've got the village nymphomaniac living among 'em, eh? Causing all sorts of interest, might even stop the war?"

Panton laughed but made a note to investigate. Never a spoilsport, Panton was acutely conscious that even his company contained its share of characters whose dedication to duty was not

THE SECOND DAY

always one hundred per cent. He had to be sure the handful of civilians remaining did not pose a threat to security in any form.

For physical reasons, the problems of November Company bore little resemblance to those of Oscar. In place of buildings to adapt, Dick Connor's men had to contend with a mixture of tree roots and stony ground when they applied picks and shovels. Of civilians to help or hinder there were none, except for a faithful caretaker in Favorite who resolutely refused to leave. Sheep grazed among the labouring platoons, their population already diminished by the cooks who were at work among the nearby trees preparing a sumptuous hot stew for the noon meal. The midday situation, Connors was able to report to Tinker, as an anxious CO came up to enquire about his most unlucky company, was a lot better than at one time seemed possible. Nearly everybody had now arrived, including one M113 which had lost a track a couple of miles from the front and whose passengers had hitched lifts forward, carrying their weapons and tools. Naturally much remained to be done; a delayed start of three hours' duration, in some instances, could not be made up by work alone. But to save time, much useful material (particularly timber from the orchards and woods) was near at hand, and the pioneers had been hard at work with their chain saws supplying ready-cut supports. Furthermore, M113s fitted neatly into some of the small, deep hollows featured in the orchards and woods. This meant that they and their machine-guns could be kept close to, and in support of the trenches their passengers were digging while protected to some extent from the heavy artillery bombardment to be expected. Everyone was aware of the limitations of the carrier's armour, and yet the vehicle's fire-power and mobility were not to be dismissed as irrelevant. Meanwhile, the riflemen dug and dug and began to lay on SKOP kits (ribbed folding sheets) as the basis of overhead cover.

Ian Linkman took the opportunity to join Tinker and Connors in order to settle outstanding matters related to the anti-armour plan. Since agreeing to put a troop in Favorite, he had been developing in his mind a way to obtain full benefit from the ambush it would spring upon the enemy. He now needed the approval of both Tinker and Connors.

"The way I see it", he explained, "is like this. Normally I want to open fire at maximum range, as you both know. Here the ground, the orchards and Förch don't let me. OK, so we let the Russians get really close before opening up. That way we're not only sure of clobbering their leading vehicles first shot, but we might even encourage the rest of their leading group into coming into the open, letting us have a crack at the lot. So my plan, if you agree, Colonel, is to hold all fire with TOWs and tanks (including those with the Vandoos on the right) until the Russians hit the obstacle. Then we'll clean up! Only 1 Troop lets fly from Favorite and stays there until I reckon it's time to go. TOWs, 2 Troop and I can then open up from back there on the crest among the trees. Only then do the TOWs behind Blickheim and, if necessary, 3 Troop over there, join in, as can the tanks and TOWs from the Vandoos, all firing in enfilade. Course, if the Vandoos find the enemy having a crack at Kuppenheim first, they may have to blow the gaff earlier. But none of us seem to expect that, do we?"

In the brief debate which took place, Linkman's plan was agreed without dissent. Tinker not only undertook to co-ordinate its execution with the CO of the Vandoos (who was expected to agree), but contributed a couple of snipers from the Recce Platoon to, as he put it: "make life hard for any Russian snoopers who might try poking around in Förch and on the obstacle outside their vehicles". He also clarified the command demarcation, designating the Favorite position as the responsibility of Linkman's squadron.

Linkman could now complete his arrangements; driving in his Jeep from one location to another – satisfying himself that the four Leopards in Favorite and their attendant infantry section and snipers were fully concealed from the front, and yet so fitted-in among the trees that they could bring fire to bear with the minimum change of ground. Satisfying himself, too, that each troop commander was aware of the latest plan; that alternative positions and routes were reconnoitred and range cards prepared – even though few engagements above 1000 metres were expected. At each TOW position, the Armoured Defence Platoon Commander carried out the same procedure, noting at the same time the progress which had been made by each detachment to comply with that weapon's characteristics. Those which were dug-in (all but one, which, to satisfy Tinker's demand that full support must be given to the Vandoos, was left mobile on its M113 on the right, able to move to fire in any direction) had required extensive labour to fit in the weapon, in addition to making room for backblast and the desire to conceal their signature as much as possible. Master Corporal Gene Petrie with November Company, had found this difficult amid the confines of

THE SECOND DAY

the orchard behind Favorite, his essential requirement for a clear field of fire reaching to maximum range to the left across the frontal boundary of Blickheim, being inhibited by trees; and the insistence of Lieutenant Eddie Leach that, wherever he put himself, he must not advertise the infantry position by the TOW's distinctive, launching signature. As Petrie put it: "It's like this. Everybody loves me when the chips are down, but there ain't no seat at the table before the play begins. I know I'll be in for it if I don't dig in, but if I do, the arcs of fire are lousy, and what hope is there of getting somewhere else fast? But if I ask to stay in the 113 and move around, every company

Right: The well-concealed TOW mounted on its M113 providing the infantry battalion's principal anti-armour capability.

THE SECOND DAY

commander gets up on his hind legs and says that will be fatal. And anyway, he wants me close by! What the hell can a guy do?"

The dilemma posed to Blowpipe operators was even more acute, and Sergeant Eddie Blake was not alone among detachment commanders in practically going on bended-knee to find anywhere to go. In no way did Leach want this weapon, with its enormous signature, anywhere near his weapon pits, knowing, as he did, that, in the primary anti-helicopter role, it would likely be among the first to open fire and advertise its presence. Gunner Jake Martin felt like a pariah while the inhospitable debate went on over his head, and not

THE SECOND DAY

BLOWPIPE
Maximum standard intercept range	3,000 metres
Minimum range	400 metres
Basic ammunition load	8 per detachment
Aiming head weight	7.2 kilograms
Round of ammunition weight	14 kilograms

Above: The too-well-exposed Blowpipe waiting for the target.

in the least bit happy when told to take himself away in solitude to a lonely knoll, higher up the slope and slightly to a flank beyond the platoon area. Even if from there he had a superlative view of the arc in which his targets would probably appear, he felt naked and unsafe from lack of infantry to protect him – even though their arcs of fire actually criss-crossed the pit he dug for himself.

Returning from a successful visit to the Vandoos, whose CO had readily agreed to Linkman's ambush proposal at Favorite, Tinker was struck as he had been previously by the way so much was crowded onto the left flank of November Company's position and yet, paradoxically, the ease with which it might be infiltrated past its left flank in ground dead to Blickheim. It was true that the road leading from Favorite to Iffezheim would soon be barricaded by the abatis the sappers would make by dropping roadside trees across it; he was pleased indeed to see that this work was about to be put in

THE SECOND DAY + 12 HRS ON

hand by US Army engineers who had just arrived to reinforce 4 CMBG sappers who were mainly engaged on the obstacle. But there was no guarantee that the enemy would let the abatis remain long in place unless it was covered by fire. So now it was Tinker's turn to revise his plans by removing half the Recce Platoon from its task of flank protection and having it cover two gaps which worried him. Fire from the Lynxes might not be heavy, but the warning they should give could buy valuable minutes for blocking forces to react.

Thus it was with blocking in mind when he stopped off in Iffezheim on his way back to HQ 3 RCR in the Bannwald. The time was just past 1400 hours. Alan Ferrier's Papa Company and its attendant tanks of Lieutenant Phil Brown's 4 Troop looked snug in the village and nearby hides, their commanders answering positively to his close interrogation regarding their alternative tasks if the enemy broke through. That they would be needed soon he doubted not, and the latest Intelligence reports awaiting him at his command post at 1445 confirmed this. It was patently obvious that 4 CMBG stood right in the way of one, if not two, Soviet tank divisions. Fight as well as the Canadians would, past study indicated that the forces against them were not of the sort to fold-up at the first sign of resistance. 3 RCR Battle Group and the rest were in for a stiff fight, the outcome of which was anybody's guess.

CONTROLLING FACTORS

★ The importance of sub-unit commanders taking measures to improve surveillance and mutual support while the troops are in the process of implementing initial orders.

★ The vital importance of integrating the control of artillery and mortars at all levels of command – Observation and fire plans must be closely co-ordinated.

★ The limitations which can be imposed by the threat of an ammunition shortage – Many battles in the past have been lost from this cause (something that often goes unrecorded).

★ The many uses of wire and mines for close-in protection of defended localities.

★ The special measures associated with the fortification of houses.

★ The compromises required to fit weapons with a distinctive signature into concealed positions, notably tanks, TOWs and Blowpipes.

★ The need to co-ordinate with flanking formations and units to obviate weaknesses at junction points.

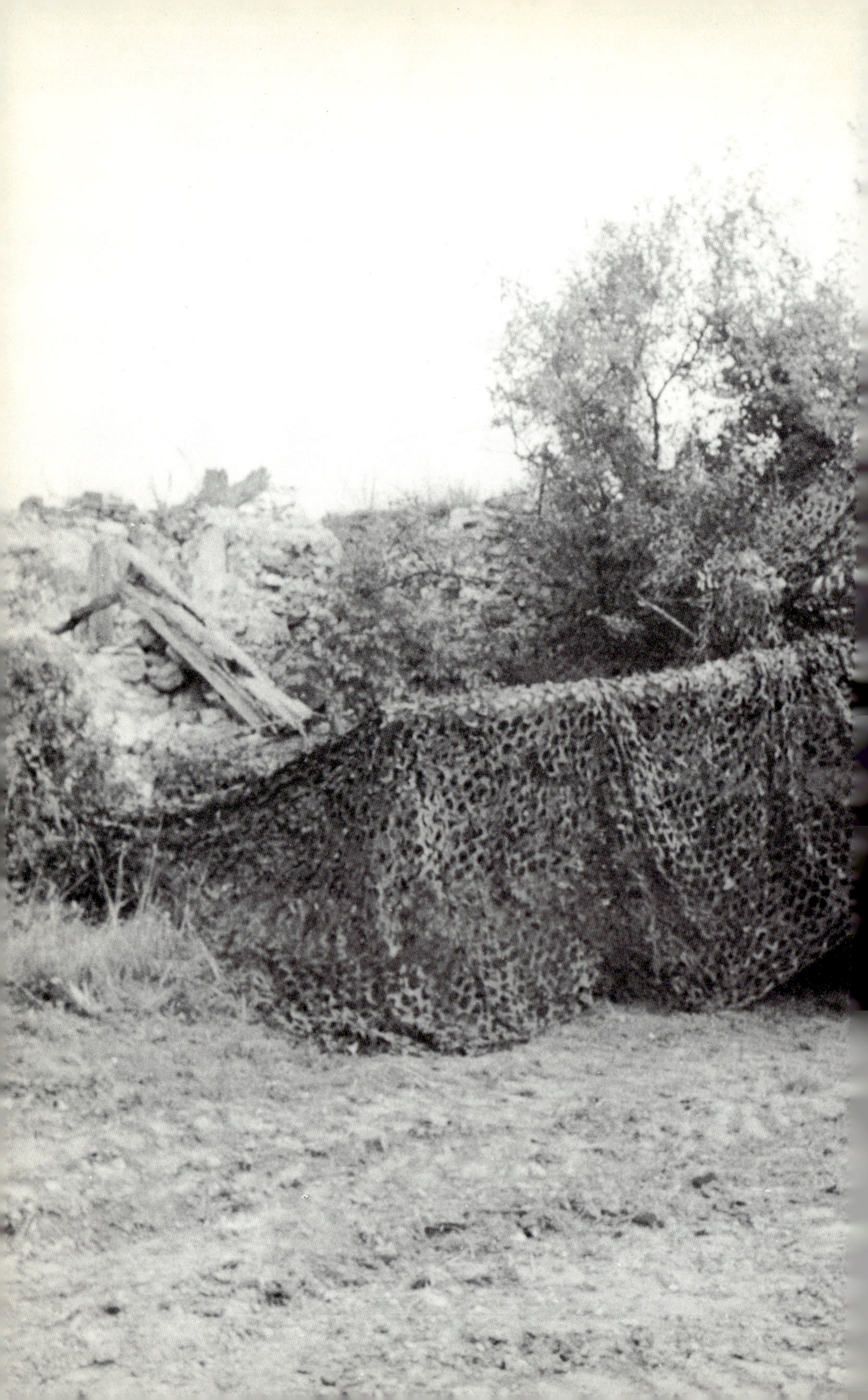

Camouflaging a Leopard among ruins and shrubbery. Complete concealment is almost impossible in the face of modern sensing equipment.

6 | Contact

The ambush
As Tinker was making the final adjustments to his plan and the Reconnaissance Platoon was redeploying to its new task (its wearied members cursing their luck at having to dig in afresh), watchers of the roads leading back from the East detected a subtle, but significant change in the pattern and nature of traffic. In place of a solid stream of administrative military trucks, there were now far more fighting vehicles, many of them combat-stained, while the proportion of intermingled civilian refugees dwindled to a trickle. Shortly before 1500 hours, movement through Förch dried up altogether, as the preliminary demolitions were blown; this meant that entry into 4

CMBG lines from the east would be restricted through the reserve demolition in front of Kuppenheim. The sappers were still putting the finishing touches to the minefield. But at 1515 hours, a series of sharp explosions reverberated along the front, and it was seen, as the smoke cleared, that craters had been blown in all the side roads and that the sappers were sowing them with anti-personnel and anti-tank mines to hinder attempts to clear the mines and repair the deep holes.

The firing of the demolitions seemed to act as a starting gun for the enemy attack on 4 CMBG. In fact, the US troops beyond the autobahn, apart from those left behind in scattered towns and villages (notably on the outskirts of Rastatt), had made quite a clean break from contact. Their rearguard was even then racing through the reserve demolition on the way to comparative safety – signs of strain on their faces. The company of US engineers who had been given the task of Demolition Guard, waved and shouted pleasantries as they passed. Thus D Squadron RCD, whose patrols with a FOO from Z Battery 1 RCHA lay in hiding beyond the autobahn, and whose attached section of Blowpipe AD missiles stood waiting on the autobahn itself, could now confidently expect the next arrivals, apart from stragglers and refugees, to be members of the Red Army.

Below: Kiowas at the ready for the first contact.

THE SECOND DAY + 12 HRS ON

Above: Kiowa in flight, nap of the earth, cautiously seeking a target.

The wait was of the shortest duration. With hardly a pause after the departure of a platoon of M60s, which had taken temporary post in this withdrawal covering the approaches to Sandweier, a tense voice came over the radio:

"Zero. This is Six. Contact! Wait! Out!" and a minute later confirmation of the grid reference and nature of enemy seen. Upon those who were monitoring the command net and heard these calls, the effect was both dramatic and executive. The pent-up expectation of action was released simultaneously with the automatic breaking of radio silence on 4 CMBG command net. From this moment, the tense reporting of enemy progress through the rear link of D Squadron would be overheard by everybody else on that frequency while, nearer the front, those who had a vital interest in picking up first-hand news switched to monitoring the forward link of D Squadron in order to read instantly the pace and direction of the enemy thrust as it pushed the Lynxes back. News of this crucial development soon reached the ears of the lowliest rifleman, for although radio silence remained in force on all the other channels, information could be passed rapidly by word of mouth among the combat teams, even when they did not have the use of the local telephone system as Oscar Company did.

In any case, signs of impending battle were almost immediately visible by activity beyond the front. Even if troops, who scanned the autobahn as if it were a frontier, had not seen the Reserve Demolition Guard taking cover, they could not help but notice a Kiowa helicopter suddenly hop up and skim at low level to hover behind cover, shifting its position from time to time as its crew searched ahead. There was also the sight of another little helicopter in the far distance, one which those with binoculars recognized as of Soviet design, probably a Hare. And after that, the flash of action as a larger helicopter, probably a Hind, was seen, its appearance greeted by the distinctive signature of a Blowpipe loosing off from the top of the autobahn, and the gratifying sight of the missile and aircraft converging with fatal consequences, and the Hind plunging to earth in flames.

"That'll discourage them," remarked Scott to his signaller in their hide on the higher ground behind Blickheim, and that, indeed was what the gunners had hoped for – the uncompromising deterrence of Soviet armed helicopters from the outset.

For Sergeant Oleg Nikolai, this was the culmination of many years of dedicated service as a regular soldier – and the shooting down behind him of the armed helicopter in no way shook his confidence in the future. Probing in his little BRDM2 along the boundary dividing 302nd and 303rd Tank Regiments, he had of necessity to skirt northwards round Rastatt in order to avoid the opposition which had manifested itself from there in a direct hit upon one of his vehicles. Driving cautiously through the paths of the Neiderwald, to one side of Neiderbühl, his progress had been further hindered by a sharp burst of fire from some sort of armoured vehicle tucked away in the trees. At once, another of his cars was ablaze and he was again forced to seek a fresh way round, reporting by radio, as he went, that the enemy seemed to be withdrawing once contact had been made. Fifteen minutes later, he saw the autobahn ahead and received confirmation of the enemy's retreat as a vehicle he identified as a Lynx evacuated a roadside position in some haste.

From his company commander over the radio came a brisk order to investigate the village of Förch, which he could see faintly

THE SECOND DAY + 12 HRS ON

among the trees with the Bühl Plateau rising up behind. The time was 1530 hours and the way ahead threatening, even if the enemy showed no real willingness to stand. But now he glimpsed BMPs either from 302nd Tank Regiment or 290th MRR, moving out of the trees to his right — and suddenly engulfed in sharp concentrations of shell fire. So he gave the order to cross the autobahn, was at once fired upon, got away with it, and dived for cover in a nearby thicket. Three minutes later, he heard the enemy driving off and deemed it safe to advance again, joining the lane some 500 yards from Förch just in time to see a couple of Lynxes moving from right to left in the direction of Kuppenheim. Apart from that, all was ominously still to his front. So he spent five minutes carefully studying the village, ignoring an insistent voice on the radio asking why he did not move or report. As he began to edge forward once more, striving to obtain observation deeper into the village, a loud bang and a cloud of smoke, erupting away to the left, denoted the cratering of the main road leading into Kuppenheim, and also drew his attention to a sudden flurry of activity in this area (which, in fact, was the demolition guard withdrawing). A moment later, he could see far enough into the village to pick out a crater there too. Discretion became the better part of valour. Working on instinct, without obtaining conclusive evidence, Nikolai reported that "Förch was held (when it was not); that the road was blocked; but that a way round could be found to the right of Favorite."

At once Nikolai was told to stay in observation. Now it was the turn of the leading battalion group of 290th MRR to take the plunge, the orders it received projecting the tanks and carriers of the advanced guard at their best speed, aiming for Favorite.

Watchers on the 4 CMBG side of the lines had been fascinated by the classical disclosure of the Red Army's presence — the stealthy appearance of their wheeled reconnaissance elements, signs of a rapid build-up of armoured units beyond the autobahn which had been duly noted by the Lynxes of D Squadron RCD, and duly shelled by Z Battery 1 RCHA when their FOO caught sight of a clutch of BMPs in the open near Bergen. Better than that, a Lynx crew, about to depart from its hide, was suddenly confronted by a Red Army motorcycle at close range — the mutual surprise resolved by a quick burst of Canadian fire which killed the driver but left the sidecar rider unharmed and a prisoner of war. That prisoner was now on his way back, closely guarded by the crew of the Lynx and destined for an escort of Military Police at Kuppenheim. They would take him away for the initial interrogation which would confirm the identity of the Soviet formation closing in on 4 CMBG's front – a formation already suspected by the Americans as being 1st Guards Tank Division.

Listeners on the radio net also sensed the enemy approach through hearing a gradual increase in the sound of Russian voices as they cut into transmissions which, up to then, had been principally American! For as the combat units of both sides converged on the Canadian front, frequencies overlapped more and more. From long exposure to training aimed to instill security consciousness, the men of 4 CMBG maintained strict radio silence and assumed that, once they did break it, they might well be jammed by the enemy. In fact, the Red Army, at this moment on this front, was far more intent upon listening and plotting enemy stations in an endeavour to supplement their own Intelligence. Any jamming which took place was the result of frequency overcrowding and faulty radio discipline.

Despite acute security consciousness, Linkman, among others, was becoming anxious to break radio silence before first contact was made by 1 Troop where it lay in ambush in Favorite. Confident as he

Below: View across the front from Favorite (left) to Blickheim (centre), with the fruit trees in between. The Soviet attack on Favorite approached from right to left, and off left.

was in his radio set's reliability and men's training, there was a natural desire to feel sure he could hear and be heard by his subordinates at this, a critical moment in the execution of his plan. To some extent he was surprised that nobody had blown the ambush plan by firing prematurely at the BRDM2 when it nosed towards Förch. The temptation among several light-triggered gunners must be severe, he guessed, and he would dearly have liked to send a steadying reminder over the air. But without the excuse of direct contact with the enemy or permission from his CO, that was forbidden. So he waited as events built up to a climax. As the side-by-side nagging of tension and excitement needled all the officers, out of duty, into carefully watching their men with special attention to reading their reactions – the men, out of curiosity, were prompted to watch their officer for their's, as well as for the comfort contributed by a positive example.

The radio dilemma was solved for Linkman by the almost simultaneous initiatives of Tinker and the enemy. Tinker, studying reports from several sources, concluded that Linkman must be allowed to speak. On his own responsibility, he sent the nickname lifting radio silence to all four company/combat teams at the front. A moment later, four T72 tanks nosed into view just beyond Förch, travelling in the open at 10 kilometres per hour cross-country. Linkman was almost the first to see them, from a splendid place of observation turret-down near the crest. His reaction at once encompassed warning and action. To Call Sign 21 in Favorite, he announced the approach of the enemy (realizing that Ron Pike's troop could not yet see the enemy); to the TOW detachments, he simply sent a reminder to hold their fire, even though they were being presented with the sort of ideal target they dreamed of, at long range, in the open. Pike and his other three tank commanders were thus fully prepared, knowing the exact line of the enemy advance and the precise range at which they would open fire. With engines running, gunners were already aware of the nature and range of the target and APFSDS already was loaded in the 105 mm guns. It was simply a matter of waiting for Pike to tell them to shift to the edge of the trees to occupy their firing positions as each commander laid his gunner on line as they moved into the open.

To Ivan Shulubin, the task of commanding the advanced guard of II Battalion of 290th MRR was routine because he had done it so frequently during training. So his mind was shut to what the

THE SECOND DAY + 12 HRS ON

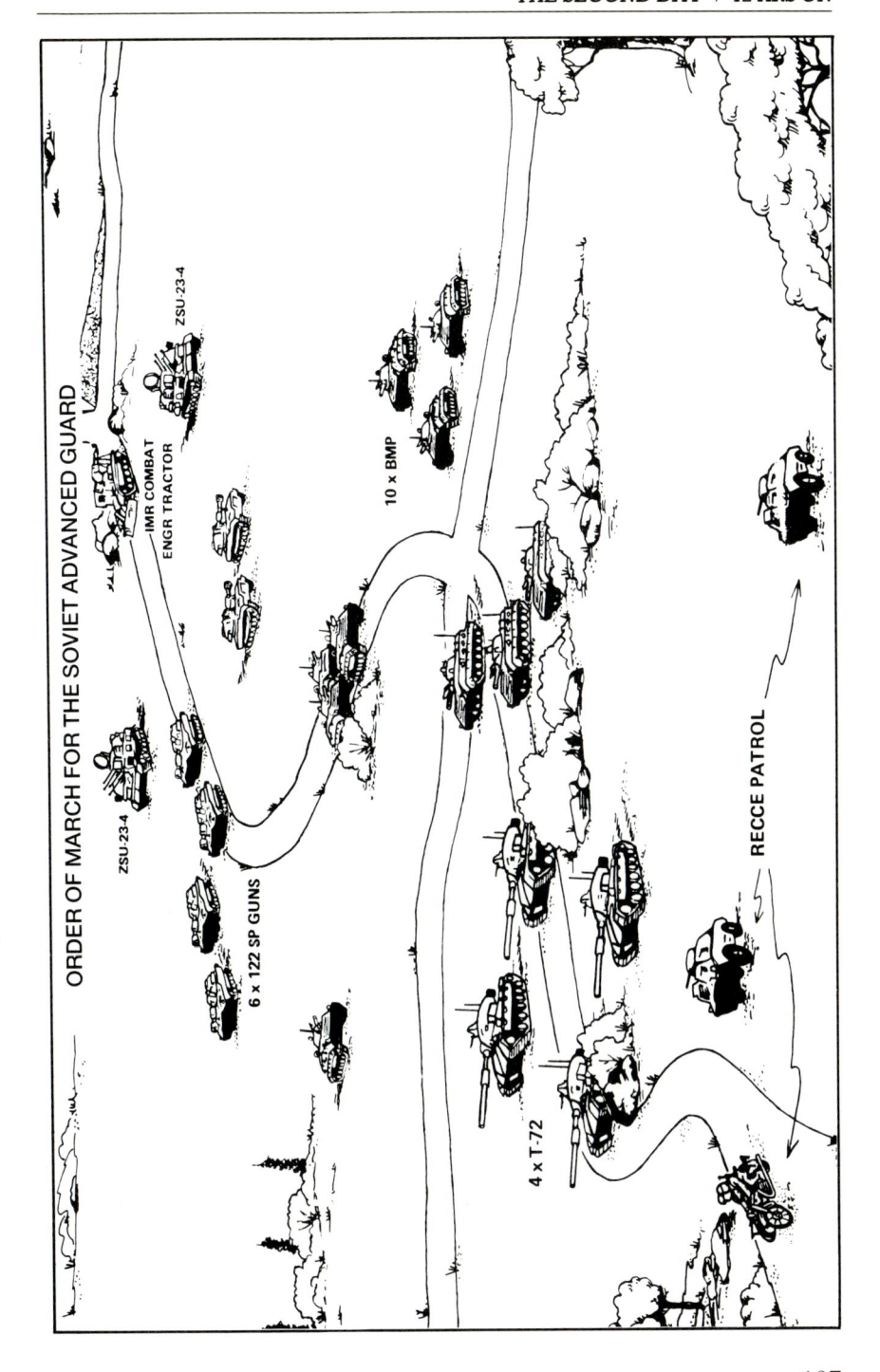

ORDER OF MARCH FOR THE SOVIET ADVANCED GUARD

ZSU-23-4
IMR COMBAT ENGR TRACTOR
ZSU-23-4
6 x 122 SP GUNS
10 x BMP
4 x T-72
RECCE PATROL

THE SECOND DAY + 12 HRS ON

consequence might be, particularly since the deployment of his team – the four T72s in front, followed by his own HQ and the ten BMPs with the FOO from the attached battery of six 122 mm SPs – had gone like clockwork. He warned the tanks to keep a wary eye on Förch and asked the FOO to hit the village with a concentration, and be ready to switch to the woods behind Favorite. Apart from that, he merely insisted upon full speed in the hope of achieving the shock effect he believed would bring success. There had not been any questions when he gave his orders over the air, for Shulubin was of the old school who expected only strict compliance and acknowledgements from out-stations; this new-fangled encouragement of discussions, such as had been tried by other units to improve efficiency, did not appeal to him. It pleased him to observe the accuracy of the first burst of 122 mm shells falling among the rooftops of Förch. He halted his BMP on a slight rise in order to watch the progress of the tanks as they neared the ground where, if trouble was to come, it might easily occur. And it did.

Ron Pike, like Ian Linkman, had decided upon minimum disclosure of his troop when the opportunity to engage came. To begin with, he allowed only a sergeant's tank and his own to leave cover. For one thing, his troop warrant officer was out of view, guarding the right flank, while the fourth tank was in depth covering behind the rear. Two Leopards were quite sufficient to deal with four surprised T72s at 600 metres. Indeed, the result of 15 seconds' point-blank fire was total annihilation.

To Captain Pat Kendal's delight, the springing of the ambush by Pike coincided almost perfectly with the arrival of some half-dozen of Shulubin's BMPs in the killing zone, close to one of the FPF tasks on which A Battery was laid. A clutch of 155 mm shells plunging down among the BMPs ruined Shulubin's composure.

There had been time for the Russian to register in his mind that the shots, which had set three T72s on fire and brought the fourth to a halt, had come from Favorite. Now, it was the safety of his company which needed his whole attention – and at that moment each platoon commander was reacting in his own way. Already the leading platoon commander, regardless of the peril to his front, was leading his three BMPs at full speed, inclined to the right, for the cover of trees and a dip in the ground. Fascinated and with sinking feelings, Shulubin awaited the outcome – his preoccupation punctuated by the sight of a nearby BMP in the second platoon erupting

THE SECOND DAY + 12 HRS ON

into flames when unluckily struck, directly, by an enemy shell. A moment later, to his horror, it was the leading platoon's turn to suffer. Before they could reach the cover (which Shulubin recognized as valueless), the first BMP seemed to cough flame and smoke under its forefoot and then swing sickeningly to one side as it came to a halt. "Mines!" he shouted involuntarily, and already the second BMP was going the same way because its commander was too slow to order a change of course.

With his command in ruins, Shulubin pursued duty, and the name of the tactics his training demanded was withdrawal. For he had automatically (and according to the book) achieved the regimental commander's aim, and now here was Colonel Oblensky speaking directly to him over the radio (by-passing the battalion commander), telling him to pull back and report what he had seen. An adequate report was not, however, easy to compose. In fact, there was precious little he had seen – just an enemy tank (he was fairly sure about that) in the Favorite area and the discovery of a minefield across the front which was well-covered by fire since both the mined BMPs were now ablaze and the crews dashing for cover. Förch, he said, seemed quiet; perhaps it was not occupied at all. And that thinking led to a plan of escape – a quick dash for the village along with a request to the FOO to shift fire to Favorite in an effort to quell further interference from there. Only later, after he had given the order and reached safety, did he realize that a firm foothold in the village was a step towards tackling Favorite.

It cost only one more BMP to get there: another of Pike's victims, seen fleetingly between the fruit trees as he was on the verge of retiring under cover again and hit first shot. But Pike's satisfaction at such a successful initial action – four tanks and two BMPs was good shooting – was almost immediately extinguished by a series of rending crashes nearby as shells burst in the wood, showering his tank with splinters, and killing two infantrymen who unwisely were standing half out of their trench watching the battle. The outburst of Russian retribution was short-lived, but it won respect and created a distinct impression that this was only a sample of what was to come.

Probably the most important contribution by the Russian artillery organization at that moment, was the spotting by its FOOs. For they noticed far more of what was opposed to them than had anybody in Shulubin's company. From an OP that only minutes previously he had established atop the autobahn, Captain Alexei

THE SECOND DAY + 12 HRS ON

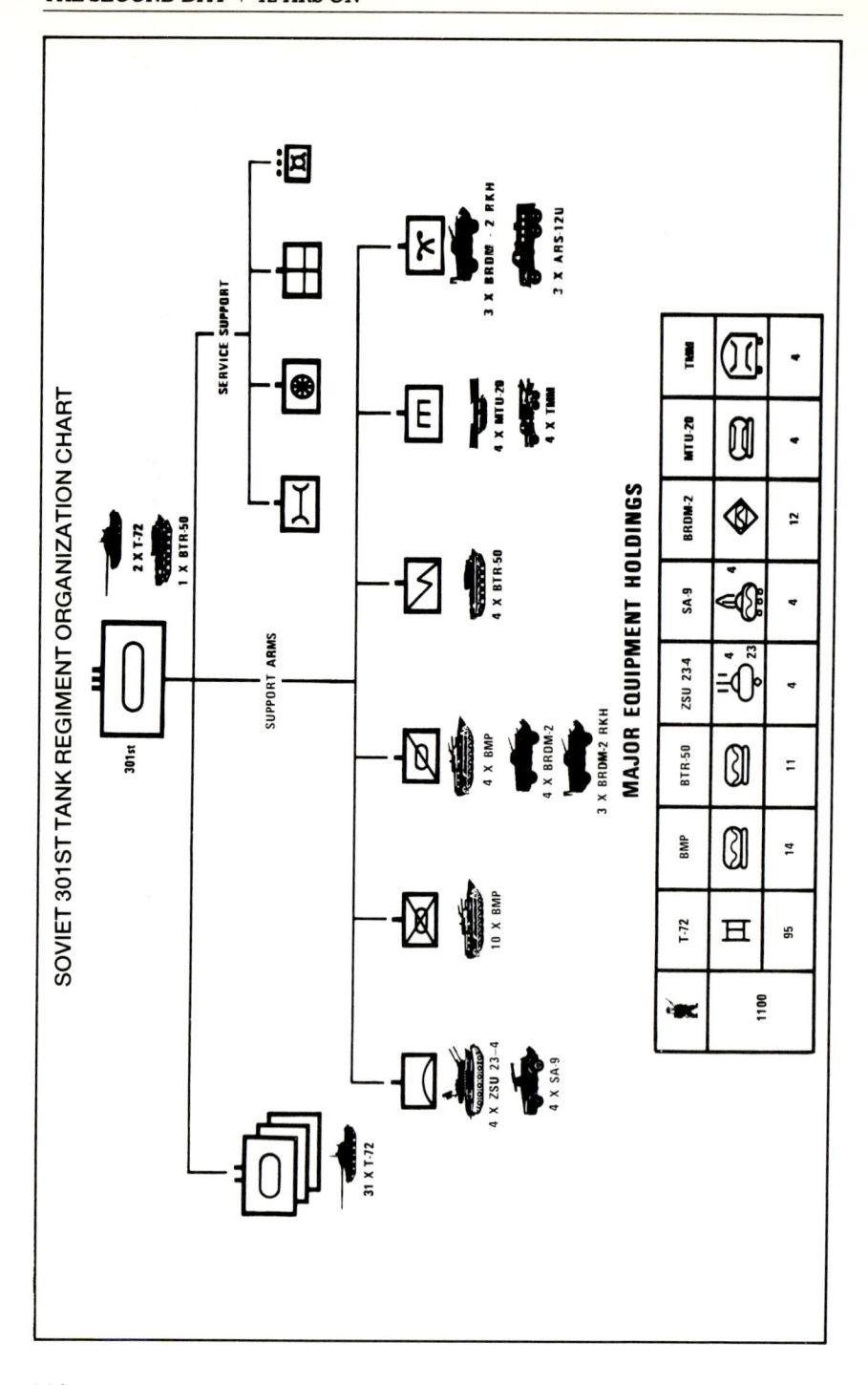

SOVIET 301ST TANK REGIMENT ORGANIZATION CHART

- 301st
- 2 X T-72
- 1 X BTR-50

SERVICE SUPPORT

SUPPORT ARMS

- 31 X T-72
- 4 X ZSU 23-4
- 4 X SA-9
- 10 X BMP
- 4 X BMP
- 4 X BRDM-2
- 3 X BRDM-2 RKH
- 4 X BTR-50
- 4 X MTU-20
- 4 X TMM
- 3 X BRDM-2 RKH
- 3 X ARS-12U

MAJOR EQUIPMENT HOLDINGS

T-72	BMP	BTR-50	ZSU 23-4	SA-9	BRDM-2	MTU-20	TMM
1100	14	11	4	4	12	4	4

110

THE SECOND DAY + 12 HRS ON

Rusalski had pin-pointed a gun flash somewhere to the left of Blickheim, and also signs of enemy occupation on the slope joining the village to the woods above Favorite. His reports, fed directly to Oblensky and passed on to Samsonov, indicated the extent of the enemy defences and helped shape the plan then being concocted to seize the heights. And they made it obligatory for an immediate assault to be launched against Blickheim, besides Favorite and the rising ground behind.

It might easily have been different if Warrant Officer George Crane of 3 Troop in B Squadron had not disobeyed orders and fired that shot from his Leopard at a lonely BMP (the survivor of the platoon caught in the minefield). But Crane, despite full knowledge of the order to hold his fire until given permission, also remembered a strongly-held theory among the pundits that single enemy vehicles might well contain Russian leaders and that, to knock them out, could easily disrupt enemy command and control. So Crane had fired and, sad irony, seen the shot miss, letting the speeding enemy escape. His troop officer, he gathered from a blast over the radio, was not pleased, but Linkman let it pass. His mind was on Favorite and the wisdom of permitting 1 Troop to remain there much longer.

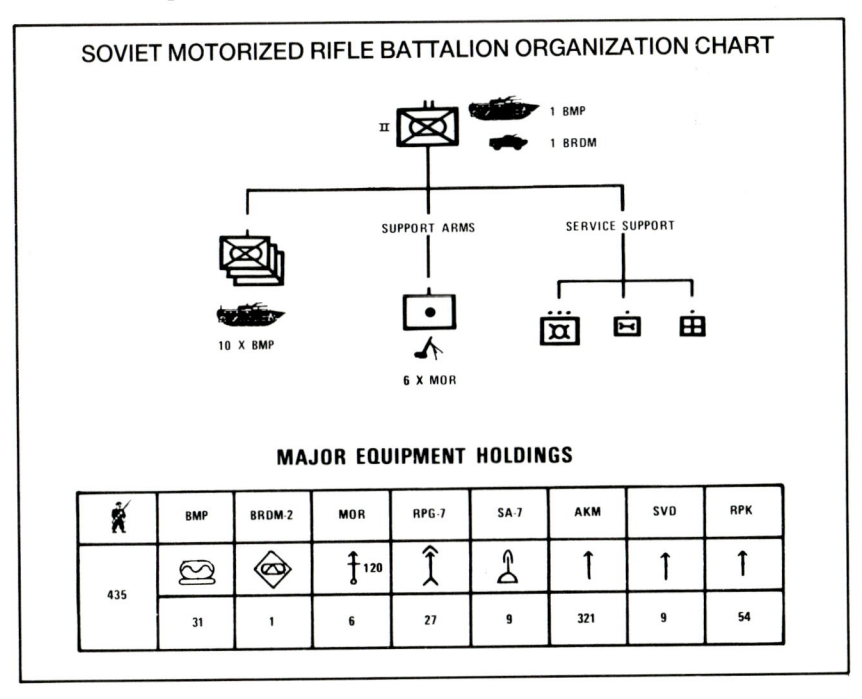

SOVIET MOTORIZED RIFLE BATTALION ORGANIZATION CHART

- 1 BMP
- 1 BRDM
- 10 X BMP
- SUPPORT ARMS — 6 X MOR
- SERVICE SUPPORT

MAJOR EQUIPMENT HOLDINGS

	BMP	BRDM-2	MOR	RPG-7	SA-7	AKM	SVD	RPK
435	31	1	6 (120)	27	9	321	9	54

111

THE SECOND DAY + 12 HRS ON

Reflecting too that if only the Canadian infantry possessed an MAW with the performance of the MILAN out to 2000 metres, or perhaps a high-velocity gun on a self-propelled mounting, there would be no need for him to risk a troop of tanks in such an exposed position as Favorite.

As at present, he thought, Connors would prefer 1 Troop to remain in Favorite in order to postpone the moment when November Company would be confronted by the enemy on the home side of the obstacle. Every instinct within Linkman told him to pull Pike out now, and chance the consequences rather than risk sacrificing valuable tanks. But to his private shame, he compromised and split the troop, telling Pike to leave one call sign on the forward edge, along with the infantry section and the snipers, and withdraw the rest of the troop to its main battle position among 2 Platoon, from where it could intervene fairly easily on the left while carrying out its main task of protecting the right flank and rear of Connor's company. Informing all concerned (including the Vandoos and A Squadron on his right), Linkman settled back in his turret to await developments, knowing very well that they would not be long forthcoming.

CONTROLLING FACTORS

- ★ Contact procedures.

- ★ The need to hamper the enemy reconnaissance without disclosing the main defensive position.

- ★ The probability that the Soviet reconnaissance will be conducted with speed, skill and determination.

- ★ The likelihood that the enemy presence will be emphasized by increased interference on radio frequencies and the use of direct and indirect speculative fire.

- ★ The great importance of commanders setting an example of calm and confidence as the moment of first contact approaches. This initial atmosphere of steadiness may well create the tone for all that is to come.

- ★ The need to plot and report all enemy movements to build-up the Intelligence picture and give ambush parties ample warning of developments.

- ★ The desirability of springing ambushes at close range with maximum surprise.

- ★ The need to remember that the enemy will report all reactions and take instant counter-measures that may have to be countered at once.

7 | The hasty attack

Neither too sure of what exactly confronted him nor keen to diverge from the prescribed procedures, Oblensky ordered the CO of II Battalion to attack Favorite at once and exploit to the high ground beyond. And the plan adopted by II Battalion was also standard in pattern. Employing the badly cut-up 2nd Company to establish a fire base centred on Förch, he ordered 1st Company to assault straight ahead through Förch against Favorite while 3rd Company worked its way around the left flank in the hope of benefiting from cover among the fruit trees. There were only 30 minutes to implement the plan, virtually no opportunity for reconnaissance and time only to create a rudimentary fire plan of 10 minutes duration with II Battalion 290th MRR's six 120 mm mortars engaging the slope beyond Favorite (where 1 Platoon November Company stood) and the 18 Howitzers from 164th Artillery Battalion, directed by Rusalski, smothering Favorite itself. Also, at Oblensky's request, a battery of 122 mm Howitzers supporting 303rd Tank Regiment firing on Kuppenheim. With hardly a pause, each company group assumed its attack formation, crossed the autobahn as the mortars and Howitzers opened fire and advanced on their objectives.

Again, it was Linkman and the two FOOs who had the best view of the coming onslaught. Connors was tucked away in the centre of his company and thus unable to see Förch because of Favorite, but to him and everybody else listening on the radio net the sequence of action was amply portrayed. They heard Linkman reporting more tanks crossing the autobahn (underlined by the start of the shelling and mortaring). Then an excited voice from the section commander in Favorite said they were under heavy fire, but that one of the snipers had shot dead a Russian who had been poking around near the crater in Förch. Next Angus Scott, realizing that his fellow FOO with N Company, might well be in difficulty from mortar fire, as well as being unable to see, reported BMPs tracking the tanks across the

113

THE SECOND DAY + 12 HRS ON

autobahn and announced that he was engaging. Soon there was the swish of shells overhead and the crump of well-concentrated bursts in the neighbourhood of the Russian column.

The TOW section commander at Blickheim was now on the air eagerly asking Linkman's permission to engage the enemy tanks to his front at 3000 metres and getting the go-ahead. Two puffs of smoke and a pair of missiles were flying to the targets, operators tracking their picked target and hoping it would not take cover too soon, wires trailing and passing beneath the overhead power lines thus obviating electronic interference with the guidance system should the power still be switched on. One struck home, the tank belching smoke; but reversing out of trouble. The other missed simply because its moving target happened to become obscured by trees at the critical moment. But there was time for each operator to reload and fire again, with the same result – a hit and a miss – the latter perhaps due to an operator's shaky hand. Linkman took charge, calculating that the enemy group was about to enter the cover provided by Förch and noticing, too, that another wave of tanks was beginning to cross the autobahn, apparently heading more in the direction of Kuppenheim, where, he knew, it would be dealt with by the Vandoos and A Squadron. Telling the TOWs to engage the latest arrivals, he warned the solitary tank in Favorite of the imminent arrival of enemy armour to its front, instructing the commander to do what damage he could and then pull back into safety.

That commander needed no urging. He could see the leading tanks – three of them heading his way with BMPs coming into view behind. Already the Leopard had suffered minor external damage without impairing its fighting efficiency as yet. Hoping the dust and smoke that was beginning to obscure his vision would also hide his presence from the enemy, he told his driver to advance and aligned the gun onto the leading T72 (or was it perhaps a T62 with a plough fitted in front?), and described the nature of the target to his gunner who instantly recognized it besides picking out another behind. At 800 metres he could not miss; both targets flashed from a sabot strike and both burned. Not so pleasing was the Sagger from a lurking BMP in Förch which penetrated the Leopard's mantlet, killed the loader and wounded the commander, besides wrecking the radio and much else besides. The gunner was yelling madly to the driver to "get back to hell out of here", and the tank was in high-speed reverse,

THE SECOND DAY + 12 HRS ON

dodging further trouble. But as a fighting unit it was finished. Now the close defence of Favorite depended on a diminished infantry section, plus two snipers and whatever effort could be applied from the artillery and flanking units.

Two centres of conflict held the attention of 4 CMBG – the drive by a company group against Kuppenheim on the right, which had become the responsibility of the Vandoos, and the frontal attack on Favorite from Förch. The latter could best be dealt with by artillery fire directed from Blickheim, since the Vandoos (who might have helped) found their hands partly full when Kuppenheim came under heavy fire from artillery and the guns of the advancing tanks and BMPs. As the action became more general, and called increasingly upon the resources of 1 RCHA, the CO 1 RCHA, with the approval of the Brigade Commander, exercised centralized control of the allocation of fire. Appreciating that this attack was merely an overture to a far greater assault to come; knowing, too, that the enemy would be keenly searching for his gun positions prior to beginning a counterbattery programme, the CO was loath to disclose every battery at this moment. For the time being, he allotted the Vandoos the use of Z Battery (which had already opened fire in support of the screen) in support, while giving A Battery the task of firing planned concentrations on Förch and letting 81 mm mortars drop bombs 20 metres in front of Favorite. Thus he kept B and C Batteries uncommitted, but asked Corps to open a counterbattery programme with their 203 mm against the Soviet batteries whose gun flashes could be detected in the distance. Dreading the moment when a full-scale Red Army bombardment of vast dimensions would be unleashed, the Brigade Commander put all his weight behind the request for CB. Outnumbered in guns and dependent upon the Allies to provide all the facilities of CB, his main advantages in the artillery battle to come lay in (hopefully) a superior fire control system and the geographical fact that, whereas his observers enjoyed an unrivalled view of almost the entire enemy deployment area, the enemy had no such sight of his gun positions or all his combat teams. Meanwhile, the group of 81 mm mortars supporting N Company was hastily shifting in its M113s to the next alternative position.

Confidence of success in holding the Soviet battalion thrust was justified. Despite the shelling of Kuppenheim and a smoke-screen laid in front of the built-up area, the Vandoos were able, quite easily, to fend off the tanks and BMPs in the open. The failure of a mine-ploughing tank to push its way through the minefield acted as the last straw, but Russian losses might have been heavier if they had not laid smoke to screen their withdrawal. The distracting effect of the attack towards Kuppenheim did, however, afford some help to the assault on Favorite. The N Company section commander there, who now maintained the only radio link with Linkman and Connors, gave a sporadic running commentary on enemy progress, having reported already the retreat of the damaged Leopard.

"Heavy enemy fire all over the place, smoke too. Very difficult to see. Looks like tanks advancing from the village."

"There's a thing like a plough on one of the tanks pushing into the minefield." – pause – "Wait. Now there's a whole lot of shells falling around there. Tanks!"

"Two enemy tanks – Oh! And now two or three smaller tracked

THE SECOND DAY + 12 HRS ON

vehicles have joined the plough which may have got through."

"Now they're all coming! We'll be able to use the Carl G soon."

Linkman cut in. He had watched the damaged Leopard retire from Favorite, its gun traversed over the engine decks, pointing towards the enemy (as a means of identification) and saw no sense in sacrificing the almost defenceless infantry who would soon be overwhelmed.

"OK, India 22 Bravo! Don't wait, come back now! We'll support!"

Thirty seconds passed with no reply. Linkman repeated the message, fearing the worst, for the volume of fire being poured into Favorite by enemy artillery, tanks and BMPs was quite daunting and there was little he could do to quell that. Then a voice which expressed triumph as well as relief came through:

Below: An M109 of A Battery 1 RCHA opens fire to initiate the battle of Blickheim.

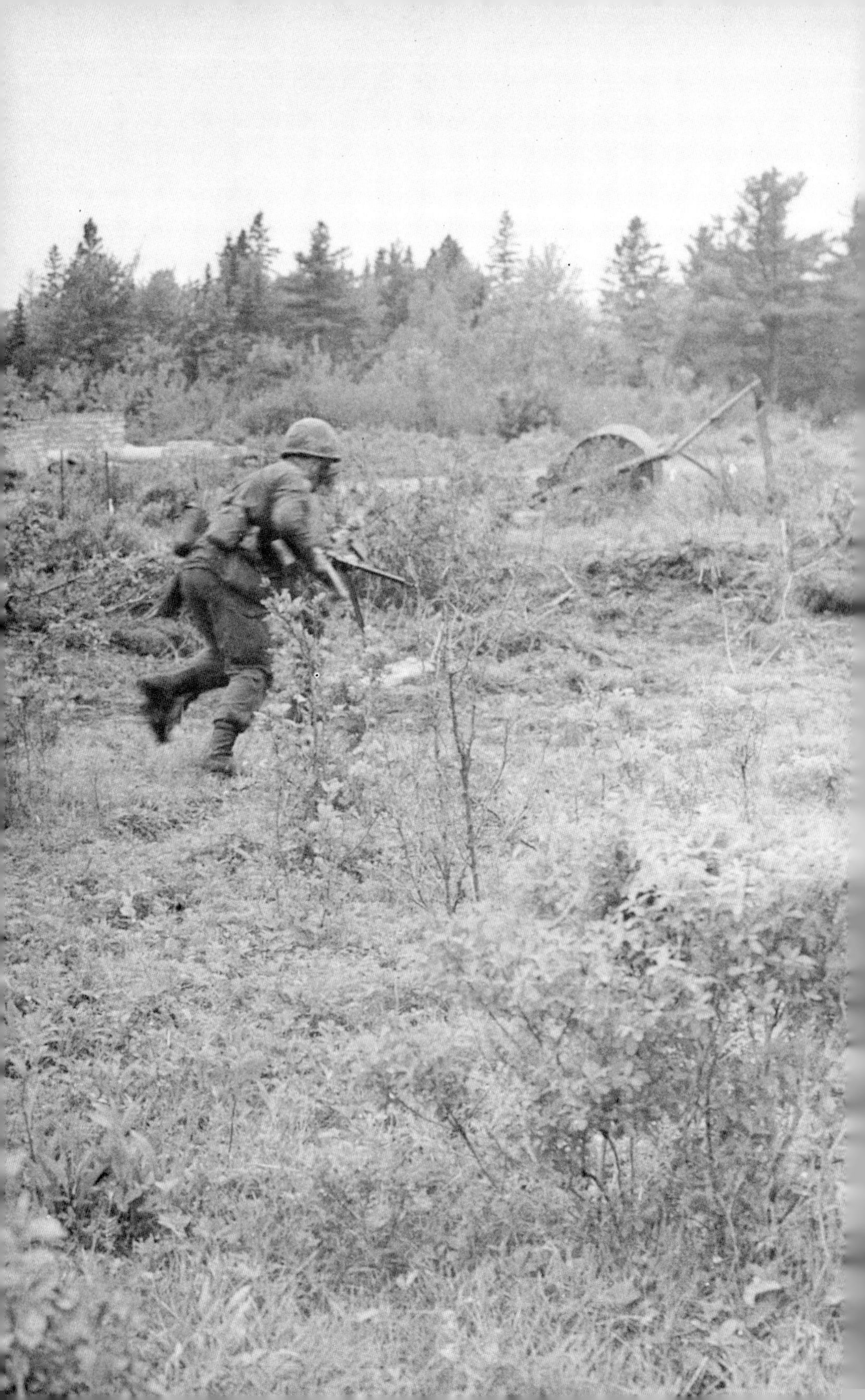

THE SECOND DAY + 12 HRS ON

"Wilco! Pulling out now, tho' looks as if we'll have to walk. 113's bust. One bit of luck. Hit one BMP with Carl G. It brewed. Enemy has dismounted 50 yards, and shaking out."

Again Linkman waited while Connors warned 3 Platoon about the withdrawal of the section and the imminent arrival of the enemy to their front. All at once, too, enemy fire against Favorite stopped and a moment later small arms fire could be heard among the trees. Then two figures emerged, one supporting the other, followed later by four running, carrying a Carl Gustav and a 50-cal gun between them in addition to their small arms. Linkman sent word to Kendal, and the gunner called on A Battery which at once opened fire on Favorite, greeting the Red Army infantry as they charged forward among the shattered trees towards the now burning buildings.

Linkman was tidying up and counting the cost. The damaged Leopard had been met behind the crest by the M113 ambulance and the wounded commander placed in it, where first aid was applied and "tagging" carried out. Now he told the ambulance to drive forward and pick up the RCR's wounded before returning with them to the Battalion Medical Station, (where triage would be completed) for onward transmission to the Evacuation Station set up by 4 Field Ambulance. None of the wounded were seriously hurt, he learned. That was something to be thankful for. For the loss of nearly half an infantry section, one Leopard put permanently out of action and one crewman killed, he had forced the Russians to deploy a battalion

Left: The infantry at Favorite pull back under Red Army pressure. **Above:** An M113 ambulance on its mission of mercy to pick up the wounded from Favorite.

119

THE SECOND DAY + 12 HRS ON

prematurely and suffer losses which might easily be in the ratio of ten against his one. On the debit side, the enemy had been given the opportunity to read 4 CMBG's dispositions and assess their strength, besides breaching the obstacle at its centre and driving in the outposts. Apparently that was the end of the matter, for no attempt had yet been made to extend the advance beyond Favorite and an almost complete silence had settled momentarily over the front. Naturally, nobody drew a hopeful conclusion from that. Indeed, Tinker took the opportunity to underline caution by congratulating Linkman on the radio, for all to hear, on winning 'a nice little skirmish'.

It would be for Oblensky, whose considerations of the state of affairs at the end of the struggle for Favorite inclined him towards caution, to make the next move. And Oblensky was a trifle shaken by the hammering his II Battalion had received for so poor a return. Not only had it lost seven out of twelve tanks committed, and a company's worth of infantry, but the battalion CO was dead, picked off at 2000 metres in his BMP by a shot from a Leopard located in Kuppenheim. It was partly for this reason that momentum had been lost in the fight for Favorite. Be that as it may, the company commander who had taken possession of that first objective had shown no anxiety to exploit his success unsupported, and Oblensky was not inclined to insist. So with Samsonov breathing down his neck again, and still with two and a half hours daylight remaining, he was left with a crucial choice prior to taking the next step: the launching of a full-scale deliberate assault employing the entire 290th MRR. Should it be before last light or after darkness had fallen?

CONTROLLING FACTORS

★   The precipitate procedures likely to be adopted by Soviet forces after meeting initial resistance.

★   The importance of counterbattery fire.

★   The importance of quick assistance to an evacuation of the wounded.

8 | Deliberate attack, flexible defence

"The Intelligence boys have had their heads together and come up with two possible ways the Russians might move," said Tinker. He was standing on the back of Linkman's tank talking to the squadron commander while they both searched the battle zone with their eyes – an expanse of ground which had almost grown still, the only movement coming from distraught animals roaming about amid drifting smoke from fires that had been lit in buildings and crippled vehicles. "They are quite sure", he went on, "that was only the prologue. There's bound to be – and I agree – a full-scale deliberate attack. We've read it before in the book, and the latest recce pictures show a lot of stuff moving up. Problem is, do they let fly before or after dark? The book says after dark, but signs are that this bunch in front of us – and incidentally, a prisoner has let it out that it's 1st Guards Tank Division – are a lot of hustlers. Might come soon, perhaps about 1900 hours; in which case they'll throw everything at us starting sometime about 1800."

"In which case," interjected Linkman, "I'd like to pull back a few TOWs to save them from the worst and for later use."

"Me too!" agreed Tinker. "But neither Connors nor Panton will be too pleased. A lot depends on when the Russians start. The General's got a hunch it will be after dark, and I tend to go along with that. So, OK, we'll pluck out a few TOWs as you want. Like one section from each combat team in front and have them vehicle-mounted, back in the Bannwald as a fall-back if there's a penetration tonight."

Linkman was relieved. That way, depth would augment his position and improve the flexibility of his combat team along with an improvement in the chances of survival for a valuable anti-armour weapon. That way, too, he avoided abandoning the long range anti-armour capability across the existing front. "I'd like to pull them now, if you don't mind," he said. "The sooner the better so as to be

THE SECOND DAY + 12 HRS ON

clear before they throw everything at us. Stands to reason they'll not start immediately, because the sort of thing they are jacking up takes at least 90 minutes."

"Do that," agreed Tinker, "but with the least fuss. I don't want the other side to get the impression we are pulling out now. Might give 'em the wrong idea. Don't forget we're buying time, so we mustn't sell short."

As they finished talking and Linkman began speaking to the TOW detachment, the battle entered its next phase. Shells of 203 mm calibre, fired by 1-40th Battalion US Army Artillery, began trundling overhead on their way to those Red Army gun positions which had already been located. The battle was being carried to an opponent whose initiative, momentarily, had been lost.

In a way, Samsonov's decision to assent to Oblensky's desire to delay the deliberate attack by 290th MRR until nightfall ran contrary to his habitual inclinations – both from the tactical angle and the considerations of ambition. The Army Commander might easily vent his wrath on any subordinate with shortcoming in aggressive intent. He had agreed only for sound tactical reasons which he felt capable of defending. The strength of the enemy position was all too apparent. The Canadians had long been rated by Intelligence (based on many years of study) as staunch and well-trained opponents. To attack them on that ground in the late evening with a setting sun in his men's eyes would be, in his opinion, operating at far too great a disadvantage. Moreover, he was impressed (and to some extent depressed) by the lessons of the past 48 hours' warfare. It had been indicated that not even the heaviest artillery bombardment would necessarily dislodge a well-entrenched opponent; the tactics of massed headlong attack supported by massed guns had been demonstrably costly and by no means a guaranteed winner. Samsonov reasoned that something more than brute force was required – and that meant the utilization of every possible technical aid; the choice of darkness as the time for movement; and the implementation of diversionary measures to distract the enemy. Unwillingly he accepted that, try as he might, he could not wholly avoid sending his men into terrain that was all too obviously selected by the enemy as a Killing Zone. There was no other way within his boundaries. Grudgingly, he had to admit that his armoured vehicles were falling prey much too easily to an enemy who fought from the cover of fortified villages and copses, and that, by implication, his preconceived tactical notions had to be modified. All the more susceptible was he, then, to the suggestion by Oblensky which offered a better chance of success than the blind charge of old.

"The Blickheim Ridge position", as Oblensky chose to call it, "is strong, but I think it has a weakness in its centre. I believe there are covered approaches leading between Kuppenheim on the left and Blickheim on the right. 290th Regiment, despite the losses suffered by II Battalion, has the strength to take it providing full support is accorded by the rest of the division, sir. I could put in a deliberate assault with I and III Battalions by 1900 hours, but that would be in daylight. On this ground, I would rather wait and attack by night. That way, I can get closer to the enemy before coming under the close surveillance of the majority of his best night-vision instruments. Also, if I attack at 2000 hours, there will be ample time to make a more detailed reconnaissance and more time for the artillery to operate. Allow me this and you will still be on the Bühl Plateau at midnight!"

Sansonov looked unconvinced, but asked a few perfunctory questions and then agreed. His mind was on the latest situation map as he worked out the supporting role for the rest of his formation; the direct aid it would give to 290th MRR; the diversions which could be employed to distract the enemy's attention; the timing and method of exploitation across the whole front and by 3rd Tank Division coming up on his left. Mind made up, he rapidly outlined to Oblensky and Romanov a scheme, and then departed to visit the other commanders to impress upon them the urgency of the new parts they must play. In its essentials, the plan was orthodox and dictated by the situation:

- *290th MRR would attack between Blickheim and Favorite (both inclusive) at 2000 hours with the intention of seizing the crest beyond by midnight.*
- *301st Tank Regiment would pass through 290th MRR and exploit to Bühl.*
- *302nd Tank Regiment would bring diversionary pressure to bear between Mendel and Blickheim (exclusive) while conserving its strength for subsequent operations.*
- *303rd Tank Regiment would seek to by-pass Kuppenheim and and Bischweier with a view to bringing pressure to bear against the rear of the Blickheim–Favorite position, as well as providing a diversion from 290th MRR's main effort.*
- *Colonel Andrei Romanov would bring to bear the full strength of the Division's artillery with priority of effort allocated to*

THE SECOND DAY + 12 HRS ON

290th MRR – a weight in field guns which would amount to the 54 SP Howitzers plus 18 truck-borne BM21 rocket launchers each with forty 122 mm projectile tubes of the Division Artillery; the 18 towed 120 mm mortars and the 18 SP guns of the 290th MRR; – a truly formidable array to which might be added, if there was time to assemble them, additional 152 mm guns from Army resources. Of the guns available to him within the division alone, Romanov, with Samsonov's approval, allotted to 290th MRR (in addition to its own 18 mortars) the entire divisional artillery of fifty-four 122 mm Howitzers, and the 18 divisional rocket launchers – a grand barrage destined, therefore, to be largely shared among November and Oscar Companies of 3 RCR and the known artillery units supporting them.

- Also in support would be as much direct air support as could be mustered, although this was not expected to be in significant quantities during the assault and might only be sent against located gun positions.

As much as anything else, it was the somewhat meagre quantity of Intelligence about the enemy to their front which prompted Samsonov and, in particular, Romanov to spread the attack rather wider than they might have chosen if they had been positive about the exact enemy locations. So far, their observers had discerned only three pin-point targets, and their counterbattery units had yet to establish their bases and begin searching for hostile artillery and mortar positions – a process which, of course, depended to a large extent upon grudging assistance from 4 CMBG if only it could be provoked into opening fire with every weapon.

It did not require the commencement of the artillery exchange to warn every man in 4 CMBG of what was in store for them. Over the years they had been warned about Red Army methods. They had been taught to expect, as a matter of course but without fully comprehending it, a massive bombardment preceding the advance of an armoured phalanx which might easily be associated with a nuclear strike or by the onset of chemical attack. Prior knowledge in no way relieved them of anxiety. There was a tightening of the nerves which were stretched from the instant of first contact. The upliftingly successful clash of arms was countered by the voices of the guns as they began to shout. The best among their leaders felt the need to speak once more to their followers, calming them, but it was no longer possible for each to go to the man in person, for the enemy could now bring down directly-aimed fire upon several sectors. Men were pinned where they were. Centres of leadership were restricted to the lowest level of command. Individuals became responsible for their own unsupervised conduct.

1 and 3 Platoons of November Company were the worst hit, situated as they were within 400 metres of the enemy in Favorite and already aware of nagging attention by a couple of snipers. The artillery bombardment, which earlier had supported the assault on Favorite, had hardly damaged them. The earth had been ripped up, trees shattered (the shells detonated in the air among them having produced a very frightening noise); but the men who remained steadfastly below ground level had suffered mainly from fear. Only one man had been buried by a near miss and one wounded. A TOW had been damaged, however, and this was one of those being withdrawn, its departure along with the others, supported at the critical stage by three minutes' gunfire upon Favorite to discourage interference by Russian small arms fire. Even so, the removal of the TOWs was noticed and attracted fire, although this local activity seemed really to merge into the overall burgeoning of fury mounting all around. Connors therefore had to content himself with talking periodically over the radio to his men, as did Linkman to his tank crews. Panton and his platoon commanders in Blickheim were still almost unharmed by the enemy. They could visit their positions in relative safety, telling their occupants how well everybody else was doing, checking for signs of over-anxiety, stiffening the morale of waverers and suppressing the careless raptures of the over-eager who had yet to come to understand the destructive realities of Red Army fire-power.

Although the variety of reactions among the men just about equalled their total number, certain categories could be found among the front-line infantry which tended to reflect the varying intensities of their employment. Sergeant Al Hobbs, of November Company (if he had not been pinned to his slit trench by fear of a sniper in Favorite who had recently nicked his helmet with a well-aimed shot), was engrossed in responsibility and therefore stimulated. The incident with the sniper had reminded him of the need for staying alert, but his attention was chiefly focused upon imposing command on the rest of his section in their nearby trenches, keeping their minds on the job in hand and rallying their spirits. Private Paul Charrier

THE SECOND DAY + 12 HRS ON

was among the inactive and in danger of falling into the category of the frustrated. Crouching in a trench where every function of living and survival had to be performed, and unable to strike back at the Russians, who dictated that he should behave that way (quite apart from frightening him), he was prey to a conflict of emotions which threatened to undermine his resistance. His companion, a stolid Newfoundlander, sought to help by indicating ways of improving the trench from within, suggesting to Charrier he might sleep, or asking him to brew coffee – anything as a means, no matter how contradictory, to occupy his mind constructively.

Also listed among the frustrated was Sergeant Bud Roach whose OP had received its fair share of 122 mm shells in the bombardment, but whose calls for fire to engage the enemy with the 81 mm mortars had been almost, but not quite, consistently refused. Both Tinker and the Mortar Platoon commander were determined to reserve the tubes for future use and protect them from premature disclosure. They now lay under nets behind the crest in the second alternative position, awaiting the opportunity, by surprise and sheer volume of fire, to save the forward infantry from an enemy charge. But while Roach grumbled at his signaller, as the latter sought to enliven the hour by a ceaseless flow of chatter (featured by nervous questions about what was going on), both FOOs were being taxed to the limit; on the one hand directing the guns, on the other endeavouring to find and report the multiplying indications of enemy build-up.

The guns, like the mortars, were being preserved as much as possible, partly to conserve ammunition and partly from the desire to save them from detection and counterbattery fire. This policy's effectiveness could be measured at the gun positions. Only on A and Z Batteries, which alone had been in action, had enemy shells fallen, while B and C were unnoticed and well on with the dumping programme which, at the other batteries, had been interrupted. Nobody could be quite sure how the enemy had located A and Z, but the CO of 1 RCHA was convinced that it was the result of enemy air reconnaissance and sound ranging, not flash-spotting, and was not in the least impressed with the current rumour of reporting by spies. The consequences of the counter-bombardment were destructive, but a hindrance rather than a total disaster: here a truck was burning and about to explode; there three gunners laid low as they handed shells into an M109; in a couple of places signallers tracing breaks in cable from the battery command post to the guns. Everybody knew that the worst was to come, and it was each battery commander's inclination to move elsewhere to escape – a suggestion the CO firmly overruled because the enemy attack was impending.

The artillery duel, in fact, subordinated almost everything else as it mounted in intensity throughout the closing hours of daylight. But although it carried with it a message of severe Russian intent, it also, to those in the know, contained a suggestion of hope. It helped that 4 CMBG's observers could actually see some of their targets, whereas the Russians saw none. Even though conditions surrounding some of the Canadian and, later, the US gun positions were made unpleasant by shell-fire and sporadic air attacks, and ammunition supply became more hazardous to arrange, at no time were the guns prevented from engaging. In the Soviet camp, on the other hand, a drop in the rate of fire was noticeable due to casualties and interrupted ammunition supply. Attempts by the Russians to find and knock out their tormentor's observation posts resulted only in temporary difficulties, and their efforts to exactly pin-point the hostile guns were inadequate.

To the soldiers in the line, watching the artillery duel remained a spectator's benefit, except when attempts to hit a suspected OP doused the crest and forward slopes with short eruptions of shell-fire. Blickheim suffered on those occasions and fires began to break out, sometimes blinding Angus Scott in his OP, but never wholly preventing him from doing his job. For the spectators, in fact, the duel in the air was the most spectacular, each sortie by aircraft drawing angry bursts of fire from the Vulcans, Blowpipes and Chaparrals, the latter specializing in guarding the gun areas. Everybody drew encouragement when hits were made on fast-moving targets. They barely noticed a certain reluctance with later enemy sorties to press home their attacks, but they did have a feeling of being cared for.

Less popular among the infantry were the Blowpipe operators at the front whose priority targets were the enemy artillery air OPs, the Hare helicopters which repeatedly popped up and had to be kept at arm's length, if not destroyed. A shot by a Blowpipe, with its distinctive signature flash, was a guaranteed invitation for retribution by enemy guns. Jake Martin sympathized with Infanteers who shouted abuse from nearby trenches when he raised his weapon to engage. But he had his orders and there was considerable satisfaction in steering a missile towards its target, watching the pilot start

THE SECOND DAY + 12 HRS ON

evasive action but succeeding in keeping track until a flash and puff of smoke culminated in flaming debris falling to earth. That the enemy response, shell clusters bursting close by, shook him and deterred further attempts for the time being, was only to be expected. He would have been happier if the neighbouring Grunts had at least cheered and not decried his prowess. He even took time off, crouching in the bottom of his trench, to wonder if the Ivan who had earlier loosed off an SA7 Grail missile at an incautious Kiowa from 444 Tactical Helicopter Squadron, had been insulted with equal discouragement by his fellow Grunt Ivans.

Above: First flash by a Blowpipe against an incautious Hare helicopter.

The nature and timing of the Russian artillery programme was an advertisement of Samsonov's intentions. Because by 1900 hours their gunners had hardly bothered to engage infantry targets in the forward zone, the command and Intelligence hierarchy in 4 CMBG drew the confident conclusion that a daylight attack could be ruled out. Messages were passed down the chain of communications informing everybody, and reminding them to prepare night fighting aids for use, along with the instruction to afford these delicate instruments protection until the need for their use arose. Already a few had suffered damage from the shelling, but that still left many serviceable under armour, particularly the tank's LLTV cameras.

NIGHT FIGHTING AIDS AND STANO EQUIPMENT

Equipment	Maximum range	Weight kg (lb)	Remarks
Survey radars:			
Short range	Vehicles 3,000 metres Personnel 1,500 metres	11 (24) less transit case	Based on AN/PPS-15(V)2
Medium range	Vehicles 6,000 metres Personnel 5,000 metres	41 (91) less transit case	Based on AN/PVS-4A
Night vision devices:			
Individual weapon sight	300 metres	1.8 (4)	Based on AN/PVS-502
Medium-range crew-served weapon sight	800 metres	8 (18)	Based on AN/TVS-502 – can be mounted on tripod
Long-range crew-served weapon sight	3,500 metres	15 (34)	Thermal imagery device. Presently available for HAW only
Medium-range NOD	1,200 metres	17 (37).	Based on AN/TVS-501
Tank gunnery equipment:			
Image intensification	1,500 metres		Low-level-light TV monitor for gunner/crew commander
Intrusion alarms:			
TOBIAS	Detects men to 50 metres and vehicles to 500 metres from geophones	8 (17)	Seismic device with up to 16 geophones connected by cable to receiver. Receiver can be responsive to 4,000 metres from geophones. Greatest detection range obtained on level ground.
IRIS	Fence length up to 200 metres	2.7 (6)	IR fence with four pairs of IR transmitters and sensors connected by cable to receiver. Receiver may be up to 4,500 metres from sensors.

There was no point, as Tinker remarked, in uselessly sacrificing valuable kit on the first day of the war. This, he insisted, would not be their last battle!

In any case, combat team commanders had each integrated a night surveillance scheme with their original defensive layout. Within the infantry companies individual weapon sights would scan out to

THE SECOND DAY + 12 HRS ON

300 metres, catering to rifles and GPMGs; beyond that, the more powerful NOD medium-range crew-served sight helped give the 50-cal HMGs vision out to 1200 metres. Superimposed on these were the thermal imaging, long-range crew-served weapon sights, belonging to the TOW detachments and ranging out to 3500 metres. Also, there were the gunner OPs' NODs; but most effective of all, the tanks' low-light TV out to 1500 metres. Some combat team commanders tended to place too high a value on the TV and depend on tanks for surveillance. The wise hoped to benefit from a broad overlap among all the passive systems, even if the more sceptical among them preferred to rely mainly upon a generous provision of white-light systems — a variety of flares from the hand-held sort to the big illuminating shells fired by the artillery. Of less importance, in these circumstances, did they hold the radar equipment and anti-intrusion devices. Men such as Panton and Connors felt they would have notice of an enemy's approach by other means long before the radar told them. Nevertheless, both had put out TOBIAS and IRIS intrusion alarms ahead of their most exposed platoon positions — and already a number of responses and alarms were being registered, mostly by stampeding livestock, only once by a patrol near Favorite.

About 1910 hours, there was a sudden brief cessation of Soviet shooting, apart from some desultory large-calibre stuff on its way towards one of the American 203 mm batteries. In several slit trenches and all the command posts, men looked up to say or think: "Hey, what's up?" and then, "This could be it!"

At 1915 hours they knew. Preceded by scattered rounds from individual guns whose gunners had pulled the lanyards before the others, a torrent engulfed the whole front as the entire gathering of Russian guns, mortars and rocket batteries let fly together and raised pandemonium along the 4 CMBG front. At once, those who sheltered in the target areas cowered, not daring to raise their heads. And for a little while, such was the effect, even those who were not at once encompassed by the expanding whirlpools of violence, were reluctant to gaze steadily through or round the bubbling cauldron of flame and smoke which erupted between the forward edge of the company positions and the line of the crest above. Thus it was some ten minutes before the coolest (and farthest detached) observers were able to judge the epicentres of attack and ascertain the pattern imposed by the Russian gunners on their plan. And no sooner had it become plain that it was the infantry locations, particularly those in woods and copses, which were targets for the heaviest load of high explosive, than it was computed at HQ Brigade that the highest proportion was falling on 3 RCR Battle Group with notable emphasis on Blickheim and the ground above Favorite; Mike Company (in Mendel) on the left and Kuppenheim on the right, in the Vandoos's sector, catching a smaller share.

There was nothing much dug-in, immobile troops could do except sit tight, take shelter, pray and hope for the best. Blickheim was in the process of being converted from the slightly-soiled state, caused by the initial exchanges of fire, into a collapsed ruin. Bricks, concrete, steel and timber were scattered like chaff before a hurricane, the roads carpeted with debris. Electricity and telephone poles were felled, their cables tangled in twisted confusion. The jumbled corpses of a quartet of civilians, who in panic had regretted staying behind and tried to flee, lay huddled and coated in dust on sidewalks. Pathetic cries from a cellar overcame Private John Grime's sense of self-preservation, compelling him to quit his slit trench and plunge among the ruins in an attempt to rescue a trapped civilian and a badly injured Canadian soldier. But mostly everybody obeyed

Below: The debris of war.

THE SECOND DAY + 12 HRS ON

orders, common sense and fear – crouching low and only occasionally, in the lulls, looking up to make sure the enemy had not come close under cover of the bombardment. Some men, such as Master Corporal Fred Terry, stayed below ground level the whole time, the terror of the moment paralyzing their sense of duty; it was for Terry's buddy, Private Gordie Miller, to take over in his particular sector, hidden powers of leadership coming to the surface in the desperation of chaos.

Corresponding rules and similar reactions governed behaviour in the different environment of November Company's position. Where air bursts among the trees scythed the surface, only the most foolhardy rose above ground level or left the protection of an armoured vehicle. True, Sergeant Al Hobbs temporarily abandoned the shelter of his trench to go to the aid of two soldiers partially buried by a near miss on a nearby trench, and got back unscathed but trembling from the attempt. But another who emulated his example was instantly cut down; he might have done better to stay where he was since both of those he sought to save were already dead. Casualties and damage mounted remorselessly where shell-fire was heaviest and prevented escape. In effect, the chink Oblensky thought he had found in 3 RCR's outer-skin was being cracked open. Lieutenant Eddie Leach worried and prayed for his platoon and himself – and was joined in his beseeching by several among his followers who had almost abandoned that habit in the relaxed days of peace. He was later heard to remark, that: "Perhaps the best soldiers are those who pray – the other sort seem unreliable" – although there were pundits who credited steadfastness under stress to the virtues of the ingrained skills from military training and a fierce belief in loyalty to regiment and self-respect.

Ian Linkman prayed, but resorted, also, to tactical mobility by encouraging 2 and 3 Troops to pull back any of their tanks which seemed in danger of suffering badly from the bombardment. In the case of 3 Troop, overlooking Blickheim, this was neither so necessary nor easy. The heart of the bombardment centred on the lower part of the village, and Warrant Officer George Crane, whose Leopard was catching it hot, found it difficult to manoeuvre among heaped rubble. He and his crew were somewhat rattled by the concussion, but he managed to keep his voice cool over the air and down the intercom – and extract a badly-scarred vehicle from the maelstrom. No. 2 Troop, on the other hand, had only to back down a hundred metres

THE SECOND DAY + 12 HRS ON

to find safety, its troop officer opting to remain and take his chances on the crest, amidst the barrage, in order to maintain some sort of surveillance to the front. Meanwhile, those in tranquil areas took advantage of the opportunity to get out the TV cameras not already mounted and ready them for the night's activities.

Surveillance, indeed, was very difficult everywhere. Long before darkness had fallen, the clouds of smoke and dust thrown up by the explosions had choked the atmosphere and seriously reduced visibility, the gentle prevailing westerly wind drifting this cloud towards the enemy lines, blanketing the obstacle and the approaches from the autobahn. Neither eyes nor night-vision instruments could see much through this screen. Nevertheless, the assembly of the two main enemy assault columns and their passage across the autobahn did not take place undetected. Kiowas, at the apex of rapid zooms from ground level, taking a quick peep, found their quarry before light had failed. Doppler radars confirmed the contact thereafter and plotted the axes of advance. But the approaching enemy, unheard through the roar of the bombardment, had arrived close by the obstacle, opposite Blickheim, before they were detected by Captain Scott's NOD; only a short time after, those moving past Förch were picked up by a TOW's long-range thermal-imaging sight.

That did not mean that the 290th MRR's approach had been permitted unchallenged. The sporadic supply of information had been sufficient evidence for the Brigade Commander and CO 1 RCHA to bring down speculative fire against likely areas of enemy presence at appropriate moments on both sides of the autobahn. In terms of damage inflicted on what, they assumed, would be a wholly-armoured enemy force, they expected but small return. The dividends they sought amounted to an undermining of enemy morale and confidence and, with luck, the injection of confusion among the Russian ranks. As a penalty for the attempt, they sacrificed an element of surprise by disclosing those battery positions which remained concealed. Yet still the guns of both sides went on firing, although, while the American 203 mm pieces still tossed a few shells at the Russian guns, the latter had, for the moment, turned to more pressing targets. Counter-bombardment, or the threat of it, had certainly laid a restraining hand on both sides and mitigated, to some extent, the weight of fire unleashed against the forward localities belonging to both sides. But now, as 1st Guards Tank Division advanced on a broad front, the artillery's participation (attenuated as

THE SECOND DAY + 12 HRS ON

it might be due to losses and damage) became merged with the evolving action in general.

Of those in 4 CMBG who quaked and were buffetted by the roaring waves of the intense bombardment, only the most dishonest could claim to be unshaken – and the dishonest were often those of loud mouth and minimal intent. The shriek and clamour of shells and rockets consumed men's resistance and, even with the bravest, tended to stun. Only a handful among the high proportion of survivors from the physical effects of bombardment, were totally stunned, however. With the rest, survival simply depended on how quickly their aggressive instincts were restored once the bombardment ended, and how soon they could recover to engage the approaching enemy. Time, of course, was needed for recovery of composure, and that could best be obtained by those who stood outside the pulverized area and who could assert a delaying influence upon the enemy – always assuming that nothing within the enemy organization had gone awry and held them back. In plain terms, 4 CMBG's dug-in infantry could only be sustained in their role as protectors of ground and of tanks and guns, if they were held in place themselves through the intention of the rest of the brigade's agents of indirect and direct action. As the 1st Guards Tank Division rolled towards its objectives, the onus on defence and the winning of time continued to depend on fire-power. But its emphasis shifted radically, with the leading role passing from the artillery to the better-armoured fighting troops.

CONTROLLING FACTORS

★ The relative immunity of men who are dug in under overhead cover.

★ The shock effect of shell-fire and the measures required by leaders to help mitigate its worst manifestations, both mental and physical.

★ The need to reserve the commitment of artillery in order to save them from premature disclosure and subsequent counterbattery action.

★ The problems of defence against enemy helicopters in the forward zone.

★ Attempts to preserve night fighting instruments from damage in daytime, allied to preparation for their use at nightfall.

★ Pros and cons of passive and active night detection of the enemy.

9 | Blickheim – defence of a village

The drive from the assembly area across the autobahn towards Blickheim had been, in the opinion of Corporal Igor Lyubshin, as difficult a piece of cross-country work as he had ever undertaken. It had been none too easy in his T72, with its KMT5 mine-plough bumping along in front, to climb the bank leading up to the highway and drop down the other side, and it was at this point that he and his crew realized, by the light of the moon and the flash of gunfire, that the precise formation in which I Battalion 290th MRR had started was disordered. With his head out of the hatch, the driver was vaguely aware that the three accompanying tanks were losing touch; through his infra-red periscope nearly everything was obscured in a green haze caused by dust and smoke; it was not a real surprise to him when the plough dipped into a deep ditch and the tank came to a shuddering halt. Curses down the intercom by Lyubshin and orders to reverse did nothing to improve matters. Shells falling nearby in clutches of half a dozen discouraged anybody from getting out to look for damage to the plough. Insistent voices over the radio between the company commander, the platoon leaders and miscellaneous out-stations indicated that confusion was rife.

As he backed out of the ditch and began once more to advance, Lyubshin found himself among the BMPs. Unable to detect the marker posts which a brave reconnaissance patrol had staked out along the route to the front edge of the enemy minefield, he nevertheless pressed on. He headed for the burning village, outlined in shell flashes ahead (which he knew to be the infantry's objective) and hoping against hope that he would notice the minefield before overrunning it. He passed a halted T72 that was shooting – the flash of its gun temporarily blinding him. Just ahead it looked as if the other mine-plough-fitted tank was also stopped, had found the minefield and was lowering its plough for use. Slightly to the right a dull flash and a heavy explosion indicated that a vehicle – maybe a T72,

THE SECOND DAY + 12 HRS ON

Above: A dismounted TOW operator seeking a target, his SMG to hand nearby.

perhaps a BMP – had advanced too far and detonated a mine. Lyubshin told his driver to halt and lower the plough, but prudently waited to see how the other plough-fitted tank progressed before starting work. From each side, as well as from behind, tanks and BMPs were opening up with their guns upon the burning village. Wildly tumultuous though the scene appeared, it did look as if a gap might be made without a serious hitch. And then they ran into the railway track, and the next moment shells rained down among the company.

Because I Battalion 290th MRR had attacked with one company up, heading straight for the narrow apex of Blickheim, the village's defenders could at first play only a minor part in their own defence, since their weapons were mainly sited to cover the flanks. Coming where it did, the Red Army attack fell chiefly to artillery and mortar tasks, and within the arcs of fire from Mike Company on the left and November on the right (although the latter was too heavily engaged itself to be able to contribute very much). It was the FOO, Scott (in response to a speculative request from OC Oscar Company) who caught the mine-ploughs at work, and the initiative of a TOW operator with Mike company, opening up at the maximum range of his night sight, which produced a hit on the right flank tank supporting the minefield breaching operation. This was all very impressive to those at the sharp end of Oscar Company who managed to see what went on, but even at 200 metres (despite the lifting of enemy artillery fire to targets towards the crest) they could still observe but little. For now they were being hammered by a new opponent – by the guns of the enemy tanks and BMPs. They had still to hang on until the enemy drew even closer – in other words, after he had got through the minefield.

Ploughing the gap was proving a frustrating business, however. The inclusion of the railroad within the obstacle stopped the leading T72 in its tracks and Lyubshin, behind, was nonplussed about how best to avert a similar set-back. He opted, eventually, for trying farther to the left, just beyond the point at which the railroad joined the minefield. This took time and, meanwhile, the infantry company commander, whose BMPs and tanks were stranded like sitting ducks, and who realized that he was losing the help of the friendly artillery barrage as it moved away from him, felt unable to wait any longer. Forgetting Lyubshin and instructing his BMPs' gunners to give maximum fire support, he ordered his men out of the BMPs, telling

THE SECOND DAY + 12 HRS ON

them to charge on foot through the minefield into Blickheim with the faint chance of reaching the objective intact and in time.

By day or night, men in battle see only what goes on in their immediate vicinity. By night, it just happens that they see rather less than by day and tend, stimulated by man's natural fear of the dark, to imagine rather more. Each of those in 3 RCR battle group who was trying to work out what was happening around Blickheim held totally different opinions about developments. Their impressions were conditioned by a combination of the intensity of bombardment to which they had been subjected, the degree of obscuration and disruption, and their physical proximity to the enemy, in addition to their ingrained staunchness of spirit and determination. Master Corporal Terry and Private Gordie Miller, for example, felt they were at the centre of the bombardment but, in fact, owed their survival to the fact that they occupied a slit trench beyond the eastern apex of the village boundary. Because they were nearest to the T72s' initial attempt at breaching the minefield, but still slightly more than 300 metres off, they were unable to pick out the target with their

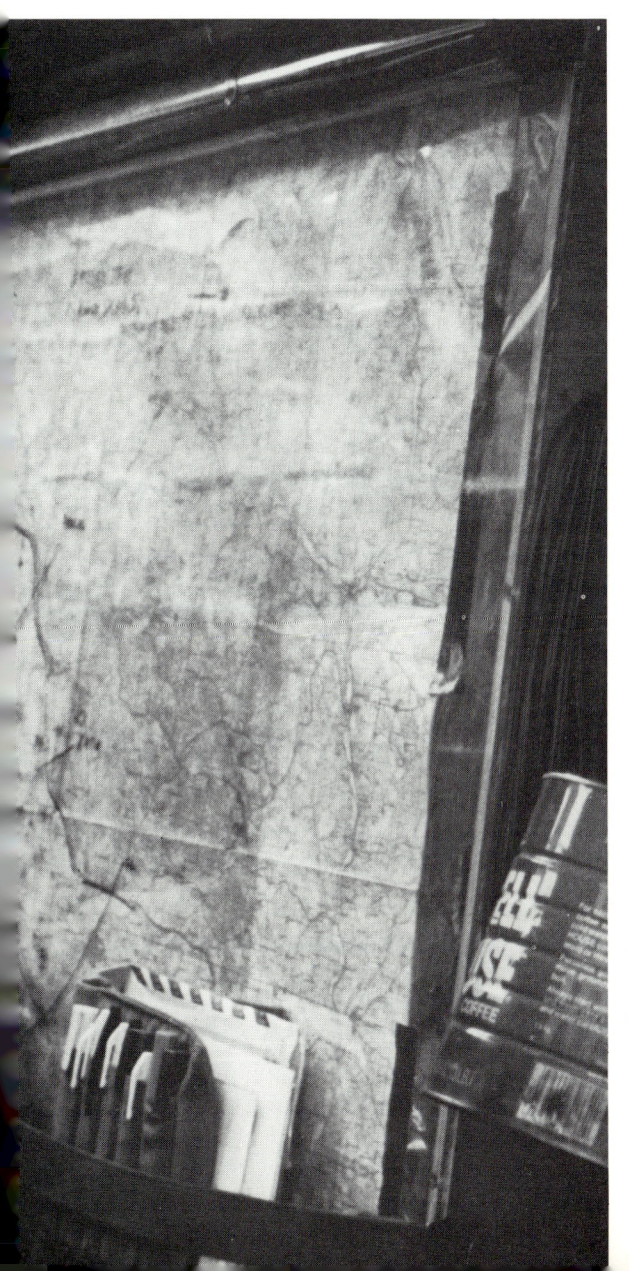

Left: Plotting the mosaic of battle in a command M113. Fire tasks can be seen plotted on the talc covering the map board, chinagraph pencils at the ready.

THE SECOND DAY + 12 HRS ON

THE SECOND DAY + 12 HRS ON

Left: An MMG team scanning the darkness and waiting for a target. Notice the overhead cover to the slip trench.

THE SECOND DAY + 12 HRS ON

individual weapon sights and only able to guess at what was going on through the sound of engines, the sight of a tank struck by a TOW and the noise of a BMP going up on a mine. Since Terry was still paralyzed by fear, it was Miller who judged the situation and reported his observations, via his platoon commander, to Panton. Lieutenant Eric Olafson, the platoon commander, who, on the cessation of the bombardment, had begun to struggle through the wreckage in an effort to assess the state of affairs, could only acknowledge on his manpack radio, leaving it to Panton to fit this valuable piece of information into the mosaic in red chinagraph that was forming on his map. Already Panton had received a warning from Mike Company, on the left, and he had only to stick his head out of the cellar to see what was happening to November. But the most useful information was coming from OC 2 Troop, via Linkman – a steady flow of reports by that officer acquired through the TV set, indicating precisely what was going on. This information the troop leader also translated into action by calling forward his other three tanks to engage the enemy vehicles piling up along the edge of the minefield.

It was Gordie Miller who took charge of Fred Terry instead of, as rank demanded, the other way about. As gun flashes to the front betrayed the BMPs and T72s, when they started to shoot overhead, into the buildings behind (the Russian gunners, to a man, not bothering to seek and find targets outside the built-up area), Miller shouted at Terry and then kicked him into seizing a weapon, calling at the same time to the occupants of the next slit trench to watch their front. His attention had been drawn to the likelihood of an infantry assault by the detonation of an anti-personnel mine down there on the lower ground. And there was another to confirm his suspicions!

"They're coming!" he shouted at the top of his voice. "Come on! Use your scopes. Don't shoot until you can see them! And shoot low!"

Miller was a trained soldier as well as a natural leader. Even Terry began to emerge from his daze and take an interest by picking up the Carl Gustav MAW. Miller's example was infectious. Not only were all the survivors of his section alerted, but the inspiration was spreading outwards through the rest of the platoon. Thus Olafson was gladdened to find his men mostly prepared for the first man to man confrontation of the battle. Calling over the radio to Panton for

THE SECOND DAY + 12 HRS ON

heavy weapon support, Olafson sensibly went to join 2 Section, the one least likely to be directly engaged and which he could employ as a reserve for blocking or counter-attack. But it was Miller, at the closest point of contact, who quite literally called the shots. Through his scope he watched the green images of men emerging – at first a handful blurred by the clutter of dust affecting the screen. Then positive identifications at a recognizable range in a recognizable assault formation. He was content to hold his fire, safe in the knowledge that, at that range, he could not miss; and, anyway, sheer volume of bullets would annihilate. But events determined otherwise. A sudden bathing of the sky to the south in light above Favorite made his scope superfluous, and at once prompted an impatient colleague to loose off with his LAR. As the illuminating shells flared brightly to the flank, creating long shadows in the approaches to Blickheim, the opening burst of LAR was joined by a ragged volley of small arms fire in which everybody else joined.

Enemy man-sized targets staggered, wavered, fell and dispersed. Shots came crackling back out of the darkness. Images rose, rushed closer and dropped – some deliberately, some not. The range was shortening. Shouts in the Slavic language could be heard mixed with the screams of a wounded man. Silhouetted to the front, the enemy

Above: Leopards night-firing.

THE SECOND DAY + 12 HRS ON

wave had melted. On the flanks, they were doing better. There an intelligent Russian platoon leader had noticed a blank spot between the places where spurts of fire indicated weapon pits. His company's charge had failed. Now infiltration looked the best method, each Russian sensing that, in a way, the closer he could get to the enemy the safer he would be. For the situation down by the minefield had deteriorated to the catastrophic.

Concentric eddies of artillery and mortar fire were striking the start line of I Battalion's assault — the efforts of A Battery 1 RCHA (less one Howitzer, out of action) and two 81 mm mortar detachments of 3 RCR pummelling Russian infantry who hugged the ditches in fear as vehicles began to reverse away. To this indirect shooting was now joined the aimed fire from 2 Troop's Leopards' 105 mm guns, concentrating on T72s before switching to BMPs — the targets visible to the gunners through rifts in the smoke and dust, and made clearer by flares and battlefield flames. Surprise was on the 3 RCR battle group side. The unexpectedly heavy volume of fire projected against the Russians, the accuracy with which it was directed and the way night seemed to be turned into day was unnerving. When tanks and carriers began to take hits, vehicle commanders sought shelter in folds of ground or where shadows might offer faint cover from view. The fire support they were giving to their dismounted infantry slackened. Self-preservation supervened. A smoke-screen laid by the tanks to help shield them from view, not only put a complete stop to their shooting but also hampered the approach of the other two companies as they drew nearer for the second phase of the attack. The smoke-screen did, however, encourage Lyubshin to persevere with ploughing, and it was in some triumph that he was able to announce over the air that he had completed a lane of one vehicle's width and that he was backing down it prior to commencing another, meanwhile circling his T72 with local smoke.

To a detached observer, the situation at Blickheim was favourable to 3 RCR Battle Group, and even to Panton (denied much detail as he inevitably was) things did not look too bad. But to Olafson, at about 2025, it looked awful when a private soldier, disarmed and limping from a wound in the calf, struggled in from the right flank and gasped out, "They're right among us! The bastards were among us before we could shoot. Goddam it, the whole of number 3 Section's had it! They're all over the place!"

144

THE SECOND DAY + 12 HRS ON

Olafson's first instinct was that of panic; his second, a recollection of something a British General called Slim had once said, along the lines of not believing the man who claimed he was the only survivor, since, probably, he was merely the fastest runner; his third, to send a quick report to Panton; his fourth, to go and look for himself, taking with him a few men to see what could be done. It was not easy picking his way through the ruins, wondering who he would meet first – his own side or the enemy. But at least the cessation of fire from the enemy tanks made life easier and the faint light still coming from flares over Favorite helped. The problem was solved by a flurry of shots, curses, screams and grenade explosions right ahead, amid the shadows of a shattered house. Apparently there were survivors among 3 Section after all – and belligerent ones too. In fact, it was the last remains of 3 Section disputing a lodgement by about a dozen Russians who had managed to enter the village and were concentrating upon securing their positions, endeavouring, at the same time, to call upon their superiors for reinforcements.

It might have been better if Olafson had waited for help that was on the way. Panton, satisfied that the main enemy threat had been contained, was assembling a small party, mostly the Pioneer Section, to drive the enemy out of 1 Platoon's position, and asking Linkman to place Warrant Officer Crane's Leopard under command to help with this very local counter-attack and also deal with any enemy armoured vehicles which might have found their way through the minefield. The Pioneers were soon on their way, with Panton's second-in-command leading them. But Crane's Leopard was again in trouble. Permission for it to advance to the attack had at once been forthcoming, Linkman reasoning that clearing up the penetrations at Blickheim would enable him to concentrate on a deteriorating situation at Favorite, where the enemy was making more progress than he or Connors liked. Crashing through heaped masonry on the village outskirts, the Leopard shed and jammed a track so thoroughly as to be beyond the capability of the crew to repair. Fortunately, Crane was able to see narrowly through gaps in the fruit trees towards a segment of the minefield, but his tank's role was strictly limited until the Armoured Recovery Vehicle arrived from A 1 Echelon – a request from Crane having been at once granted by Linkman who wanted every tank at his disposal to be mobile.

So the Pioneer Section counter-attack went in unsupported, except by Olafson and his small party. Of necessity, it was improvised and aimed at an ill-defined objective with a minimum of Intelligence about the enemy. In the event, it amounted to a wild rush behind a short blast of preparatory fire from a Carl Gustav, an LAR and two rifles. Scrapping with grenade and SMG in the half-light conveyed no great advantage to either side, both of whom were desperate. After fifteen minutes, a breathless Company 2IC was able to report to Panton that he thought the position was clear of the enemy and that Olafson was dead; and suggest that, perhaps for the moment, he should remain in command of 1 Platoon himself since he could not find the Platoon Warrant Officer. "In any case," he added two minutes later, "indications are that the enemy is starting something big out there in the direction of Favorite. Where's that tank? Over!"

CONTROLLING FACTORS

★ Problems confronting a Soviet minefield breaching party.

★ Problems caused by dust and smoke obscuration.

★ The value of the tank LLTV set.

★ The likelihood that a few leaders will fail and that their place will be taken by junior ranks of unrealized quality.

★ The need for quick counter-attack by small forces to deal with local enemy penetrations of a platoon sector.

★ The manner in which the battlefield becomes illuminated by fires.

★ The importance of smoke at night.

10 | Break-in

November Company under pressure

Lieutenant Leach's 1 Platoon in November Company, like its opposite number in Oscar, had its back to the wall from the start of the attack by 290th MRR's III Battalion; but unlike the men in Blickheim, found itself almost alone at first in holding its ground.

III Battalion 290th MRR attacked with two companies up – the left one using Förch as cover and driving through Favorite in its attempt to seize the high ground to the left of the Förch-Hügelsheim road hitting 3 Platoon; the right one crossing the open ground to the north of the road, taking in 1 Platoon. At first the attack on 3 Platoon made little headway, even though it easily found and negotiated the gaps in the minefield at Förch, and crossed the start line at Favorite in reasonable order. Trouble did not break out until it left the cover of the trees, but then the intense fire which poured down upon the closely-grouped tanks and BMPs, from an arc that included Kuppenheim on the left to the crest immediately ahead, precluded further progress. The company commander discreetly withdrew his vehicles under cover and instructed them to deal with the enemy by fire-power, concentrating on knocking out the Canadian weapons while the infantry endeavoured to infiltrate among the trees leading to the crest. The wisdom of his choice was necessarily slow to become apparent, and a certain chilliness in the voice of his battalion commander gave warning of disapproval from on high. But this company commander was not the kind to sacrifice men uselessly. Moreover, encouraging news from his colleague on the right gave hope that it was there that leverage would be applied to loosen resistance along the entire front.

No. 1 Platoon was in a rather bad way before the Russians put in their assault. Quite apart from the fact that vital support from the tanks and TOWs near Blickheim had been denied due to the obscuration and losses (one of the three remaining dug-in TOWs at

147

THE SECOND DAY + 12 HRS ON

Blickheim had been destroyed by a direct hit from artillery, another damaged), the barrier of trees separating it from its right-hand neighbours placed it in semi-isolation. Furthermore, its own losses from the well-directed artillery concentrations were dire: two out of three TOWs were wrecked along with half the Carl Gustavs and 50 cals and many of those weapons which had not been damaged needed cleaning. Sergeant Roach's radio had been smashed, so the FC was temporarily out of action. Until he could find another radio, the 81 mm mortars would be directed either by the FOO or somebody else within the infantry company. Kendal had survived in his OP, but his view of the front was impeded by smashed trees and the smoke and dust. The tanks, on the other hand, had got off lightly with only minor damage. So, although 2 Troop was distracted by the need to give support to Oscar Company on the left, its intervention along with Linkman's two squadron HQ tanks was reasonably assured.

The weight of attack which III Battalion was able to throw against 1 Platoon amounted to four T72s and ten BMPs plus the close-range fire of assorted infantry vehicles and their dismounted occupants of II Battalion lodged in the much-battered Favorite. This amounted to a superiority in the region of that magic figure of three to one which military pundits commend as minimum necessary for the prosecution of offensive operations. What was more, III Battalion managed to open with and maintain momentum; its journey from the autobahn to Förch had been unchecked and hardly interfered with; its passage through the breaches forced in the minefield (which

BATTLEFIELD ILLUMINATION

Equipment	Maximum illumination diameter	Remarks
Tk searchlight white light	1,200 metres	To provide direction and reflected battlefield light capability for main battle tank – LLTV
Trip flare	300 metres	Burns for 55 seconds
Projector C1	70 metres	Burns for 10 seconds
Flare signal handheld C3	350 metres	Burns for 30 seconds
Bomb ILL 81 mm mortar	1,250 metres	Burns for 60 seconds
Shell ILL 105 mm	800 metres	Burns for 60 seconds
Shell ILL 155 mm	1,000 metres	Burns for 120 seconds
Flare AC para AN/Mk 8	1,250 metres	Burns for 180 seconds
Flare AC para M8A1	900 metres	Burns for 180 seconds

had been widened by II Battalion in the interim) uninterrupted and its fanning out into attack formation, beyond the gaps, accomplished smoothly despite a gradual growth in hostile fire. It was only at this moment, indeed, that resistance in this sector began to bite.

Both November Company and the adjacent elements of Linkman's combat team were being drawn into the sort of attritional slugging match they would have preferred to avoid, a condition exacerbated by Linkman's decision to illuminate the battlefield with white light. Linkman's call to Kendal for illumination from A Battery was in part based on a long-held conviction as to its value, and partly through necessity. Over the years, Linkman had held a preference for the clarity of white light in illuminating targets (particularly those beyond 2000 metres range) compared with the mistier visions depicted in the various types of active and passive night vision instruments, with their restricted ranges of acquistion. The conditions of obscuration now presented to him for the first time in battle, simply reinforced that opinion. But there were disadvantages and risks involved, since the order that directed his tank commanders to occupy positions from which they could open fire at the instant of illumination, compelled them all to forfeit the protection of hull-down positions. For the configuration of the ground near the crest was convex, and therefore, in order to obtain crest clearance for their guns against targets at the bottom of the slope, they had to drive their Leopards forward into the open.

The anti-armour attack by Linkman's B Squadron failed to achieve its maximum potential. For one thing, 3 Troop was largely preoccupied by supporting Mike Company against the diversionary attack by 302nd Tank Regiment and in the defence of Blickheim. In any case, it was not at all easy for this troop to pick out targets in the current conditions fronting November Company. Similarly, No. 1 Troop on the right could not afford to disregard entirely what was happening to its front at Favorite and in the direction of Kuppenheim, where 303rd Tank Regiment was staging its demonstration. This left only Squadron HQ (with its two Leopards) and the four Leopards of 2 Troop to tackle one advancing enemy company group. Unfortunately, these six tanks, by moving farther down the slope, had lost sight of many targets among the splintered remains of trees lying all over the place. Moreover, despite retaining the useful background cover provided by trees and slope, they nevertheless came into full view of enemy tank commanders who, at the critical moment when the flares burst into light above them all, had halted with a view to giving aimed fire support to the BMPs as they motored at full speed up the slope onto 1 Platoon positions.

The exchange of fire which broke out and the roar of engines as the BMPs charged was both spectacular, awe-inspiring and destructive. Within three minutes, an area some 250 metres square was dotted with burning vehicles and populated by men at each other's throats. Where tracer ammunition slashed to and fro, and guided missiles roared both ways, up and down the slope, the BMPs' infantry passengers opted for discretion and took to their feet, hunting through the felled trees and torn ground for the survivors of 1 Platoon whose trenches were exposed to view by the brilliant flares dangling from their parachutes overhead. Neither side was shooting well. The excitement and terror of the moment, transmitted to darting eyes and unsteady hands, down-graded the performance of even the best marksmen.

Each weapon's discharge inevitably disclosed its location and attracted retribution. Vehicles which had been struck once and destroyed, continued to receive hit after hit from gunners who were quite unable in the confusion to separate the living from the dead. When Linkman called to Kendal cancelling the illumination, much damage had been done to both sides. One TOW had been knocked out (after scoring one indecisive hit at 100 metres) along with all the 50 cals, whose close-range shooting had badly damaged at least two BMPs before their positions were overrun. Two Leopards – the dozer tank from squadron HQ and the warrant officer's tank from 2 Troop – were in flames, the unprotected ammunition within their fighting compartments exploding volcanically; a third Leopard was limping out of action with a jammed turret and a wounded gunner from enemy fire – and numerous hits from a Canadian 50-cal gunner who had mistaken his target.

With Russian infantrymen hunting among the dug-outs with SMGs and grenades, their Canadian opponents had to look more to their own defence than to dealing with the vague shapes of enemy armoured vehicles. When anybody boldly exposed himself in order to fire a Carl Gustav or an M72, the chances were he would miss, even at close range; and it was no guarantee that a kill would be achieved if a hit were obtained. Frequently, those men caught in the act of tank-hunting were shot down by the Russian riflemen whose prime task at that moment was just that. Nevertheless, one BMP was

THE SECOND DAY + 12 HRS ON

disabled by a Carl Gustav and finished off by M72, and several received hits or were badly scarred. But groups of Russians reached the crest and took shelter there.

Leach had gathered seven survivors and was attempting to conduct a rearguard action as he backed off to merge his force with 2 Platoon in rear. Private Charrier was among those who joined him, a Carl Gustav in his hands and an exaggerated claim to have knocked out two BMPs. In fact, he had damaged one that had already been hit and put the wind up a 1 Platoon M113 which was trying to extricate itself from the surrounding brawl. Of the M113s, only one had been lost, but the gunners of the mounted HMGs of the three which escaped, provided a smattering of fire as they withdrew. Two of these were quite severely damaged by near-misses from shells and one had received a glancing blow from an RPG7 whose operator had then paid the price for missing.

None of this was plain to Connors who was anxiously trying to find out what had happened to Leach and his men, while endeavouring to fill the hole which seemed to be opening wide in his company's centre. Leach's radio was out of action, but 3 Platoon was reporting renewed activity by enemy infantry infiltrating along the road. Next moment, sounds of firing down by the abatis confirmed this. So, without totally writing off 1 Platoon as a dead loss, Connors ordered 2 Platoon to take sole responsibility for the defence of the abatis and instructed 3 Platoon to deal with the infiltrators from the flank. In fact, most of those close to the threatened point of confrontation were taking steps on their own initiative to deal with the situation. Kendal was seeking permission to bring down the fire of A Battery on 1 Platoon's position, but Connors, lacking positive information about the state of affairs there, vetoed the suggestion for the moment. Linkman was telling 1 Troop to send a Leopard to block the road and cover the abatis. The CO was heard on the air telling the Recce Platoon to deal with any enemy who might now penetrate the gap and plunge towards Iffezheim; and warning Papa Company, too, of an impending blocking task coming its way.

The state of play, as Tinker saw it, was to say the least, critical. Although Oscar had apparently held firm at Blickheim, and November Company was still in possession of the major portion of its sector, with no immediate sign of the enemy resuming his advance, it was patently obvious that the pause could only be temporary. He had discussed the situation with the Brigade

THE SECOND DAY + 12 HRS ON

Commander on the air and had been told that Tactical Air Reconnaissance had just reported a considerable body of enemy armoured vehicles moving towards Blickheim from Rastatt, with indications of a gradual envelopment of both flanks of 4 CMBG.

"You can expect them to exploit between Blickheim and Kuppenheim," said the Brigadier-General. "You must hold fast! Keep a grip on the flanks and deal with the penetrations as and when they occur in the usual way."

At the same time the Brigade Commander prepared for the worst. To begin with, he asked the US Artillery, through CO 1 RCHA, to start paying less attention to counterbattery work and more to harassing the enemy armoured column which had been detected, his staff indicating the likely assembly areas on the gunner net. Also, through the TACP at the battalion FSCC, he asked for support at first light from the company of TOW-armed helicopters which had been promised – to be told that only the equivalent of a platoon could be found, so heavy had been the losses already incurred by these machines. As compensation, it was mentioned that air strikes from A10 aircraft might be provided – information that was disseminated throughout the battle groups of 4 CMBG as much as a morale booster as a stimulus to the planning of targets for them. Believing that God helps those who help themselves, the Commander stiffened up 4 CMBG's organization, instructing CO 1 RCHA to continue giving priority of support to 3 RCR Battle Group and, of essential importance as the front began to strain, reinforcing the Brigade Reserve under Lieutenant-Colonel Cowdray, CO of RCD. To the existing force of C Squadron, with its attached platoons from 3 RCR and the Vandoos, he now added the Field Squadron from 4 CER in the infantry role, relieving it of its continuing task of preparing demolitions in rear. This gave the sappers their first chance to rest in nearly 36 hours. Their withdrawal now to Sinzheim came as a welcome respite for the weariest troops in a formation, most of whose members were suffering in some considerable degree from overwork, an irregular feeding routine and the stress of battle.

From Major-General Samsonov's point of view, operations appeared to be developing reasonably satisfactorily. At 2100 hours, he had joined Oblensky on the outskirts of Niederbühl, and brought with him Colonel Pavel Podduyev, commander of 301st Tank Regiment. Uppermost in his mind was selection of the moment to unleash the 301st through the gap pried open by 290th MRR. But for the moment he had to wait. The gap was not yet fully open and, in the back of his mind, there persistently lurked the cautionary thought that at no time dare he collect too dense a concentration of vehicles at one spot. True, there was as yet no evidence to suggest that the NATO powers were about to launch nuclear weapons, but everybody knew that a state of desperation might easily act as the final provocation – and who was to know when that condition had been reached? And what, if any, warning might be received?

Impatiently, Samsonov listened to Oblensky adjusting his plans to suit the situation at the front as it became plainer. Regretting that Blickheim seemed as far from capture as ever it had been, and that the left-flank company of III Battalion had failed to make the progress expected of it, Oblensky drew comfort from those incursions which had been achieved, and determined to close down on failure while exploiting success in the classic manner. Telling I Battalion to call off its assault on Blickheim and attempt merely to pin down the enemy in that area, he diverted its left-flank company group through the gap in the minefield ploughed by Corporal Lyubshin, and told it to widen the penetration of the enemy defence

---

CONTROLLING FACTORS

★ The methods adopted by Soviet forces in a deliberate night assault on a narrow frontage.

★ The need for infantry and armoured commanders to assume direction of artillery and mortar fire in the event of a breakdown in fire support communications or through obscuration of OPs.

★ The possible counter-productive effects of white light illumination of the battlefield.

★ The high speed with which a charge by enemy armoured formations can close with and overrun a static position.

★ The deterioration of shooting by soldiers under fire and pressure. Enhanced value in these circumstances of the nerveless weapons – submachine-guns and grenades.

★ The value of the M72 in a mêlée between infantry and AFVs.

★ The perils of engaging friendly forces in error.

★ The method and pace at which Soviet forces may be expected to exploit a break-in.

THE SECOND DAY + 12 HRS ON

already made by the right-flank company of III Battalion. Smoke was to screen off Blickheim as this company advanced. Simultaneously, III Battalion was to persist in its operations to seize the crest (he was not sure if his men had reached it or not) as a secure start line for subsequent operations by 301st Tank Regiment. II Battalion, meanwhile, was to launch an attack inclined leftwards, into the Vandoos sector, aimed at expanding the main penetration and cutting across the rear of the enemy strong-point in Kuppenheim.

Embracing this plan, Samsonov instructed 302nd and 303rd Tank Regiments to persist in their diversionary activities on the

Right: The A-10 Thunderbolt close air-support aircraft of the US airforce. A potent, highly-manoeuvrable, well-protected ground attack aircraft – invaluable when available.

THE SECOND DAY + 12 HRS ON

flanks and warned Colonel Romanov of the impending operations, telling him now to shift the weight of his artillery fire deeper into the enemy rear. Harassing of known enemy gun positions was once more in order, along with random concentrations on likely forming-up places for counterattack, such as Iffezheim. The preponderance of fire would still be reserved for support of 290th MRR, however; the bombardment of the crest line of principal importance and geared to III Battalion's requirements on call to Captain Rusalski who would travel with the assault. Speed, as everybody knew, was of the essence and so the launching of attacks by individual companies tended to be

THE SECOND DAY + 12 HRS ON

at their own discretion, acknowledged by battalion commanders and vetted by Oblensky.

Oblensky, as was his way when the climax of any operation approached, took control even more closely himself. For that reason, he moved his command BMP 78, along with the command group of his tank battalion and a T72, to the vicinity of Favorite in order to be on hand to co-ordinate the final, crucial phase of 290th MRR's attack. He had hoped it would begin at 2130 hours, but there had been a hold-up in the deployment of I Battalion's company which was due to by-pass Blickheim. Its leading BMP had exploded a mine, which somehow had been missed by the plough in the gap, and enemy artillery fire had hindered the recovery operation to re-open the way. He figured that the enemy presence in Blickheim might prove fatal to his main assault if it were not contained. The mere threat of an attack against his flank from there worried him; it could not be ignored.

So he fixed 2200 hours as the jump-off time, but allowed II Battalion to begin its advance on the left flank at 2120 hours.

B Squadron Combat Team stretched and regrouped
Major Linkman was delighted when Tinker seized the opportunity, during the lull in the fighting, to visit his command tank. He felt the need to discuss problems man to man, rather than in public over the air, and to demonstrate that B Squadron combat team was becoming over-stretched. Three tank troops (not one of which was still at full strength), the Reconnaissance Platoon of 3 RCR, and a greatly reduced Armoured Defence Platoon, were weak enough as a force to cover a frontage of about 4000 metres which was beginning to bulge in the middle. The expanding enemy wedge which was being driven between Oscar and November Companies had not only pressed a fairly deep dent into his own area of responsibility, but was threatening to split his combat team into two pieces. It was an acknowledgement of this danger which had prompted Tinker to drive forward, not only as an expression of his concern but also to make advanced preparations for some relief by Papa Company's combat team of B Squadron's responsibilities.

Right: In action, the feeding routine is irregular. You take meals as and when you can – and as often as possible.

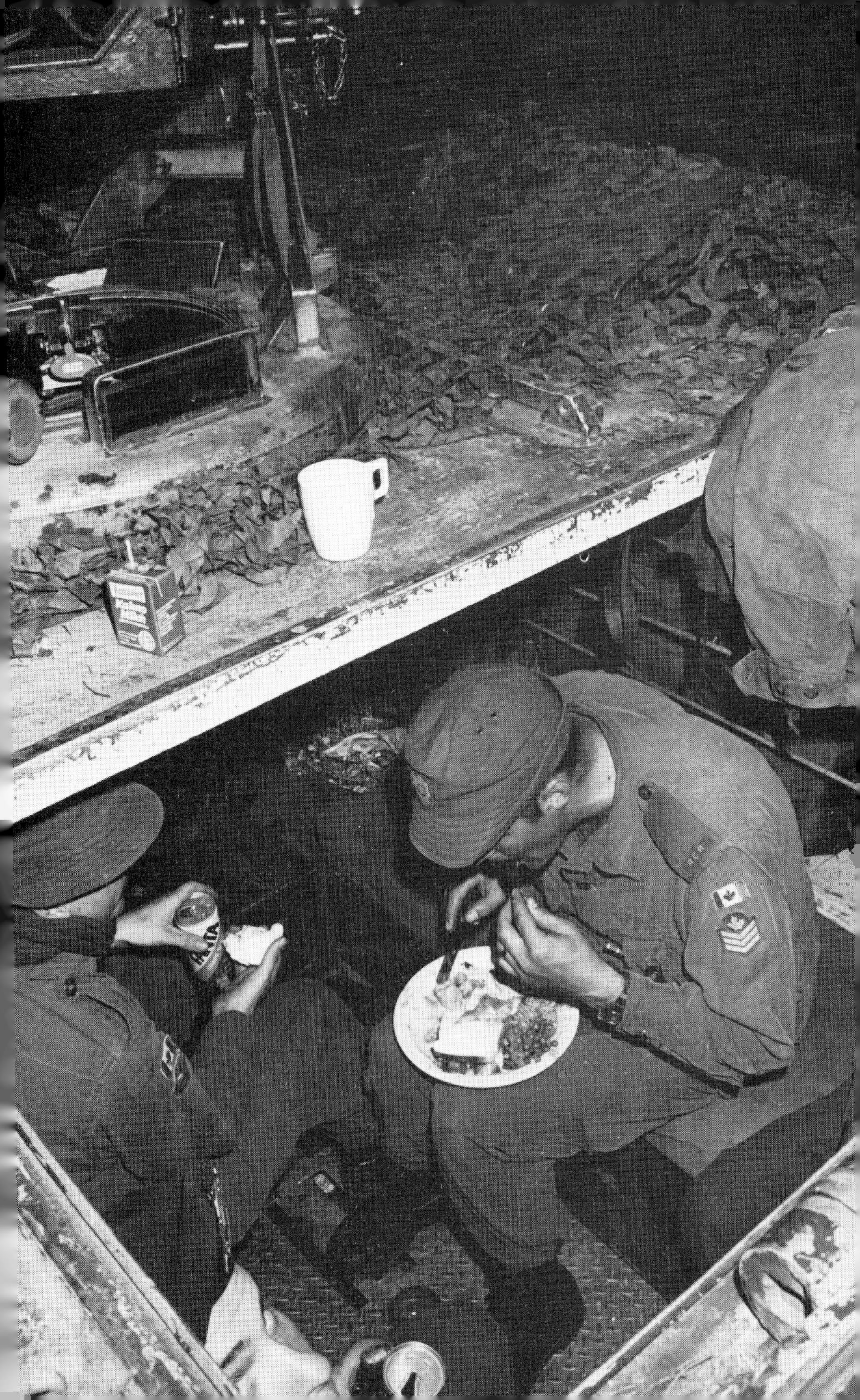

THE SECOND DAY + 12 HRS ON

Even as Tinker approached in his M113, Linkman could be heard on the radio giving notice of his intention to cope with the next phase of the battle in greater depth — a clear indication, to all who heard, that he was about to give ground. In his own way, he was preparing Tinker, besides his subordinates, for the worst — and it came as a welcome encouragement when Tinker broke in at the end of the exchange of radio messages to give tacit approval. Already, the CO of 3 RCR Battle Group had appreciated that, as Linkman was pushed away from Oscar and November Companies, he would stand in need of infantry protection — thence the transfer of the Reconnaissance Platoon to his command. It remained to be seen, if and for how long, even this arrangement would last under pressure.

As he discovered when he arrived at Linkman's hide (in a clump of trees adjacent to the road and with access to either right or left flank of 3 RCR's position), the tank leader had opted to deal with the enemy threat, whenever possible, by flank attack. 3 Troop on the left, while retaining only one Leopard in support of Mike Company on the extreme left, would manoeuvre its other three tanks against the enemy from behind the crest line overlooking Blickheim. At the moment, in fact, two tanks were fit for the task, but the ARV's crew was straining and heaving to dislodge the jammed track on Crane's Leopard and it was hoped it would soon be mobile again. In the meantime, Crane could still participate as a pillbox in an immobile role. 1 Troop on the right had been relieved of assistance to the Vandoos; in fact, it was the Vandoos who were now increasingly responsible for helping the RCR with an arrangement to reinforce Linkman with a troop from A Squadron in extreme emergency. So 1 Troop, in the manner of 3, could be employed from the right flank against the enemy threat, while still maintaining a presence in support of November Company.

As to 2 Troop's future and his own, Linkman was in some doubt. He wanted to move to one flank or the other since to fall back on Iffezheim would merely break his combat team into three portions and hinder Papa Company combat team in assuming its allocated tasks. He was tempted to move in with November Company, whose position looked the strongest, but rejected that because, if the worst came to the worst, A Squadron RCD and the Vandoos would secure that flank. The left flank was more attractive since, from there, he could continue to bolster the intact stronghold at Blickheim and at the same time reinforce Mike Company if the enemy should effect a penetration there. As to the yawning gap that would open up as he withdrew to the flanks, that could only be taken care of by the nine mobile TOW detachments under their platoon commander, Captain Goodhart. It was a bit thin, even though the ground promised reasonably long ranges of engagement, for the TOWs had already demonstrated in action, what had always been anticipated before the war, that their long time of flight and the ease with which they could be baffled by smoke and enemy fire were serious handicaps.

There was one other deficiency in his squadron that Linkman had need to face: the lack of a 'personal' FOO, now that he was becoming divorced from the front line where all three FOOs were located. Tinker had foreseen this difficulty as well and already had discussed it with Major Pat Vivier, the BC. If time had been available, it might have been possible to bring up a fresh FOO from another battery, or perhaps employ one of the FCs – or in emergency get infantry or tank officers to call down fire using the prescribed procedures. None of these courses appealed to Tinker, mainly because everybody, in a moment of crisis, already had his hands full, but also because a first-class FOO was almost on the spot. He had put it to Vivier, and the BC had agreed that this was the time for him to join in personally. Now he was on his way.

Unfortunately (and caused directly by the immediate enemy threat), Tinker was forced temporarily to reduce the firepower at his

Below: Leopards in firing position behind cover, as armour begins to dominate the battlefield.

THE SECOND DAY + 12 HRS ON

disposal just when it was most needed. A reminder from the mortar platoon that "the enemy are almost blowing down my tubes", left no choice but to evacuate them from their too-exposed position just behind the crest. No sooner was the word given than their M113s were racing hell for leather from the nearby hides to the mortar pits, crews throwing weapons and ammunition on board and then jumping in to make their escape in the nick of time. But, for the next 20 minutes, at least, they would be out of action as they took up position again well to the flanks and rear.

Meanwhile, the mechanics of regrouping were being engineered by the signallers, each affected call sign, or group of call signs, making arrangements to leave the radio net to which they belonged and join the one to which they were assigned. Sticking fastidiously to the drills which had been hammered home throughout the years of training, senior signals NCOs studied the Signals Operating Instruction to ascertain the frequency in use by their new control; then, using the allocated nickname, instructed their out-stations to change to the frequency of the combat team they were to join and, themselves, having received acknowledgement from all their out-stations, told them to 'change now' and switched to the new frequency. Finally, each control asked permission to join the new net and, having received it, carried out a radio check to ensure that each of his own out-stations had complied. Simple and often repeated though the drill was, this was always a tense moment for all concerned. So many things could go wrong, particularly among tired and scared signallers; and when they did, Sunrays frowned and fumed, signal NCOs reproved and cursed, and signallers wished they had picked another trade. This time, the operation went well. The hiccups were small and soon cured. Five minutes was usually enough to complete all transactions. Once more, Sunray could talk to Sunray as if on the office telephone.

Vivier had a brief exchange of information with Tinker as they passed, and the BC joined Linkman only a few minutes before the next enemy attack – one that conformed to the familiar pattern with an intensive blasting by artillery of the ground ahead and to the flanks of the moving armoured phalanx. In reply, 4 CMBG used its own guns, also in the manner prescribed, striking at the located enemy artillery positions and bringing down concentrations on known or suspected assembly areas. Yet variations by both sides were noticeable.

On 1st Guards Tank Division's part there was a measurable slackening of artillery output brought about to a significant extent by 4 CMBG's counterbattery programme. Minimal time for the Russians to switch to the new plan impaired communications and a threatening ammunition shortage (caused by delay along disrupted lines of communication leading to a failure to replace immediately second-line stocks) also imposed difficulties. The directing of fire was somewhat less well-contrived by an unavoidably speculative plan due to ignorance of what lay beyond the crest. But the smoke-screen which blanketed Blickheim, even though it was instrumental in subtracting effort from the delivery of high explosive, produced an effect transcending that of blinding the defenders. As the smoke shells fell with a plop upon the ruined village, and their white vapour gushed forth, a shout went up in Oscar Company of:

"Gas! Gas! Gas!"

Many there were who doubted the authenticity of the alarm but none could afford to ignore it. The dread of chemical and biological attack which, of necessity in order to reinforce training, had been impressed on them over the years, induced an automatic reaction at the slightest mention of the danger. By the light of fires, waning moonlight and thickening fumes, everybody groped for his respirator, and started the time-consuming business of sealing himself from head to toe in equipment which, by its very nature, reduced each man's combat effectiveness by a distinct margin. As the left flank company of I Battalion 290th MRR was beginning to by-pass Blickheim, the defenders of that village, one of whose task was to threaten the flank of just such a move, were neutralized. Again it was only 4 CMBGs artillery and the tanks which could intervene. Once more shell-fire could only hamper and cause little direct damage to an armoured opponent. Inexorably, the Leopards (the only nearby fighting vehicles whose crews were protected by an NBC-proof, pressurized air system and thus able to fight at near-full capacity) were drawn out of their shielded positions in order to engage the enemy in the open.

Much depended on Lieutenant Ron Pike, the leader of 3 Troop, at this juncture. With one tank committed to guarding his left flank, two (including his own) available for mobile intervention on the right, and the fourth (Warrant Officer Crane's) still immobilized by track trouble, Pike was deeply conscious of the conflicting priorities demanded of him.

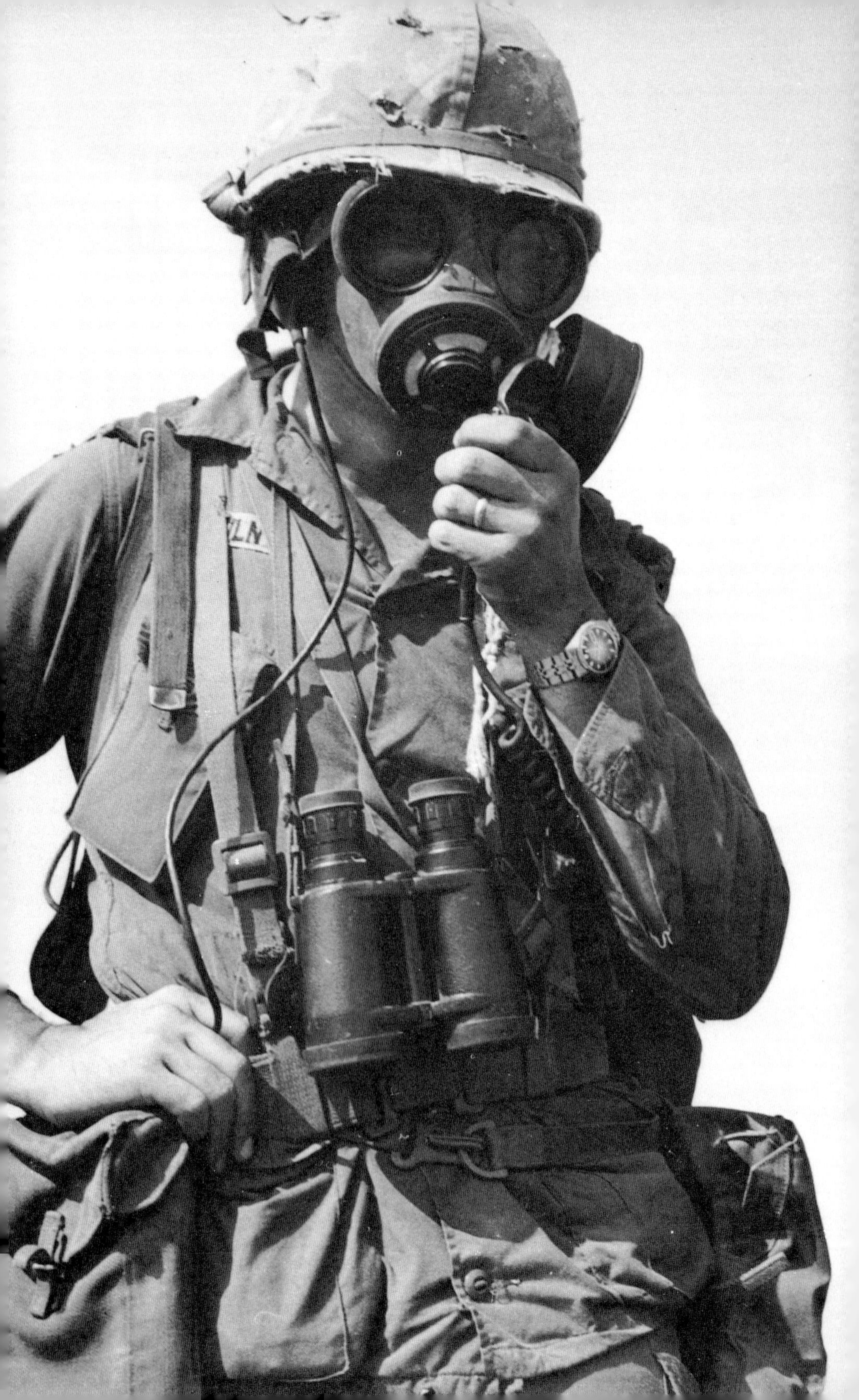

By-products of the gas alarm — a certain clumsiness and problems of intercommunication. Notice the man-pack radio on the right.

"Deal with the bunch coming up on your right!" Linkman insisted over the air. "And get call sign 25 Bravo (the ARV) back to me quickly. I can't afford to lose that."

Setting aside his squadron commander's implication that troop officers are expendable, Pike initiated the manoeuvre he had foreseen must some time come. As a message from Crane announced "Ready to move in Figures 5. Call sign 25 Bravo moving in Figures 10", he instructed Crane to: "Go east, close alongside village boundary, tackle enemy in rear. Then rejoin me back here. Do not, I say again, do not go beyond the end of the village for fear of coming into view of the enemy beyond. I will be operating up here, also against the enemy flank." Informing Panton of his intention and asking him to warn his men what Crane's tank would be doing, Pike (with a sergeant's tank in attendance), vacated the village precincts and drove a hundred metres southwards behind the crest before turning left to occupy a pre-reconnoitred hull-down position clear of the smoke-screen, thus dominating the enemy thrust line.

It was well done. The leading enemy tank was only two hundred yards short of the crest and moving at eight miles an hour when Pike caught sight of it on the TV screen. A quick alignment of the gun sights; a brief command to the gunner, without the need to lase; the swift fire order "Sabot-tank – On!" and the equally swift gunner's reply: "On!" followed by "Fire!" and "Firing now!" At once the scene was obliterated by the flash and smoke of discharge, the bright impact of the APFSDS round on a T72's armour obscured to the crew – but was all too apparent to those with an unobstructed view of the target.

Once more the routine job of manoeuvre, shoot and manoeuvre of mobile armoured combat held sway in the approaches to the crest. Seeking to use all his weapons to maximum anti-tank effect, the Russian company commander disembarked his infantry with instructions to stalk the enemy tanks ahead, and told his T72s and BMPs to take what cover they could, to shoot, lay smoke as necessary, and then charge to the crest line. Then his luck began to run out. By chance all his vehicles had, in the first rush, avoided the local minefields laid by Oscar Company. Now a T72, followed shortly by a BMP, struck some. Armoured momentum died in the instant. Private Rudi Leshko, one of those recently debussed onto his feet from within the cramped BMP, was among the handful who at once tried to move ahead, as much for self-preservation as of aggressive

THE SECOND DAY + 12 HRS ON

intent. Several others came with him and did not stop when a corporal stepped on an anti-personnel mine which neatly removed his foot. Thus there was mixed response to the check. While some on the Russian side cringed, others went bravely forward.

Taking advantage of the enemy's initial surprise, Pike and his sergeant each got off a couple of well-aimed shots (accounting for a pair of BMPs) before shifting their ground. By the time they were redeployed, smoke was billowing around, and each knew the enemy must soon reach the crest. Hopefully, too, Crane would soon be in action against the enemy rear, as a hasty message from the ARV, whose crew saw no future in tarrying amidst a tank battle, proclaimed they were "Moving, Now."

Of course, Pike's application of manoeuvre automatically sacrificed ground, territory which he alone, along with a section of 3 RCR Reconnaissance Platoon which happened to be there, could be called upon to deny the enemy. The sudden resurgence of fighting away towards Kuppenheim and Favorite, even as Pike was changing position, made it all too plain that the rest of Linkman's squadron and Connor's November Company were otherwise engaged. Containment was all that Pike could hope for while endeavouring to wear down the enemy and save his own vehicles from destruction. It was cat and mouse stuff – the Russian T72s, BMPs and RPG7 men trying to pierce the gloom and the Canadian infantry shield in order to stalk the Leopards; the Leopards endeavouring to ambush the Russians and batter their flanks.

As so often happens in battle, the soldiers' aims were interwoven with a race against time as well as the enemy, each leader at every level trying to achieve mastery over the opposition before the march of events overtook the demands of the moment and imposed the need to re-plan and act on revised lines. Foremost in the thoughts of the men of 290th MRR, was the insistent need to seize and hold the crest line sufficiently long for 301st Tank Regiment to break through, unchecked at the start line. All Pike had to do was contribute to 3 RCR battle group's aim of delay by hitting the enemy so effectively that he might be forced to hesitate – even stop or abandon his efforts – short of the objective. Every little effort on his part, or by one of his subordinates, could contribute to that aim; an accumulation of minor episodes frequently had a bearing out of all proportion to their size. For example, trivial and sacrificial as Warrant Officer Crane's role in harrying the enemy flank down on the lower slopes might

THE SECOND DAY + 12 HRS ON

have appeared to him, its potential was considerable within Pike's overall scheme.

Prior to the battle, Crane had reconnoitred the southern approaches to Blickheim. The course he now steered was charted to avoid the local, protective minefields sown by Oscar Company and, at the same time, contrived to carry him along a covered thoroughfare between fruit trees to the easily recognizable track junction at which he could turn right to face the enemy flank. Praying that nobody in Oscar Company would fire on him in mistake for the enemy (and answered in full because Panton had managed to pass a warning to those who were in a position to do so), he reached the turning point in safety and emerged from the tree-line. Nothing happened. But through the II periscope he could see a single T72 broadside on, and, beyond, on the move towards the crest, a BMP. A single shot was enough to make the T72 burst into flames, while it took two to hit the BMP when it took evasive action. Of the two targets destroyed, the T72 gave Crane satisfaction. But it was the BMP which was of most importance, containing as it did the commander of I Battalion, who was at that moment on his way to take charge of the battle on the crest and confirm to Oblensky that the way for 301st Tank Regiment was clear. The skirmish Crane had started, and which now was prolonged as nearby infantry survivors from the I Battalion's leading company either ran away or hunted Crane with RPG7s, had grown into something more telling than the harassing operation Pike originally had in mind. Now the fireworks display engineered by a long burst of tracer machine-gun fire, followed by the lurid bursting of multi-barrelled smoke grenades Crane employed to cover his retreat, added to the exaggerated doubts and fears plaguing Oblensky and his colleagues as they watched the situation at Blickheim burgeoning.

All along, of course, Oblensky had been worried about the danger from Blickheim, his initial dread of fortified villages inflated from the start by evidence of their menace to leading Soviet formations and by the impact the defence of Förch and Kuppenheim already had on his own deployment. His delight at reports of I Battalion having reached the crest were now modulated by a fear that it might soon be cut off and exposed to destruction by forays from the village, and from anti-tank fire ripping to pieces the men and vehicles which stood, stranded and bewildered, on exposed ground. The failure to gain a foothold within the village and the dreaded

THE SECOND DAY + 12 HRS ON

Above: A Leopard moving in the open in aid of the threatened infantry. **Below:** An RPG-7 man and his comrades continuing to advance after the BMP has been halted by a mine.

167

THE SECOND DAY + 12 HRS ON

expectation that the Soviet artillery would not be able to maintain its protective smoke-screen indefinitely, impinged heavily upon his thoughts. Romanov had already warned him that the supply of smoke ammunition at the gun positions was far from inexhaustible. He had been within minutes of telling Podduyev that the way from 301st Tank Regiment was open when Crane struck. The sight of vehicles burning at the lower end of the slope was one thing (to both regimental commanders), but the abrupt loss of contact with the CO of I Battalion at the very moment they needed his affirmation of the feasibility of use of the right-hand axis by 301st, was a serious deterrent – particularly when a garbled report from an over-excited infantry company commander suggested that his CO's command vehicle had been destroyed.

Matters became still more intimidating when a BMP struck a mine further down the slope where mines were not thought to be. In fact, they had just been delivered by a volley of 155 mm carrier shells (each sowing nine anti-tank mines) called down by Captain Angus Scott.

Below: The Red Army's artillery continues to pound, but an ammunition shortage threatens.

168

THE SECOND DAY + 12 HRS ON

CONTROLLING FACTORS

★ The need to disengage some forces in order to prolong resistance, even at the expense of ground and position.

★ The value of flank action against an enemy wedge, balanced against the difficulties of regrouping for its implementation.

★ One way to provide an extra FOO for short durations in an emergency by employing the BC in person.

★ How temporary reductions in fire power are likely due to enemy incursions towards mortar and artillery emplacements.

With Podduyev fidgeting beside him and anxious to throw in the armour whose columns were already beginning to bunch near the gaps in the minefield, Oblensky was impelled into a quick and unwelcome decision.

"I do not think it would be wise for you to use the right-hand gap," he announced at last. "You have heard and you can see for yourself that things are uncertain over there. I think you should use only the left-hand gaps here at Favorite. Do you agree?"

Podduyev replied that he did not entirely. He was already disposed in two battalion columns – I right and II left, with III in reserve – and, on principle, preferred to advance on as wide a front as possible. On the other hand, he could not ignore the danger lurking on the right or reject the evidence of the latest situation reports that the three lanes now open at Förch were the sole, unchallenged thoroughfares through the minefield. Linkman and Pike, by their resistance, had achieved their aim by compelling the enemy to pause for the reassessment which would bring about an unwanted change in plan and, perhaps, induce confusion. By insisting upon his I Tank Battalion, on the right, entering the minefield gap but only tentatively trying to force its way past Blickheim, Podduyev in effect, shifted his main blow to the left! II Battalion was now the centre of gravity and leading bearer of hope. He was encouraged in the belief that, in the light of the situation as presented by Oblensky and his staff, this plan might work. Although the attack on the right at Blickheim had only achieved partial success and the attempt by II Battalion 290th MRR to cut in behind Kuppenheim seemed to be meeting fierce resistance, there apparently was an enlarging hole of some 1500 metres opened up in the centre. In daylight against an unshaken opponent it would not have been enough, but in the existing conditions of poor visibility it might suffice. And then, there was Samsonov getting more and more impatient! He decided to agree with Oblensky, and gave the orders that placed emphasis on concentration through the left axis.

November Company squeezed

If Major Connors could have consulted with Colonels Oblensky and Podduyev, he would have reached a marked degree of agreement with their estimate of the situation in the neighbourhood of Favorite. Purely from November Company's point of view, the threats to its flanks were only contributory causes for concern. Indeed, the oblique attack into the Vandoos sector seemed more like an act of folly than a considered operation of war – and his men had been delighted spectators of fire pouring down on an enemy whose progress was both hesitant and wilting. It was matters on his left flank which were getting out of hand, as pressure from dismounted enemy infantry, backed up by several well-handled armoured vehicles, produced a strain close to the breaking point. By now his men had been scanning the front through their image-intensification instruments for a considerable length of time and, as everyone knew, 30 minutes at a spell was the longest they could undertake without needing relief. In any case, the majority of the rank and file were short of sleep, while none of the officers had closed their eyes for more than a couple of hours in the past 48.

The renewal of the bombardment shortly before 2200 hours acted as a warning, and the reactivation of fighting over by Blickheim coincided with fresh movement in front of both 2 and 3 Platoons. Standing among trees at the junction between the two platoons, overlooking the abatis, Connors attempted to judge the direction and weight of the enemy effort before deciding what to do next. He did not want – indeed, he was not permitted – to withdraw. On the other hand, he was not meant to sacrifice his command if a more flexible and economic kind of resistance could be devised. But flexibility implied manoeuvre and the likely abandonment of carefully prepared shelters. Eventually, the choice was virtually taken out of his hands by the aggression of III Battalion 290th MRR. Unable to obtain clear fields of fire against an assailant who skilfully stalked rather than blatantly charged; deprived of close heavy-weapon support because the mortar platoon, as it changed position, was out of action; the M113s with their HMGs parked in rear; and 1 Troop away back on

THE SECOND DAY + 12 HRS ON

the crest, 3 Platoon's two, exposed forward sections became embroiled in the close combat style of small arms and grenades against an enemy with the initiative and who was superior in numbers. Fight as hard as it would, 3 Platoon was doomed unless Connors did something dramatic to save it. And soon it was borne upon him that 2 Platoon might be equally in peril. For the renewed enemy attack in its direction (also on foot but closely supported by armoured vehicles) oozed over the crest as the shelling lifted, thus immediately threatening the frontal section.

The counteraction Connors employed was of a defensive and an offensive nature. With the aim of extracting what remained of 3 Platoon from its predicament, he sent forward the M113s from their hides in rear. Firing their HMGs for all they were worth and supported by HE and machine-gun fire from two of 1 Troop's tanks, hull down on the crest, they charged to the rescue. Linkman was helping for all he was worth – pulling out the last TOW in that area, making 1 Troop give unstinted support to 3 Platoon, and joining in himself with 2 Troop to sweep the crest line in front of 2 Platoon with 105 mm shell and machine-gun bullets.

Sergeant Al Hobbs in 3 Platoon had all but given up hope when the orders to withdraw came over his manpack radio. Half his section was finished, and he felt remarkably lucky still to be alive himself, for it had been pure reaction when he shot dead the Russian who had suddenly appeared at close range spraying wildly with a submachine-gun. With enemies all around, and the slightest movement an invitation to destruction, the task of shouting warnings to his men to get ready for as he put it, "the quickest skedaddle in history", was perilous and by no mean foolproof. Such was the noise and distraction of battle, even his powerful voice did not get through to men who were intent on killing and trying not to be killed themselves. When the M113s did come lurching down the slope, guns blazing, and the tanks up on the crest plastered the surrounding orchard, it took a sublime act of courage to stand up to attract his own 113's attention. The chances of being hit by Canadian fire were quite as high as that from the Russians, since the latter at once cowered in face of the heavy weapon's shooting, while 3 Platoon's desperados went on shooting.

Connors watched from his own M113, unable in person to influence the outcome, but admiring the behaviour of 3 Platoon Commander and Hobbs as each used their voices coolly over the air,

THE SECOND DAY + 12 HRS ON

Above: A hull-down Leopard holding the line.

guiding vehicles to the right place, reporting the pick-up and arranging the withdrawal under smoke from 60 mm mortars. That the two forward sections' M113s got back was a tribute to skill – and luck; that neither contained its full complement of men and equipment an almost inevitable consequence of staying too long and indulging in hand-to-hand combat with a ferocious enemy. As they reported their depleted states, Connors did two things more before pulling back himself. He gave Kendal the word to bring down artillery fire on the position just vacated, and instructed the remnants of 3 Platoon to amalgamate under Lieutenant Leach, with the survivors of his 1 Platoon, and occupy a new position in their M113s in rear of 2 Platoon, thus providing a mobile reserve in November Company's location while maintaining contact with the Vandoos on the right – but doing nothing to fill the gap opening up on the crest. In a way, in fact, the gap was filled momentarily by the action of the gunners – their 155 mm VT fuzed shells burst scything the slope, slaying the dismounted enemy infantry and temporarily bringing all movement to a halt.

THE SECOND DAY + 12 HRS ON

In consequence of November Company's withdrawal, the task confronting Linkman and his B Squadron was becoming increasingly unmanageable. 3 Troop was committed to the left, 1 to the right with 2 stretched wide in the centre. The nine TOW detachments were spread out in a thin line to the rear, where Papa Company combat team stood centrally placed, ready to perform its important blocking role. Thus B Squadron's task was becoming merged with that of other combat teams preventing Linkman from retaining control over all its constituent parts without prejudicing those combat teams. Tinker had already recognized this and had contemplated making a change when he visited Linkman at the front. Now, as it became clear that 3 RCR battle group was strained to bursting, he resolved to bow to an accomplished fact. Over the air to Connors, Linkman and Major Alan Ferrier (OC Papa Company), he gave fresh instructions, basing them upon the assumption that neither 2 Platoon of November Company, nor the two Leopards of 2 Troop, B Squadron RCD could hold out much longer where they were. When the time came to give way – and Linkman would be the one to judge that – the remnants of his command (less 1 Troop) would swing sideways to form a flank guard capable of attacking the flank of the likely enemy thrust. Ferrier's Papa Company would then fill the gap, dealing as it thought best with each enemy move and taking under command the nine TOW detachments which were located within its boundaries. 1 Troop, meanwhile, would revert from Linkman's to Connor's command and help the survivors of November Company providing what, by then, might amount to little more than a flank guard to the Vandoos. To Linkman and Connors, Tinker laid down the strictest injunction that under no circumstances were they to evacuate the crest line prematurely.

"Every minute counts!" he called into the microphone. "Hold on until first light. Don't give 'em an inch more than you must."

It was the sort of exhortation their CO was only rarely accustomed to give, and that fact in itself lent emphasis to the desperation of the occasion.

The selection of tactics was not the only pressing matter for Linkman. Logistics also were beginning to have their say, in the form of reminders from all three troop commanders that their supply of main armament ammunition, in particular, was running low. The routine, after dark top-up by A 2 Echelon had been unnecessary in the light of expenditure up to then. In the present conditions only

173

THE SECOND DAY + 12 HRS ON

A 1 held close in rear under the SSM was needed. There was no prospect of sending soft-skinned M548 load carriers with their vulnerable loads into the troop positions at this moment and good reason not to bring the tanks back to the carriers when an immediate enemy attack was impending. The most Linkman would permit was replenishment of one tank per troop at a time, starting with 1 and 3 Troops (who had fired slightly more) and leaving 2 Troop and his own tank to the last, despite the likelihood of their being called upon at any moment to fire at top rate. The danger of running out at a critical moment began to haunt Linkman, the more so because it came as a surprise, an event such as peacetime training had rarely taken realistically into account.

CONTROLLING FACTORS

★ The problems of fatigue exacerbated by the use of night vision devices.

★ The value of APCs in extracting dug-in infantry forced to move.

★ The value of bringing down own artillery fire upon recently vacated positions in order to catch a following up enemy in the open.

★ The value of a cool voice over the air in steadying men under pressure.

Below: Commander and gunner of a Leopard of the RCD intent upon the acquisition and engagement of an abundance of targets.

11 | Blocking – Papa Company Combat Team

Shortly after midnight, Major Alan Ferrier felt assured that the testing moment of Papa Company and its attached sub-units which composed the team was nigh. The news from Oscar Company, November Company, and B Squadron was worrying but not in the least unexpected, coming as it did from a part of the front over which the flames of battle had flickered almost continuously over the past hour, the all-consuming gunfire stoking its attendant conflagrations. All around, the guns of 1 RCHA and their American companions had raised their rate of shooting to a crescendo, and now came reports of a fresh influx of enemy armour funnelling through gaps in the obstacle and making for the crest line.

The seizing of the crest line by the Soviets had been a victory for "the bigger battalion"; the holding of Blickheim by Oscar Company a triumph for static forces. Two obvious factors, long acknowledged by Ferrier, had been underlined. Troops, even armoured troops, were at a distinct disadvantage in the open to infantry and guns which were concealed and well dug-in; while those entrenched in open terrain were less likely to prevail than those in woods or, better still, a built-up area. On the other hand, mobile armoured troops which managed to retain their mobility and took pains not to be trapped or drawn into the open, had a good chance of survival and also of inflicting heavy blows on the enemy, whatever his posture. In determining to keep his two platoons of infantry in Iffezheim for as long as possible, while employing, in the mobile role, only the five Leopards under Captain Peter Cummings (backed up by Captain John Goodhart's TOWs). Ferrier sought the best of both worlds. In a sense, he adopted the classic form of defence by having mobile armoured forces pivot on a secure locality. At the same time, he permitted the specialists in armoured warfare quite a free hand. While reserving the right of veto, he nevertheless encouraged Cummings to deploy and manoeuvre his own tank and 4 Troop, in conjunction with the TOWs, much as he pleased. That way they would take maximum advantage of their matching characteristics of protection, fire-power and mobility. As long as Cummings obeyed the firm injunction given to him verbally by Ferrier at midnight, that "No enemy must be permitted to cross TOP HAT – a line drawn one thousand metres to the west of Iffezheim to Oos", there would be no interference on the combat team commander's part.

It looked a tall order to Cummings. All the evidence pointed to an imminent assault in darkness by a complete Soviet tank regiment, well supported by the customary artillery barrage. On a frontage of between three and four thousand metres he could be faced by 95 enemy medium tanks along with at least 10 BMPs, plus any other fighting vehicles which had survived the initial assault and were in fit condition to join in. Pitted against his five Leopards and eight TOWs, there was little doubt that sheer weight of numbers would prevail, no matter how well his side shot or managed to preserve itself from destruction. That, however, was not the complete equation. The openness of the ground; the restrictive and distractive effect of the Iffezheim stronghold; the ability of the mobile armoured vehicles to choose alternative positions for long-range engagement from unexpected directions, which might easily (due to the incalculable variety of their locations) escape the enemy preparatory bombardment, were factors in favour of Papa Company combat team. Added to this would be the impact of aggressive operations from the flanking forces contained in the other combat teams, whose anti-armour effort would converge on the designated killing zone in the vicinity of Iffezheim.

It was not entirely without hope, therefore, that Ferrier and Cummings contemplated the oncoming struggle, even as preliminary shelling of Iffezheim began to pummel the village. Ferrier took comfort from the knowledge that his men were still fresh (if unblooded) and that Oscar Company in Blickheim had not suffered excessively from even rougher treatment. The compact built-up area of limited perimeter had been relatively easy to place on a defensive footing, although not as elaborately as at Blickheim. For a start, not all the accesses had been blocked off because Ferrier foresaw a possible need for forces to sortie outwards, or retire inwards, when engaged in mobile operations. Also, there was a more difficult civil affairs problem here; the local administration had broken down and there was good reason to suspect that a hard core of the suspiciously high proportion of the population who had opted to stay behind were more hostile to the NATO powers than to those of the Warsaw Pact. Ferrier had laid down strict rules for his own men, as well as for the people, concerning the consequences of subversive activity. Already, there had been an unfortunate incident in which a civilian had been caught slipping away from the village carrying on his person compromising information about the defensive layout. Resisting the immediate inclination to shoot the man out of hand, Ferrier had called for the battalion's Military Police to remove the spy – and was sorry he left shortly before the hostile bombardment began. The inevitable effect, needless to say, was to make everybody "spy-conscious" and, therefore, all the more jumpy and prone to rumours whenever they started.

Watching the shells bursting on Iffezheim's roof tops, Cummings and Goodhart, tucked away behind the village in woods, thickets and hollows adjacent to their pre-arranged firing positions, were able to complete their final arrangements virtually uninterrupted. "Surely", remarked Goodhart to Cummings, as they surveyed a perfect field of fire stretching some 3500 metres to their front, "they can't honestly try coming over that! We'll massacre them!"

"Maybe they will, maybe they won't," replied Cummings, comfortably. "Who knows, they may have problems too. Having got so far, in this direction, which way can they turn without starting all over again? Forget it. Each to his own battle and don't take anything for granted. We think we're going to shake him. Who knows what he's got up his sleeve?"

In point of fact, Podduyev had very little up his sleeve, except brute force. It was perfectly obvious to him, as well as 301st Tank Regiment's battalion and company commanders, that the plateau onto which they were being sent had the look of an ideal killing zone – if the enemy chose to make it one. He reasoned that open country was not necessarily ideal tank country, despite the pontifications of pundits. Such terrain flanked by woods and built-up areas, as history told him, might easily turn into a death-trap. So Podduyev selected a method of attack which habitually had been favoured by the experts of the past – the massed thrust on a narrow frontage at top speed, in the hope of bursting through by sheer momentum, despite the high losses incurred. "Tanks will lead from the start", he insisted, "and the infantry company will be held back either to clear out any

THE THIRD DAY

Right: A Carl Gustav team awaits the 301st Tank Regiment onrush on the outskirts of Blickheim, its field somewhat obscured by the town's nameboard.

pockets of resistance among the woods, or take out Iffezheim should it prove troublesome. There must be no pause. Keep moving!"

At no time, after 301st Tank Regiment squeezed through the lanes in the obstacle, was its deployment unnoticed or unharried by 4 CMBG. NODs and tank television cameras in Kuppenheim, as well as on the high ground above Blickheim, detected each group of vehicles, which instantly became the target for artillery of all calibres – Canadian and US Army. Fanning out quickly, the two leading tank battalions were able to steer clear of the heaviest concentrations of shell-fire and escape serious losses. But naturally, cohesion was loosened and the forming-up process below the crest hampered. It was, moreover, confused still more by Panton's initiative. He had by now concluded that the gas alert had been a false alarm and had cancelled it. His men's combat worthiness, tired though they were by the strain and exertions of the night, was considerably restored. Determined to do what damage he could to the gathering enemy phalanx, and anxious to sustain morale through offensive action, he sent out a tank-hunting patrol armed with a Carl Gustav and a few M72s to see what damage they might inflict.

Private John Grimes, carrying an M72 along with his FN rifle, brought up the rear, behind his section sergeant and the two other private soldiers (who carried the Carl Gustav and its ammunition), as

THE THIRD DAY

they stole forth on their mission. Good cover was to be obtained among shattered trees, long grass and shallow folds in the ground. It was a creepy business stalking an unseen enemy, the sole evidence of whose presence was a rumble of engines to the front. Using the Individual Weapon Sight, the sergeant was able to pick out suitable targets, out to 300 metres, and plot a course which avoided the obvious danger spots. Awe-inspiring though the armoured formation ahead might seem, the patrol's principal worry was that of falling into ambush by enemy infantry. There was one scary moment when shots to one flank hinted that they might already have been detected. Then a random illuminating flare (although it exposed several tanks ahead) made them freeze for fear of being spotted. Grimes had to admire the skill with which his sergeant led them — the care taken, without loss of pace or apparent determination, to find a suitable target, get within range and then with luck — get out!

At a range of about 250 metres, the patrol leader spotted two tanks — T72s, he thought. Doubting the Carl Gustav's operator's ability to hit one at much above 150 metres; preferring to attack such a tough target from flank and rear, where the thinnest armour was; and aiming to obtain a position from which subsequent evasion seemed feasible, he continued to crawl towards a selected point of attack alongside a felled tree whose profusion of foliage offered excellent cover. He was just in time. Grimes heard the sergeant's soft order to the Carl G man to fire at almost the same moment as the tank revved its engine to advance. The discharge of the weapon, and the bang of the hit on target, caught everybody by surprise — the tank commander, who was concentrating hard on the way ahead; the other nearby Russian tanks — and the patrol leader who called out in unfeigned astonishment: "My God! You've hit her!"

At once everybody became extremely busy. Soviet tanks sprayed wildly with their machine-guns, hitting nobody; one turned on its exhaust smoke apparatus to blind and add confusion to the assault formation. The stricken T72, penetrated to its engine, stood where it was, fuel leaking profusely. Infantry of the 290th MRR searched warily for the source of the attack, and a moment later were rewarded by the flash from another discharge as the Carl Gustav fired again. This time it missed its target but spread further uncertainty among I Battalion, 301st Tank Regiment as it started again on its journey to the crest. Ambitious to make a contribution (and also be rid of an encumbrance) Grimes took a pot-shot with his

180

M72 in the general direction of the enemy tank mass and was rewarded by what looked like a hit. There was no time to check, however. He and the patrol were now the hunted. Bullets were flying all around; the Carl G operator gave a cry and his companion went to ground.

"I'll cover! Rest of you scram!" shouted the sergeant, and Grimes heard long bursts from an SMG as he took to his heels and ran for all his worth towards the village. He was the only one to reach it and through forgetting, in his terror, to use the prescribed recognition procedures, was lucky not to be shot by his own side.

The incident had its effect upon Lieutenant Yuri Tursov, a tank platoon commander in 3 Company, I Battalion, 301st Tank Regiment, whose T72 had been hit by Grime's M72. The shot had struck and wrecked the searchlight, without damaging anything else, but Tursov, with his head above the cupola ring, had taken some of the blast and was shaken. He remained in control, striving hard to overcome the ringing in his ears and to find his way through that confounded smoke-screen and keep contact with the column as it moved, by fits and starts. The sensation afflicting him, as they advanced, was one of being pecked at all the way. First the shelling, then the infantry ambush and now, as the slope began to level out, more shelling and the sight of tanks ahead being fired at from the flank, and firing back. The battalion commander had told them that the crest ought to be crossed at 0030 hours. That had not been achieved. Already it was 0100. The company commander had said that, given two hours' hard driving they ought to be somewhere near Hügelsheim, deep in the enemy defences at the crack of first light. That remained a possibility – but not if there were many more halts such as the one which occurred as he topped the crest and found, revealed before him, a scene sparkling with gunfire and shimmering with vehicles and buildings aflame. It dimly occurred to Tursov that the pecking might be over and that "running the gauntlet" might be a better term for what was in store. Excited voices were coming through the radio net, telling of shots from the flank tearing tanks apart. When the company commander spoke on the air to Tursov it was in a pitched tone, filled with authority, but a trifle distraught.

"Iffezheim is strongly held and stopping our advance," it said. "The infantry company is to clear it. It will join you in 15 minutes, perhaps sooner. You will go with it and support its assault. Report when moving."

THE THIRD DAY

The order overlooked the full portent of events along the road to Iffezheim, failing, as it did, to mention that not only the village but also certain localities on either side of it were centres of resistance. Both B Squadron and Papa Company combat team had been enjoying a useful shoot at the stream of armoured vehicles debouching into the open ground of the killing zone. With a clearly discernible array of targets passing across their front, the Leopard and TOW gunners were able to pick their shots. And with a sense of security, too, since their commanders reckoned that, from covered positions, they were unlikely to expose their vehicles to a bewildered opponent. As the tanks of the leading Russian companies staggered and burst into flames under a fusilade of shot and missile, those which survived sought safety behind a smoke-screen generated from their exhaust manifolds. Conceal the stricken leaders as the screen, for the most part, did, its billowing clouds, blown back upon the second wave of attackers, simply prevented their drivers and commanders from picking out the way ahead. As a result, the advance came to a virtual standstill, some vehicles straying off course and others, in a few instances, colliding.

Typical of the experience among the RCD's troop leaders' was that of 4 Troop's Lieutenant Phil Brown. Lying in wait with a sergeant's tank and a couple of TOW detachments behind Iffezheim (while his troop Warrant Officer and the fourth Leopard stood ready still farther back and on the opposite flank), Brown was content to let the TOWs open fire at the leading enemy tanks as soon as their night sights clarified the targets at about 1800 metres. He joined in at about 1200 metres, and soon the ground in front was nicely lit by burning tanks, without a single shot coming in his direction at any time – the enemy having failed to detect his location. Naturally, the smoke-screen put an end to easy practise, but fleeting targets were sometimes silhouetted and then engaged, usually with unspecified success.

But with confidence, Brown could report to Cummings (who could see it all for himself) that the enemy onrush was, for the time being, halted. But Ferrier, keeping an eye on the outskirts of Iffezheim, had a jolt when he heard a TOW commander report, over the air, another batch of vehicles – some of them BMPs, approaching fast, perhaps heading straight for the village. Simultaneously, the shelling which had eased off temporarily, started again and intensified. Shouting on the microphone a warning to all his out-stations,

THE THIRD DAY

Ferrier retired rapidly to his command post to await the direct assault upon his stronghold that was all too obviously on its way.

BMPs closing fast through dispersing smoke and rising dust, with shot and shell whistling among the buildings, all combined to keep Canadian defenders' heads down and help the Russian infantry company reach the village with meagre losses. Pausing only long enough for their men to debus, the BMPs drove among the houses and brought direct fire to bear from their 73 mm guns against those Canadians who showed themselves. Close behind the first intruders came a T72 from Tursov's platoon. Shaken by the suddenness of the assault. Papa Company found itself, quite literally in many instances, with its back to a wall. Unable to manoeuvre in such confined surroundings, Ferrier and his two platoon commanders had to simply fight where they stood, the battle spreading forwards and sideways as assailants grappled with defenders in streets, gardens, cellars and upstairs rooms.

When determined defenders possess the advantage of prior knowledge of ground over their attackers, the momentum of the assault should fall off. Having steered their way to possession of a useful foothold in the eastern corner of Iffezheim, the Russian company was bound to pause to consolidate, prior to pursuing a more deliberate reduction of the garrison, block by block and, if necessary, house by house. Meanwhile time was passing and the illumination by fires would soon be superseded by daylight – which might well benefit the defenders. Using armoured vehicles as a spearhead, the Russian company commander attempted to blast a way through. With 33 degrees of elevation at their disposal, the BMP gunners were able to fire into upper stories from close range, thus subduing many defenders who fought back from above. Nevertheless, the efforts of Soviet infantry to protect the BMPs completely was unavailing. Carl Gustavs, 50 cals and M72s, fired at close, if not point-blank range, not only knocked out or crippled BMPs, but, in consequence, blocked the narrow streets to further progress by armour. Tursov's tanks were thus largely confined to the outskirts, shooting up the perimeter buildings and seeking to prevent any 4 CMBG attempt to mount an armoured stroke against the company's point of entry into the village. And in this respect his tactical sense paid off. A Leopard tank (from 4 Troop), seen creeping up, was despatched before it fired a shot – its funeral pyre a monument to the folly of probing unsupported; and yet another example of the fighting superiority of a stationary weapon system over one on the move.

News of the foothold in Iffezheim suggested to Podduyev that the village, even if still in enemy hands, might at least be neutralized. Peremptorily, he insisted that the advance be resumed; not unwillingly his subordinates complied, if only because they reasoned that they might just as well be shot at advancing as standing still – as was currently the case. Furthermore, they, like everybody else, were only too conscious that the cloak of darkness would soon be lost and that, if they had not fought their way into the open by then, the opportunity might be permanently denied them. It was going to be all or nothing: I and II Battalions, on the right and left respectively, were to attempt to widen the lodgement area and give flank protection. III Battalion, which was already through the obstacle and feeling its way among the debris of battle that cluttered the slope between Blickheim and Favorite, would charge the centre, making for Stollhofen via Hügelsheim. Artillery would prepare the way, but in view of the confusion that had earlier been caused by the laying of smoke, this means of protection was, for the time being, forbidden except for strictly local usage. Podduyev calculated that III Battalion might be taking up the lead at about 0230 hours. That would give it only 45 minutes darkness before first light at 0315 hours. It was tight, far too tight for comfort, but possible!

> **CONTROLLING FACTORS.**
>
> ★ The distinct advantages enjoyed by dug-in troops over those moving on the open ground.
>
> ★ The expected density and method of exploitation by a Soviet tank regiment.
>
> ★ The need for routes through a village that is being used as a base for mobile action.
>
> ★ An SOP for dealing with spies.
>
> ★ The need to review NBC countermeasures at frequent intervals.
>
> ★ Value of small infantry tank-hunting parties.
>
> ★ The importance of holding villages and woods as a means of distracting the enemy armour from its main aim, and deflecting its relatively limited infantry force into clearance operations.
>
> ★ The folly of single tanks attempting to advance without close support.

12 | Sitrep – the stabilized situation

Lieutenant-Colonel Tinker was anxious, although careful not to show it. Pleased as he was that the enemy thrust had been brought to a halt, there was ample evidence to suggest that the pause was again only a temporary one. The gathering of III Battalion, 301st Tank Regiment in the approaches to the killing zone at Iffezheim was plainly revealed by the usual sources at the same time as SITREPs he had called for from his hard-pressed combat teams exposed the fragility of 3 RCR Battle Group's overall situation.

- *Mike Company – Intact on the left flank at about 85 per cent strength; managing to hold off such pressure as several enemy tanks were exerting, without feeling over-extended; sufficiently supplied with all natures of ammunition. In a word, to quote its OC: "Comfortable."*
- *Oscar Company – Hard-pressed on two sides by an opponent who was making life unpleasant from all manner of weapons, and whose efforts had worn down a weary Company to about 70 per cent strength; secure, nevertheless, within its village stronghold (in Blickheim) and marginally capable of offensive action; ammunition situation satisfactory, except for the single Leopard (Crane's) in location, which was down to only a few rounds and calling frantically for replenishment.*
- *November Company – Battered, forced out of its original position and therefore worth little more than a flank guard to the Vandoos. Strength about 40 per cent, of whom nearly everybody exhibited signs of considerable fatigue. Virtually bereft of an offensive capability, it could only look to the two remaining Leopards of 1 Troop for close support, and these, although recently topped-up with ammunition, were crewed by men severely strained by the erosive effects of prolonged night action in a confined space.*

- *B Squadron – A shadow of its former self, with only one tank at its HQ and five others split between 2 and 3 Troops (excluding Crane's in location with Oscar Company) plus the Lynxes of the Reconnaissance Troop. Delighted though Linkman was with the score of enemy vehicles knocked out for the loss of only five of his own team, and relieved as he was that the Echelon was managing, somehow or other, to supply him with just enough ammunition, the fact remained that his force was almost at the limits of its effectiveness. No sooner had the enemy pressure relaxed than he had decided to take the remaining tanks of 2 Troop under direct, personal control and pull back Crane's tank, as well as the other 3 Troop tank that remained in location with Mike Company. That way Crane could be replenished, and some sort of concentrated mobile force would be reconstituted.*
- *Papa Company Combat Team – Somewhat breathless in its reporting, but in better order than the sights and sounds from Iffezheim suggested. While Cummings and 4 Troop of B Squadron had succeeded (with the loss of one Leopard and three TOW detachments) in holding their ground (and were in the process of replenishing with ammunition), Papa Company was beginning to feel on top of a nicely-balanced contest amid the shattered environs of Iffezheim. "Despite the presence of a couple of T72s and half a dozen BMPs prowling about and making life very uncomfortable," said Ferrier, "we've made the bastards smart. Am about to try shoving them out!" – an intention which he reinforced with a request for artillery fire on the enemy-held part of the village (risking the shots landing among his own side) and the commitment of armour-hunting teams armed with M72 and Carl Gustavs to clear out the BMPs.*
- *1 RCHA – At about 90 per cent strength and efficiency, but living from hand to mouth with ammunition. A Battery, directly threatened by the closeness of enemy armour attacking Iffezheim and therefore under orders to withdraw to Stollhofen, before first light, while the remaining three batteries continued to fight, with C Battery providing the support for 3 RCR.*

As these facts became known, it was obvious to the Brigade Commander, as it was plain to Tinker, that 3 RCR Battle Group was close to the breaking point and that the crack might appear before

THE THIRD DAY

first light if the enemy's next attempt were not held up. In the shadow of fatigue, men's sharpness of perception and execution declined; errors crept in, marksmanship fell off, the giving of orders and compliance with them became blurred; endurance and even courage were sapped. A relatively clear and none-too-threatening incident might assume a menace out of all proportion to its real size – a type of reaction which became multiplied in its impact when information was sparse or misleading. These were the germs of decay which could only be nullified by the constant updating of information, and by a deeply-probing insight into their followers' condition from leaders at all levels.

What Tinker was not aware of, at that moment (and the Brigade Commander was), concerned the changing situation elsewhere on his own front and those adjoining. To the north all was well, but to the south the Vandoos no longer felt able to hold Kuppenheim much longer. And still farther south, a significant enemy penetration (by 3rd Guards Tank Division) looked as if it were achieving a breakthrough of extensive dimensions.

Before the enemy thrust against 3 RCR Battle Group had been brought to a standstill, the Brigade Commander had laid plans which were adaptable to either success or failure. His principal instructions were addressed to Lieutenant-Colonel Brian Cowdray, CO of the RCD, and to the CO of 1 RCHA.

"Brian," he said, "I don't like the look of things up there on the right any more than you do. But my orders are to hold and hold I will. Any time now, the Corps Commander might tell us to vamoose. So . . ." and a long pause as he studied the map again in order to gather maximum rhetorical effect: "this is what we'll do. With the aim of restoring the front to its original alignment, I want you, Brian, to move C Squadron RCD into the Vandoos Sector with a view to help bring the enemy advance to a halt and finally destroying him where he stands. You will have under command not only your D Squadron but also the Field Squadron of 4 CER. In direct support you will have C Battery, 1 RCHA, and Z Battery at priority call and, – and I am sorry its not more – at first light the under-strength company of US Army TOW Cobras working with 444 Tactical Helicopter Squadron, less one section. So much for your party. Now, I intend to have the Vandoos move the armour reserve from their combat team to strengthen their left flank. That troop will bring pressure to bear against the enemy who are operating in that part of

THE THIRD DAY

the front. As for Doug Tinker's lot – well, they are going to have to do a bit better! I intend telling him he must prevent the Ruskies breaking out before first light – and I don't care how he does it or if it means doing something really desperate. Are you with me?"

They were – most of all Cowdray, who recognized in his Commander's manner an intention – several times discussed by them in the past in private – to sacrifice something of intrinsic value in order to maintain the overall aim. And that something would very likely be B Squadron RCD, along with a fair-sized slice of 3 RCR's infantry. He therefore made no comment. Decisions of that sort were not easy to make, he knew. Nor did Tinker comment when the orders reached him over the air, spoken in person by the Commander in his firmest tone. Their onward transmission to his combat teams, moreover, were only slightly delayed by the need to formulate a quick scheme (instinctively, in his mind, Tinker formulated an aim, tripped off factors and debated courses, before fixing upon his plan) of how to put it over convincingly to his subordinates, so as best to overcome their doubts, which was an important factor. It went out verbally and tersely as a collective call, and, in its essentials, told each company/combat team (for all to hear and understand) that they could work in unison:

"Mike Company, stay where you are!"

"November Company, hold on! Help coming from Delta Zulu Foxtrot (the Vandoos) and later from Whiskey Hotel Juliet (the RCD)."

"Oscar Company, do the same, but do what you can to delay that bunch of armour moving up the slopes."

"B Squadron, I'll buy you a beer after, but enemy group now approaching from Blickheim must, I say again, must be stopped and prevented from reaching Papa Combat Team line until first light at least. Attack his flank!"

"Papa Combat Team, clear enemy from your location Alpha Sierra Alpha Papa and do not permit enemy to get beyond TOP HAT."

Upon B Squadron and Papa Company combat teams the burden fell heaviest and the way they received it was a measure of their commanders' inner confidence at this, the most demoralizing hour of the night. Keyed up by the excitement of a bout of close combat which seemed to be going his way, Ferrier merely replied with a loud "Wilco" and then got on with the battle. Linkman, on the other

THE THIRD DAY

> **CONTROLLING FACTORS**
>
> ★ The occasional need to sacrifice units or sub-units for the maintenance of the aim.
>
> ★ The importance of commanders stationing themselves in due time at the vital point and stiffening morale and determination through personal example.
>
> ★ Every likelihood that not all mounted support will be available because it is engaged elsewhere.

hand, weary beyond belief, downcast over the size to which his squadron had been reduced, and exceedingly anxious about the ammunition state, prevaricated. He needed more time, he said, and went on to imply that any aggressive effort on his part would lead to disaster for what was left of his command. Which is just what the General expects of him, reflected Tinker, as he grasped the microphone and spoke uncompromisingly to the tank squadron commander: "Those are your orders. Comply. Out," giving the proword an expression that brooked no denial.

"The trouble with these tankmen is that they care too much about their tanks," ruminated Tinker to himself, but to Andrew Barton his operations officer, sitting in the M113 beside him, marking up the maps and writing down the exchanges in the Operations Log, he said, "I think we'd better go join B Squadron Commander. He may need a little encouragement," and they set off round the right flank, behind embattled Iffezheim, to look for Linkman as he prepared for the presumably fatal mission.

There was no sudden blaring of the battle from the diminuendo into which it had fallen when I and II Battalions of 301st Tank Regiment had come to the end of their first onrush. Instead, the splutter of combat which persisted, along with the rancorous street scuffle in Iffezheim, mounted slowly and spread wider as the combat teams of 3 RCR Battle Group complied with their latest orders and began to harry III Battalion on its line of march.

THE THIRD DAY

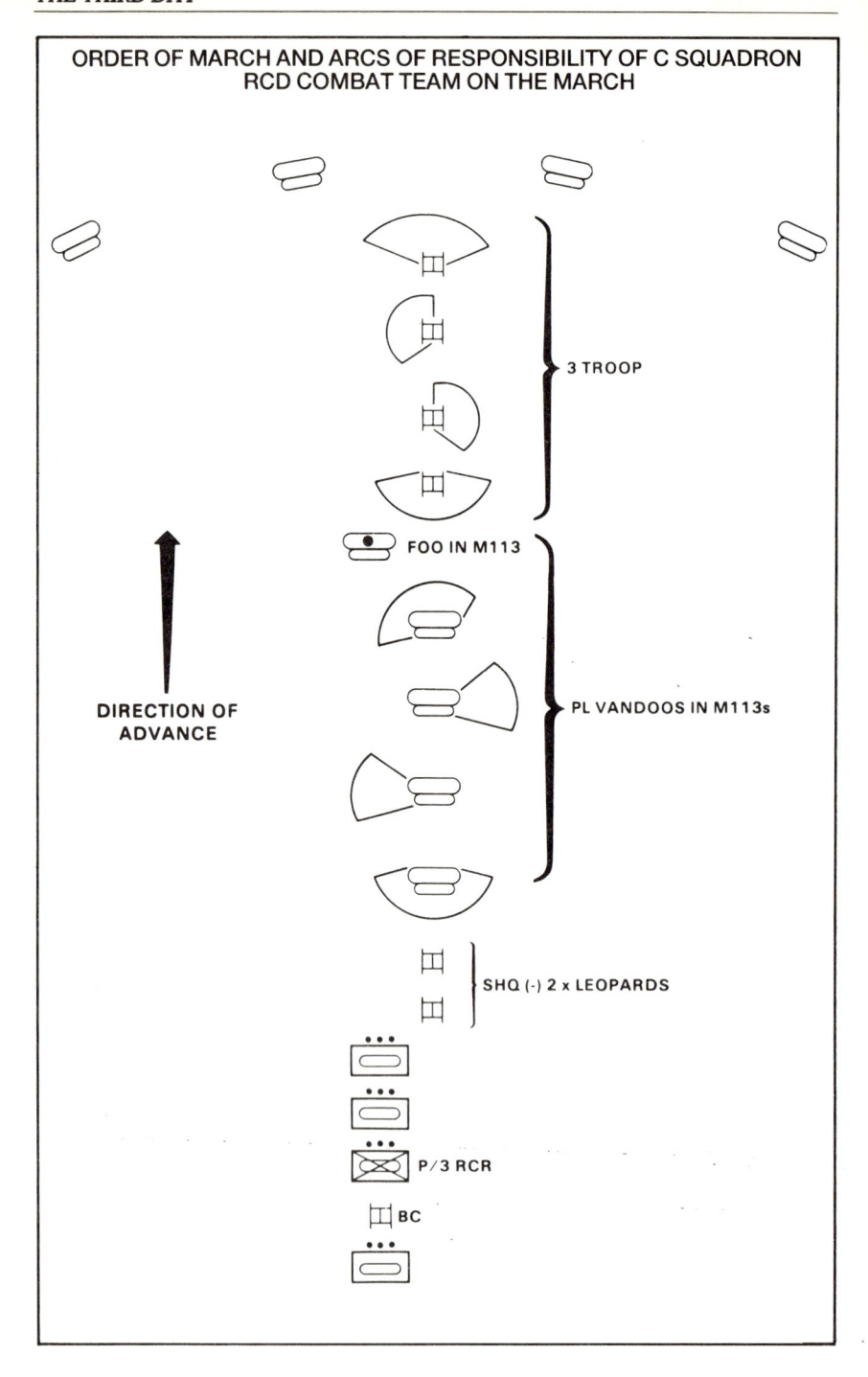

ORDER OF MARCH AND ARCS OF RESPONSIBILITY OF C SQUADRON RCD COMBAT TEAM ON THE MARCH

DIRECTION OF ADVANCE

3 TROOP

FOO IN M113

PL VANDOOS IN M113s

SHQ (-) 2 x LEOPARDS

P/3 RCR

BC

13 | Counter-attack plans

For most of the time since battle had been joined on the Blickheim feature, the tanks and infantry elements of Major Lionel Grove's combat team had remained undisturbed and engaged in working on their equipment and seeing to their local defences. While the recently joined members of C Squadron RCD endeavoured to bring their tanks to the top line of efficiency after their time in preservation, the infantry commanders from the platoon of 3 RCR and from the Vandoos made contact with their armoured opposite numbers with a view to co-ordinating the plans and discussing procedures they might be called upon to put into operation together. The infantry, who had long been resident in Germany, wanted to be sure that the tankmen, who had so recently arrived from Canada, were aware of the latest methods of infantry tank co-operation as practised by themselves. And the tankmen were only too happy to pass on to the infantry the latest techniques which had been developed at the Combat Training Centre.

Groves had been given to understand by Lieutenant-Colonel Cowdray that the most likely role demanded of 4 CMBG Reserve – of which C Squadron was the principal and most powerful sub-unit – would be counter-attack to restore the front should it be broken. To this role might well be tacked on somewhat less demanding blocking activities. But, in Cowdray's opinion, there was always a likelihood that the Brigade Reserve would find itself embroiled in that most testing of all operations of war, the execution of a withdrawal in contact with the enemy. Nevertheless, Cowdray had instructed Groves to reconnoitre and study two possible directions of approach should counter-attack prove to be necessary – one route via 3 RCR's left flank; the other along the line of the inter-battle group boundary within the Brigade Group's sector with a view to being able to operate either from 3 RCR's right flank or the Vandoos' left. Without doubt, thought Groves, the second course was the one to be expected. Moreover, the approaches to the vital ground in that sector would also be suitable should his combat team be called upon to cover a withdrawal. So he carried out the initial reconnaissance of the centre sector himself in a Jeep, along with the Vandoos platoon commander, and sent his second-in-command with Lieutenant Dougal McGregor (the 3 RCR platoon commander), to study the other route.

Cowdray assumed, and Groves took it as assured, that the aim of the RCD Battle Group in the counter-attack would be occupation of vital ground leading to destruction of the enemy within the Group's boundaries. To some commanders that sort of directive might have led to an interpretation along the lines of a headlong charge. But not to Cowdray or Groves, especially in the light of the lessons they had learned within the past few hours through understanding the significance of 1st Guards Tank Division's fate when it attempted precisely that kind of method. When Cowdray arrived at Groves' headquarters and gave verbal instructions which were to despatch C Squadron combat team up the centre route in order to re-establish the line along the crest between Blickheim and Kuppenheim, which he now designated vital ground, the theme was one of subtle infiltration rather than blunt confrontation.

"There's a fine covered approach most of the way to the crest line, as you know, Lionel," said Cowdray. "And for most of the way the RCR and Vandoos have something in the woods and villages. No doubt the enemy will push in among them, so we can't expect to move about as we please up there. So I'm going to have D Squadron lead off and search for the soft spots and give what warning they can of any Russians who've perhaps got across the Kuppenheim–Bischweier Road. You'll follow, and what I want you to do is wriggle through those woods to the northeast of Oos. Try to get there without being shot at, move into fire positions, chop off anything trying to get through from the east and then let the Ruskies come at you. Don't go for him! Be cunning, draw him out. Keep hidden and surprise him!"

In principle, Groves concurred, although how he was to "wriggle through" undetected remained to be seen. It might work if time were available, but chances were that, with the best will in the world, the higher command might be tempted to hustle him if the situation deteriorated any further. These darker thoughts he put aside in favour of implementing the routine attack procedures,

THE THIRD DAY

employing the order of march and grouping he had previously settled with his subordinates. Now that the Lynxes of D Squadron were to lead the way, the task of his own leading sub-unit – 3 Troop's Leopards under Lieutenant Harry Owens – was simplified. Hopefully, that troop, with the platoon of Vandoos in close attendance and an FOO from Z Battery travelling among them, would be given sufficient warning by D Squadron of an enemy presence to enable them to find covered approaches among the woods from which the threat to the enemy flank could, unobserved, be sprung.

Protected though the passage to their operational area was by the strongholds of 3 RCR and the Vandoos, the approach by the RCD Battle Group was conducted as if it were an advance to contact in a void between unembattled forces. To maintain control, Cowdray had imposed report lines and bounds at well-defined critical points along the route. D Squadron, which was on the move before first light as the battle flared to north and east, reported Oos clear at 0300 hours as 3 Troop's leading Leopard nosed up to the town's western outskirts. In the threatening circumstances, Owens had opted to advance in line, ahead of the Vandoos' four M113s which moved in convoy, one tactical bound behind the tanks and only just ahead of Squadron headquarters from where Groves aimed to keep the point troops under his eye.

Watchfulness was, indeed, the prime consideration among everybody on the move, no matter where they happened to be. Even when D Squadron was reporting all clear, the suspicion of danger lurked in the minds of the rest. Each tank's commander, gunner and driver concentrated upon specified areas of search, their arcs of vision interlinked by Owens so as to give all-round surveillance with priority to the front and the more threatened left flank. Eye fatigue from constant gazing into night vision devices soon began to accumulate, but as D Squadron emerged from the environs of Oos, and began to probe among the woods to the north-east, the first grey traces of dawn appeared to the eastward. Gradually and thankfully, the soldiers switched from electronic optical instruments in favour of natural vision, through optics, or more comfortably, using the unassisted eyeball with heads above cupola rims.

At this moment, too, the men of 301st Tank Regiment were beginning to bless the return of daylight. Rusalski and his fellow artillery observation officers could pick out targets with far greater facility. Ivan Shulubin and the other infantry leaders felt more able to

THE THIRD DAY

infiltrate the close country on the flanks than previously, while Tursov, in the enclosed space of Iffezheim, and the surviving tank commanders who were endeavouring to blast their way across the Bühl Plateau, at least had the advantage of full vision instead of the restricted arcs inflicted on them by optics. Somehow the confidence of them all was revived once they could see by natural means, and this confidence was enhanced by initial gains almost everywhere in the final minutes of darkness.

Unexpectedly, a platoon of tanks belonging to I Battalion (on the right) penetrated a chink in the defences of Oscar Company and found itself, as daylight broke, moving northwards across the rear of Blickheim and Mendel in quite exhilarating fashion. Similarly, the combined efforts of 290th MRR and II Battalion, 301st Tank Regiment, drove back the remnants of November Company and put

THE THIRD DAY

still further pressure on the Vandoos, while offering temptingly obvious opportunities to expand their exploitation towards the south and south-west. And if this news was enough to gladden the hearts of Colonel Podduyev and General Samsonov, a company belonging to III Battalion made a dramatic leap forward which carried it across the Iffezheim – Oos Road in the grey light preceding sunrise.

It came about due to the difficulty 4 Troop's commander and gunners found in differentiating between the dead vehicles (many of them burning littering the foreground) and the live ones entering that area. Eyes and brains, which were jaded from excessive peering into vision devices, failed to interpret early enough the nature and pace of an indistinct clutter of shapes on TV screens and periscopes. When,

Below: M113s infiltrating close country, with everybody on watch.

THE THIRD DAY

at the last moment, gunners in two Leopards, which stood squarely in the way of the T72s, were ordered to open fire, the flash of their guns vividly exposed their positions to T72 gunners who had halted in order to give support. Only one T72 was hit, but in return two Leopards were disposed of, along with a TOW detachment before it could complete any engagement at all. Thus a hole was torn in the thin green line established by Captain Peter Cummings, one which could not at once be filled except by the fire of the batteries of 1 RCHA, lying back in depth – a task of engaging armour over open sights which they had no great relish to attempt. With just two Leopards (including his own) and four TOWs left at his disposal, Cummings could only tackle the flanks of the enemy phalanx and hope that somewhere, somebody else would do something drastic to save what looked like a lost situation.

For all that, the shooting by Cummings' surviving vehicles did have an effect. The sight of gun flashes from his right flank, as the Leopards opened fire, imposed prudence on the Soviet tank company commander, impelling him to halt one platoon of tanks and tell it to give support to the one in the lead. Already another T72 was stopped dead and seemingly inert in all respects, and so momentum was reduced without being lost. But when the commander of a TOW detachment, his M113 lying hidden and by-passed by the Soviet tanks, screwed up all his courage and, with a quaking heart, gave the order to fire at 100 metres at a T72, a deadly blow was struck. It was a risky shot, just outside the minimum effective range of the guided weapon, but the operator, despite a shaking hand which made the crosswires tremble a little on target, scored a hit. The cheer which went up from the TOW crew might, however, have been even more heartfelt if they had know that their victim was the Soviet company commander – but their main concern now was to slip away, leaving behind an opponent whose control system had been stunned by a shot to the brain. Indeed, the TOW crew's relief was almost undone by the narrow escape they had from an RCD Lynx (which had become detached from D Squadron in the dark). For this vehicle's commander, acting in the belief that, if anything came from the enemy's direction it must, of necessity, be hostile, had opened fire and scared the daylight out of their own countrymen with a burst of 50-cal that, luckily, glanced off the side armour.

The loss of the Soviet tank company commander imposed a hesitation in the progress of III Battalion which was to be of immense

THE THIRD DAY

value to 4 CMBG. For 15 crucial minutes in which the six surviving T72s paused, awaiting orders from above, the first streaks of daylight denied them the full cover of darkness and provided time for the defenders to use a card which, until now, had been unplayable. Already, scouting Kiowa helicopters from 444 Squadron were forward in readiness to seek out what they could of the probing enemy tank forces. Standing by in a holding area (HA) were six TOW Cobras of the US Army, fully armed with their engines running, and awaiting calls from the Kiowas which would manoeuvre them to their fire positions from where the Kiowas would point out their targets. Top of the list of targets to be engaged were the ZSU 23-4S then the T72s, which threatened to break loose south of Iffezheim. But also the gap between Iffezheim and Oos was to be covered. Important to the Canadians was the desire to prevent the Cobras engaging friendly tanks in the complex area of the KZ.

Apart from the bulk of D Squadron RCD and C Squadron RCD, there was scarcely a combat sub-unit of 4 CMBG which was not now engaged in combat, and the fact that the enemy was now poised on the brink of the breakthrough, he so earnestly desired lent a mood of desperation to every action by each member of the brigade. Even if Papa Company in Iffezheim was seemingly on the verge of ejecting the enemy infantry (having confined them to the eastern corner of the village), its by now somewhat attenuated pair of platoons was in no fit condition to come to the support of the remainder of Papa Company combat team – that is, Cummings' struggling handful of AFVs. And even if Mike and Oscar Companies of 3 RCR held firm on the left flank in their fortified areas, their purchase on the forward slope (along with the hold of Vandoos combat teams to the extreme right) was being undermined by penetrations behind the crest line. For I and II Tank Battalions, as they slowly fanned out, were pushing aside, respectively, B Squadron and N Company. Moreover, a similar disaster to the one which had that moment afflicted the leading company of III Battalion in its drive westwards, was visited upon 3 RCR Battle Group. Tinker, on his way round to join Linkman (for encouragement's sake) had fallen foul of the enterprising platoon of T72s which had filtered among the woods between Iffezheim and Mendel. The 125 mm shot which went in one end and out the other of his M113 killed everybody on board (including the Intelligence Officer) except the CO himself. He now crouched low in a ditch, cut-off completely from his battle group and bent mainly on survival

THE THIRD DAY

with the intention, so frequently drummed in to his officers and men, of evading capture if possible and returning to the fray.

In effect, the future well-being of 4 CMBG mainly rested in the hands of Lieutenant-Colonel Brian Cowdray's RCD Battle Group and, to the largest extent, upon the efforts of Major Lionel Grove's C Squadron combat team. But unfortunately, their task had been made harder by the incursion southward of II Tank Battalion into the woods to the east of Oos. Their presence there had narrowed the frontage and reduced the number of options open to the battle group in its effort to occupy vital ground, between Blickheim and Kuppenheim, unopposed. They would probably now have to fight for that ground, and that might be self-defeating; at best a pyrrhic victory, at worst the destruction of 4 CMBG's last hope. Abandoning his initial idea of moving as far east as possible before turning northwards against the enemy flank, Cowdray now told D Squadron to give flank protection to the east (where a troop of A Squadron RCD and the Vandoos along with the remnants of Oscar Company, were putting the brake to further Soviet penetrations), and have C Squadron emerge obliquely from Oos, among the woods, steering the axis of advance towards Blickheim, with the intention of driving a wedge into the centre and rear of the advancing enemy mass, thus cutting the spearhead from its shaft. Telling D Squadron to pinpoint every visible enemy position (for the benefit of C Squadron combat team as it searched for fire positions), Cowdray asked for maximum artillery support. He was given an additional battery at priority call, and call on every gun within range.

CONTROLLING FACTORS

★ The importance of counter-attack tasks being carefully considered prior to commencement of action, and for commanders to study the approaches and plan the execution on the ground.

★ The need for counter-attacks to be economical. Only by seizing key terrain (by means of subtle manoeuvres as opposed to a costly head on charge) is a secure fire position, from which the enemy can be destroyed effectively, likely to be achieved.

★ The deterioration of eyesight among men who have become tired from over-use of night vision instruments.

★ Delays which can be inflicted on the enemy as the result of surprise action by relatively small but boldly-handled forces.

14 | Counter-attack – stabilizing the situation

4 CMBG's counter-attack evolved as an article of many pieces derived from several brains instead of a co-ordinated packet put together by one mind. What the commander had conceived as a cohesive attack against the major enemy penetration, was denied that closely-interwoven pattern by the steadily expanding enemy incursions and the disappearance of Tinker as the directing force within 3 RCR Battle Group. Certainly Cowdray could exert an influence which would compensate for the loss of Tinker, but his assertion of authority was inevitably gradual because it was some 20 minutes before Tinker's disappearance was confirmed and 3 RCR's Deputy Commanding Officer, Major Mycroft Brent, began to assume command. Combat team commanders, sticking to their initial orders and the ground they held, made things work out the way they did – a process as much the product of sound discipline and determination as it was of planning, ingrained military instinct and training.

Of course, the intervention of RCD Battle Group was of fundamental importance since it alone possessed the power of a closely clenched fist hitting the enemy in a soft spot. Nobody realized this more, in the first instance, than Lieutenant Harry Owens of 3 Troop of C Squadron. Groping ahead, due to shortage of Intelligence of the enemy until a patrol of D Squadron reported the small copse on the eastern outskirts of Oos to be clear, he made a quick, confident dash for its cover, and ran his troop across the open ground intact. But when it came to contemplating a further step forward to the next, much larger wood, the proposition looked daunting. True, a Lynx had announced its safe arrival at the northern tip of the wood, but equally evident was the sight of its companion burning, not far off, apparently hit by fire from the southern-most edge of the same wood. Groves had seen it and was addressing all stations on the air, having already asked his FOO for fire missions on the hostile localities in the wood, on call.

"Call Sign 31 and India 41 will occupy wood now. Call Sign 32 is to give direct fire support on the right flank, Call Sign 33 on the left. Call Sign 31 will be in readiness to advance to the northern tip of the wood at 0345 hours, which is H Hour. Golf 31 will provide fire on enemy locations on call from H Hour. Call Signs 34 and India 42 will stand by to reinforce 31 on my orders, probably at completion of his task."

These short orders engineered the use of concentrated force with all arms co-operation on the narrowest of fronts – and took a chance in that time for implementation was short, to say the least. But, for one thing, Groves feared that delay would allow the enemy too much time to prepare a reception and, for another, he had no wish to forfeit the momentum of the initial drive. The fact that the execution of the attack would coincide with the intervention by TOW Cobras was purely by chance – distracting as it was likely to be to friend and foe alike. Good timing, indeed, was the essence of the counter-stroke, but, in the turmoil of a fluid situation, it was as much a matter of luck as of judgement.

To Colonel Podduyev, of course, the sudden eruption of enemy activity at three points at once, took on the nature of a carefully co-ordinated counter-attack of considerable danger. Standing with his head out of his command vehicle on a small pimple overlooking the plain stretched out before him, with Iffezheim in sight but Oos obscured by the woods, he was able, nevertheless, to formulate a fairly complete impression of what the enemy was doing even without much reference to the startled reports that started pouring in from hard-pressed units. The timing of the Canadian attack caught his 301st Tank Regiment at a bad moment since nearly all its battalions were not only somewhat depleted, but also committed. The only reserve immediately free to counter what looked like a blow to his centre, was a single tank company of III Battalion which had already lost three of its ten tanks. Although 290th MRR's leading elements stood close behind, they were in no condition immediately to move to his aid. He put in a call to Samsonov and was at once granted full artillery support, and within 30 minutes, assistance from Sagger-armed Hind helicopters. For the moment, however, Podduyev had to look to his own salvation.

Right: M113s keeping under cover before making a dash into the open.

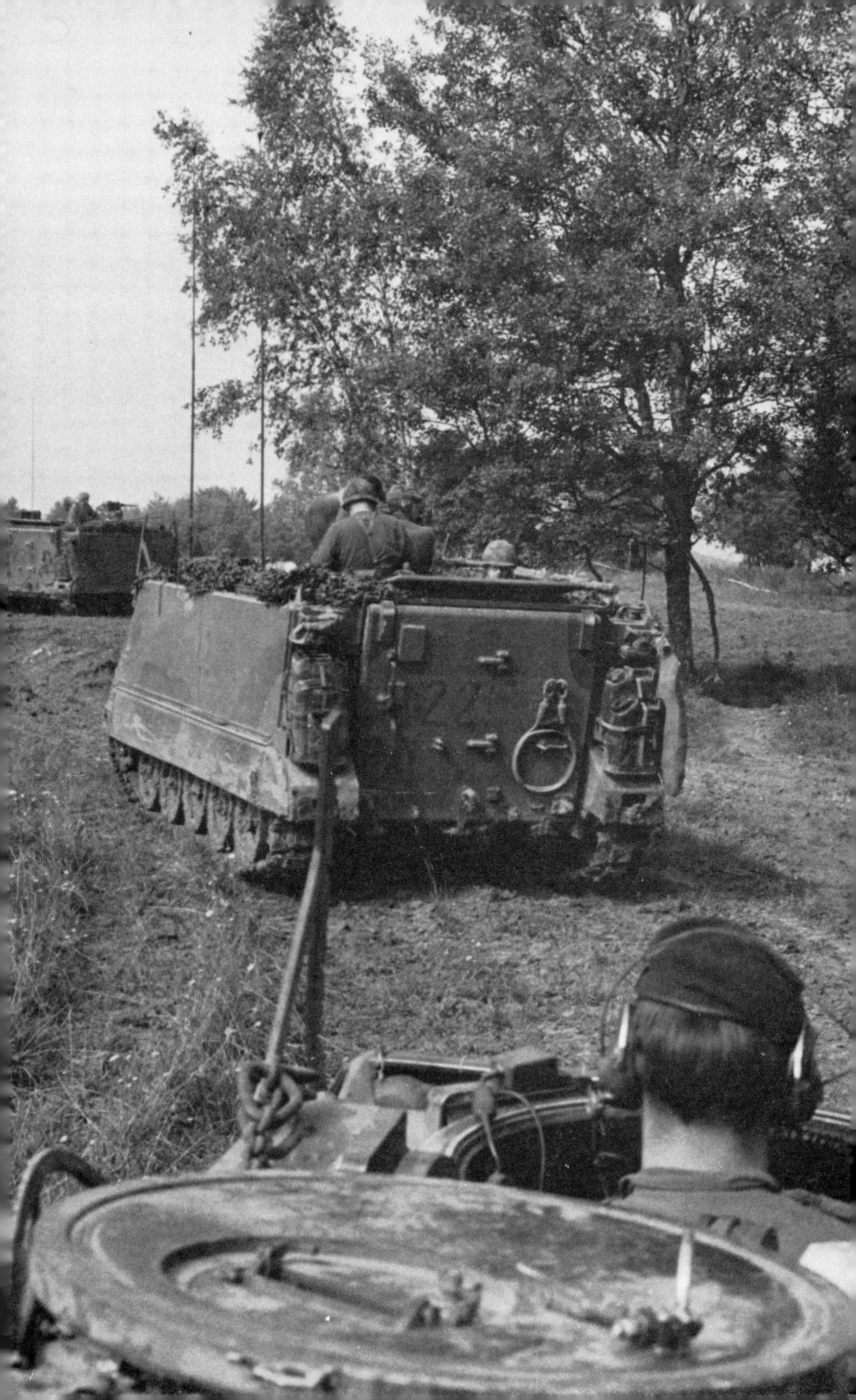

THE THIRD DAY

Groves' combat team formed up as so often it had on exercise, the leading tank troop in front of the assaulting M113s (whose gunners were ready to fire on the move as they advanced); Squadron headquarters in observation, with the two supporting troops nearby in their hull-down positions and already picking out likely target areas. On hand, too, the FOO, directing operations from the top of his M113. Looking round to satisfy himself that forming up was complete, Groves muttered a quick prayer for an operation he did not fully believe in, and spoke the executive order into his microphone.

"Charlie Charlie 3! This is 39. Move now! Move now! Good hunting, Out!"

Right: The point of the counter-attack force, well dispersed in the open. In the foreground, the infantryman has his 66mm LAW slung. The M113 is ready to give support with its MMG, while the Leopards dominate the scene.

THE THIRD DAY

Gritting his teeth, Lieutenant Harry Owens ordered his warrant officer and second sergeant's tanks to advance on the objective he had already described to them. One hundred metres behind, the four M113s of India 41 had assumed open formation and were revving up. C Battery's fire was already falling on the wood some 300 metres distant. 2 and 3 Troops were opening with HE and machine-gun fire. He had decided not to lead in person because it was essential for him to retain full control of his troop as a whole and engage targets to its front with fire – something he could not do satisfactorily while on the move. The two Leopards seemed to leap out of cover on full acceleration, and shot across the ground towards the objective in fine style. A flash somewhere to the left revealed a T72 which had seen them coming. But the shots fell short, kicking up dirt; and already 3 Troop was lasing on that target at some 1500 metres, and obtained a hit with its second shot. The M113s were roaring flat-out on his tail, their 50 cal gunners spraying the surrounding countryside wildly. Three minutes later Owens, in profound relief, was joining the rest of his troops on the objective, at the same time as India 41 halted, dropped ramps and decanted infantry among the trees to hunt out the hidden enemy with grenades and small arms. Groves, who watched it all a tactical bound in rear, was already telling Call Signs 34 and India 42 to comply with their orders and reinforce the position. Meanwhile, 1 Troop was taking steps to guard its flanks from anybody within the wood who might try to stalk it through the trees and paths; and inching forward, in conjunction with the infantry to its northern perimeter, with a view to implementing Cowdray's principal aim – the domination by direct fire of the enemy corridor stretching westwards past Iffezheim. Speedy, mounted action had won the day, cost-free in casualties except for two M113 gunners shot in their exposed, unarmoured posts.

A grim situation now faced Podduyev. The enemy had managed to seize positions from which he could be ejected only by direct attack; and the means of direct attack available to him were severely limited. He could and did have heavy artillery fire dropped on the woods now in Canadian possession. He asked, and received quick compliance by Oblensky, for occupation by 290th MRR of the wood, close to the west side of the one in enemy hands. But a tentative attempt by his reserve tank company to throw back the hostile counter-attack attracted such a blast of fire that it barely got started. Summing up to Samsonov, Podduyev had to admit that, although his I and II Battalions were threatened, and should be able to survive, both the infantry company in Iffezheim and the entire III Battalion were in serious trouble and might face annihilation if they were not relieved or, unthinkably, he assumed, withdrawn. Already Podduyev was witness to the attacks being launched by TOW Cobras led into action by Kiowas, and knew there was little he could do to stem this systematic picking off of the tanks and BMPs scattered about the open plain. For the anti-aircraft units – SA-9s and ZSU-23-4s – which had pushed forward in the final hour of darkness had hardly got beyond the crest line, and those which now tried to find covered firing positions on top of the plateau were more vulnerable to hostile fire than the tanks and infantry carriers. Armour could not

The Red Army forward defences. **Above**, an SA-7. **Below**, an ZSU-23-4, its search radar in operation.

live in the environment of the forward edge of battle or receive help from the few SA-7s that were held back on the crest. Moreover, those which did try to enter the killing zone were often the target of artillery directed by the Kiowas who scouted ahead for the Cobra pilots.

Quite apart from the heavy damage being inflicted upon his division, Samsonov had to accept the conclusion that its relative lack of success was depriving him of the sympathy of the ever-watchful and predatory Army Commander. While 1st Guards Tank Division struggled ineffectually amidst the meshes spread out by 4 CMBG, his rival on the left flank, Major-General Igor Gandalfski with his 3rd Guards Tank Division, was making significant inroads into a US Army division. When it became apparent at dawn that the 1st was not going to attain its objectives, the Army Commander had come through on the air with a sour message saying if, within the hour, 1st Guards Tank Division had not broken out, its activities would be curtailed and used only to apply leverage on the right flank of the 3rd, which was doing so well. Since the prospects for a breakout had

THE THIRD DAY

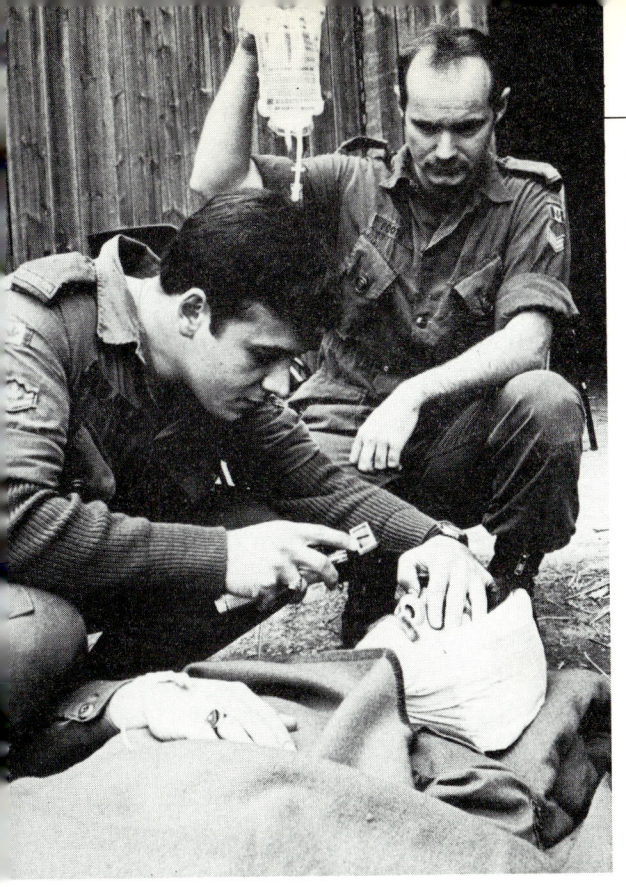

Far left: M113s concentrate in Blickheim for withdrawal.

Left: Meanwhile, the collection and treatment of the wounded continues, each man who reaches the medical officer having a high chance of survival.

virtually evaporated, and the Army Commander was obviously only too well aware of that, Samsonov was inclined to interpret the exhortation to "get on or get out!", as a warning order to shift his main effort from the Bühl Plateau side of Oos – Sinzheim, employing 303rd Tank Regiment in the leading role.

It was also running through the Commander's mind, at HQ 4 CMBG, that there might soon be a distinct change of emphasis and alignment of the enemy's main line of thrust. Already, in the closing hours of the night, information had reached him from the Vandoos, from a Canadian liaison officer with the US division on his right, and from HQ VII (US) Corps, that things might be going awry beyond his right flank boundary. From Corps, in fact, came a broad hint that another realignment of the front was in prospect. But, lacking positive instructions to call off 4 CMBG's attempt to re-establish the original line, the Commander felt bound to maintain his existing aim. Nevertheless, a nod to the Brigadier-General was as good as a wink. At any moment, he guessed, orders for a withdrawal might suddenly replace those which demanded unyielding defence of vital ground.

207

That would make it difficult for the hard-pressed combat teams at the front to extricate themselves, and it would place a considerable responsibility on RCD Battle Group to cover that withdrawal. And always too, at the back of his mind, he had to remember his special responsibility to his own Government for the unique force under his command and the need to maintain its integrity.

As matters stood, shortly after 0400 hours, something rather like a stalemate had descended upon 4 CMBG front. Before Hügelsheim, the leading elements of III Tank Battalion had come to a halt due to a combination of command indecision (through lack of a leader at the front), the fading efforts of Cummings, and the attention of TOW Cobras which buzzed, nap of the earth, unchecked from defiladed firing points on all sides. The squabble for Iffezheim was unresolved. On the flanks, the menacing penetrations, which had taken place at dawn, had also been blunted. T72s and BMPs, which had seized positions in the rear of Blickheim and Kuppenheim, were demonstrating an unwillingness to surrender their gains without exacting a price – and the 4 CMBG combat teams confronting them were in no state, just then, to offer very much for any attempt at ejection. Only in the centre did sufficient strength exist within the RCD battle group to pursue offensive operations. But there, too, the cost was likely to be exorbitant and unacceptable because, confronting C Squadron RCD combat team was a distinctly well-prepared Soviet infantry position, guarded by Saggers and tanks. The situation had been pointedly indicated when a Leopard from Owen's 3 Troop had indiscreetly shown itself at the edge of the wood. From the next wood, barely 150 metres distant, a couple of Saggers had been launched, one of which struck the Leopard without penetrating. And when a section of the Vandoos, in an endeavour to seek out the Sagger operator, exposed themselves too flagrantly nearby, they were at once treated to a volley of machine-gun and mortar fire which left nobody in any doubt about the reception that was to be expected in that wood. From that moment, the two sides glowered at each other and awaited orders from above. For the first time in more than twelve hours of almost non-stop battle roar, a strange silence settled over the Blickheim feature, as the principal activity was transferred to the realms of higher command.

To the west of the Blickheim feature, however, the noise of battle persisted with the crack of high-velocity guns, the clatter of helicopter rotor blades and the roar of guided missiles predominating. In the triangular killing zone bounded by Iffezheim, Hügelsheim and Oos, the rapid execution of the doomed vehicles of III Battalion went on without remission. In Iffezheim, the last stand of the invading infantry company was ended when its commander received orders to escape with whatever could be saved. Just as soon as it was realized by the defenders that resistance within the triangle was at an end, a troop of sappers from 4 CER, mounted in their M113s as infantry, drove cautiously among the burning or abandoned enemy vehicles, to round up stragglers who had baled out and were either trying to make their escape or thankfully surrendering. And these same sappers, as they carried out the duties of infantry, also examined the now-deserted enemy vehicles and completed with explosive charges the destruction of those which were merely disabled.

Hand-in-hand with tidying up the battlefield – the search for and evacuation of the wounded of both sides, the removal of PWs by the sappers and Military Police, the recovery of slightly damaged equipment, the replenishment of those sub-units which now found themselves separated from the firing line, and the feeding of tired men whose need for sleep was rather more urgent than eating – there also proceeded, with extreme urgency, preparations for the next phase of this defensive action. For even as the killing zone ceased to be the scene of fighting and the last Red Army infantry (along with Tursov in his T72), screened by smoke, made a bolt out of Iffezheim

---

CONTROLLING FACTORS

★ The vital importance of reconnaissance in advance of and to the flanks of the main force while out of contact.

★ The vital importance of ample fire support against likely and located enemy positions.

★ The need for commanders to be well forward in the advance to take advantage of fleeting opportunities.

★ The vital necessity for speed when moving from one tactical bound to the next, and of entering fresh fire positions without delay – all the products of careful consideration before giving the order to advance.

★ The value of attempting to separate enemy supporting units from their associated armoured troops.

★ The importance of completing the destruction of immobilized enemy equipment and of collecting prisoners.

THE THIRD DAY

(thus, to some extent, relieving HQ 4 CMBG and 3 RCR of some part of the concern they each felt for those combat teams almost cut off in Blickheim and Mendel), a new Warning Order was sent personally by radio from Commander VII (US) Corps to the Commander 4 CMBG:

"Lima Romeo Zulu on your right cannot hold on much longer," he said. "I am pulling back before last light to Intermediate Position along the Arizona line. I realize this means you must pull now in daylight. If you stay, the alternative, as I see it, is envelopment. Present position will be denied to enemy until 1000 hours. Thinning out can start as and when you choose. Over!"

The details had yet to be settled, but argument with the uncompromising order there could not be. Time spent on that would be better employed extricating 4 CMBG from under the enemy's nose.

15 | Withdrawal

The dismounted infantry in Blickheim
In planning the execution of a withdrawal by daylight in a situation in which three of his combat teams – Mike Company and Oscar Company of 3 RCR and Alpha Company of the Vandoos – were dismounted and in close confrontation with the enemy, the commander 4 CMBG had to pay careful attention to the details of what promised to be a complicated and hazardous operation. A period of five hours in which, unmolested, to make the arrangements would normally be sufficient, but if the enemy took it upon himself to mount further attacks within that period, the difficulties posed could be tremendous. In rapidly putting together a plan that, of necessity, had to be simple, HQ 4 CMBG had to bear in mind the essential importance, in all phases, of keeping control, ensuring security and retaining mobility – simple to state but difficult to implement in the circumstances against an aggressive opponent in daytime under the threat of air and ground attack. Moreover, the fatigue of the troops and the shock to their morale which might ensue when they were told to give up something for which they had fought so hard to hold, were factors that were not to be dismissed lightly. The power of leadership at company and platoon level would therefore be taxed to the limit.

The orders in the standard form were received by battle group commanders over the air, followed and confirmed by a visit to each of their command posts by the Brigadier-General in person. With time so short, written confirmatory orders were not going to be issued; only an overlay, showing check points, RVs, routes, recovery, and giving timings, such as those for Denial, No Rearward Movement, Thinning Out, Final Abandonment and Clear of a Line. In diluted form, these basic details would percolate down to each level until the individual rifleman at the front became aware of what was expected of him.

THE THIRD DAY

Each combat team was confronted by its own peculiar set of problems, and the closer they happened to be to the enemy, the more diverse they seemed. The OC of Mike Company in Mendel could envisage problems in breaking away in complex country, hustled, perhaps, by the attentions of a Red Army Tank Regiment (even one which had shown no great inclination to press its attacks). But Major Panton (who would depend to some extent on support from Mike Company as well as the remnants of Papa Company combat teams) had the worst job of all extricating his Oscar Company from the ruins of Blickheim where almost every move would be hard to conceal from a foe who lay close on three sides. Panton's task was quite different, therefore, from that confronting Major Groves of the C Squadron RCD combat team whose task would be that of covering troops designated to provide delaying positions across the entire 4 CMBG front as soon as the forward infantry positions had been vacated.

Panton and his men were taken by surprise by the order to withdraw. Nothing had seemed less probable after a night of stolid resistance and, for the moment, nothing seemed less feasible. Curbing his anger, he sent a warning to his subordinates, along with the injunction that secrecy was vital. Nothing overt was to be undertaken, for fear of intimating to the enemy what was being planned. Then he carried out a review of his command's condition and layout. The latest SITREPs from platoons indicated that, apart from the possibility of a rogue enemy party of two or three men which had got in during the night and might be hiding in one of the cellars, the nearest opposition was dug in, supported by a few tanks and BMPs, somewhere between 100 and 300 metres distant, and showing little inclination to attack again. Fortunately, the outer ring of largely wrecked buildings prevented the enemy from seeing what went on within Blickheim. It was possible for dismounted men to move about among the rubble without disclosing themselves to view or direct fire. Only on the northern face of the village had his men stayed in slit trenches beyond the built-up area; elsewhere they had retired to the houses. Pulling back the men to their M113s, Panton therefore assumed, would not be too difficult. The worst problem would be first how to remove the vehicles and then how best to get clear without exposing them to fire in the open ground outside.

A reconnaissance by Panton on foot, in the course of which he took the opportunity to talk to as many officers and men as he could

THE THIRD DAY

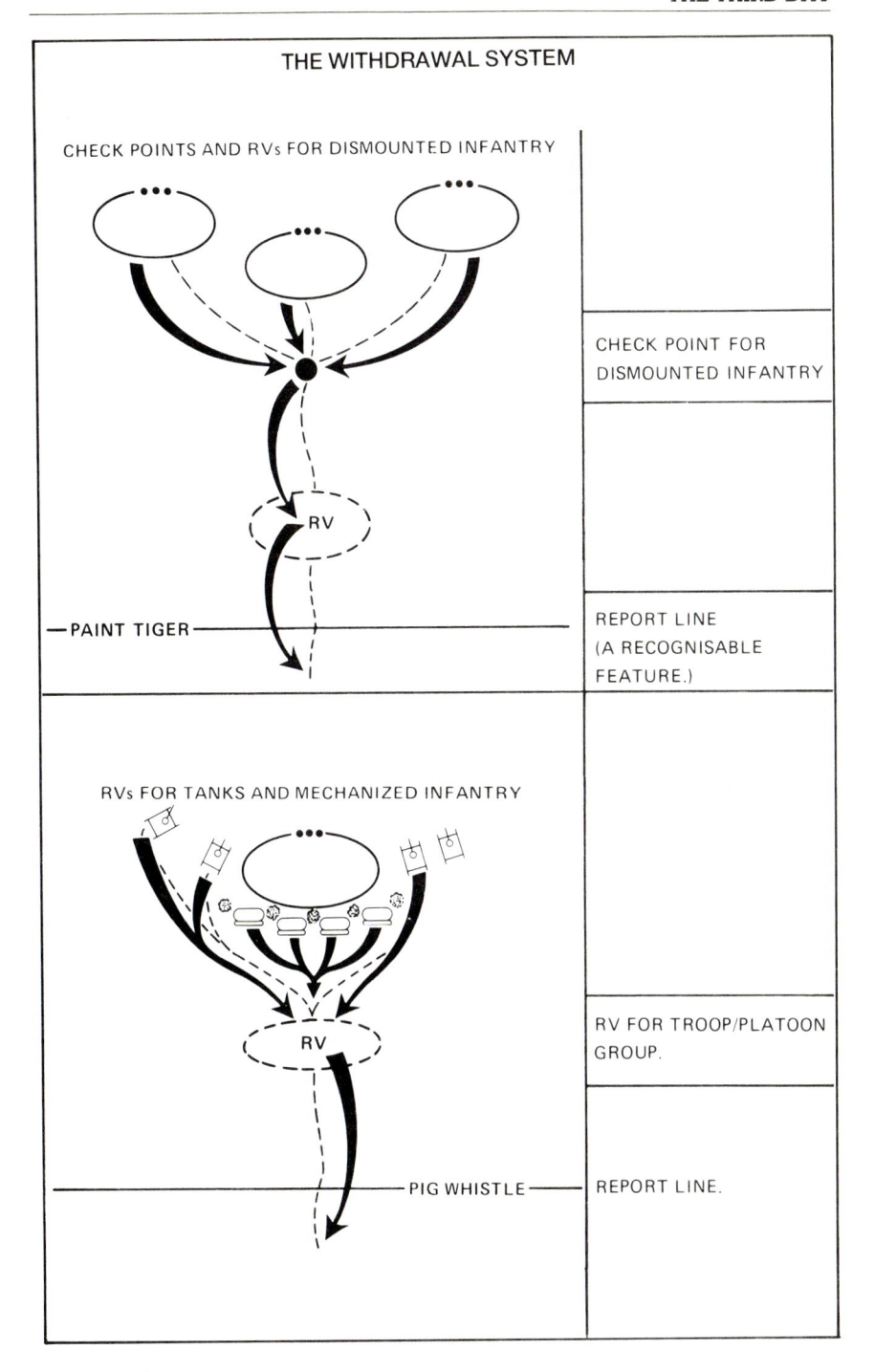

THE WITHDRAWAL SYSTEM

CHECK POINTS AND RVs FOR DISMOUNTED INFANTRY

—PAINT TIGER—

| | CHECK POINT FOR DISMOUNTED INFANTRY |
| | REPORT LINE (A RECOGNISABLE FEATURE.) |

RVs FOR TANKS AND MECHANIZED INFANTRY

—PIG WHISTLE—

| | RV FOR TROOP/PLATOON GROUP. |
| | REPORT LINE. |

THE THIRD DAY

in order to explain what he understood to be the reason for leaving at all, revealed the extent of the problem. Of the original thirteen platoon M113s, two had been totally wrecked by the shelling and four, belonging to the most exposed platoons, were so deep in rubble that their extrication without a major excavation (which was bound to notify the enemy of what was intended) was out of the question. One of the company HQ carriers was also a complete loss. In sum, therefore, Panton could raise about 50 per cent M113 strength to lift 65 per cent of manpower. A picture in his mind of the sequence and system of withdrawal (as described in all the manuals) was readily translated into a plan. Those M113s which could be made to run would be assembled at the last moment at a check point near company HQ in the centre of the village. Previously, every unnecessary man and the walking wounded would have been "thinned out" in small parties. Next, those of the soldiers who were not immediately confronting the enemy would be pulled back to the M113s. Finally, the handful of men occupying the most exposed positions would make a run for the vehicles under cover of an intense artillery bombardment and such support as might be provided from higher up the slope by the two remaining Leopards belonging to Major Linkman's squadron.

Simple as it looked in notes on paper, Panton assumed the risks and could only keep his fingers crossed and hope not one of his men would fail when the test came. Above all, he prayed the enemy would not discover what was going on until it was too late to interfere. The process of moving the men to the check point was only a beginning, of course. Then would come the most nerve-wracking part; that of driving, in general view of the enemy, northward along the forward slope towards Mendel (as the route providing best cover from view and fire available), to finally cross the crest on the way to a combat team RV outside Iffezheim. By night, thought Panton, the chances of getting away with it might have been quite good, but by day... So he had a short talk over the air with Linkman, explaining the route he intended to follow, and then fell into a long discussion with the FOO, Captain Pat Kendal, in order to devise a local fire plan which would:

- *delude the enemy for as long as possible;*
- *cover the initial thinning-out and collection of vehicles and men;*
- *cover the final abandonment; and*
- *screen with smoke, as much as possible, the cross-country dash.*

214

With details settled, Panton went round his platoons again, this time giving each leader detailed instructions, questioning and re-questioning each weary individual to ensure that he had grasped what was intended. Underlining, too, that, if radio communications failed, each leader should carry out his orders to the letter and not stand around waiting. Over and over again he repeated:

"There are no second chances in this business. Get left behind and there's damn all I can do. It'll be salt-mines for you and that's for sure!"

The old hands, knowing their leader's brand of humour at times like these, took the remark at face value; the newly joined soldiers were not too sure. Fatigue had blunted the sharp edge of the sense of purpose in some individuals. Panton sensed among them a kind of apathetic acceptance of the prospect of defeat and surrender. It worried him, as he strove harder yet to warn officers, NCOs and the well-known hard characters in his Company to use their influence: "You'll recognize defeatism in old buddies," he said. "Remember what some of 'em were like that day last winter when November Company beat us at hockey? Those you can cope with. But watch the new men. They're jumpy – some of 'em – so watch them. They'll give no warning."

By 0900 hours he was back at his command post, having done all that seemed possible. Already the handful of men designated eligible for thinning out had departed, and so far the enemy seemed to have noticed nothing unusual. Kendal had taken one opportunity to bring down a short concentration on a couple of BMPs observed moving from left to right beyond the obstacle. There had been quite a whine of engines out to their front at one time, and a sharp exchange of fire behind them near the crest when Linkman had spotted a T72 changing position and frightened the life out of its crew commander with a shot that glanced off its glacis plate.

If it suited Panton that the Red Army had assumed a slightly less belligerent attitude, it also suited the men under General Samsonov's command. The night's combat had left them battered, quite as weary as their opponents, only too pleased to eat and sleep, and with a sincere respect for 4 CMBG combativeness. They were ready, for the time being, to let the Canadians rest, and happy to steal a little sleep themselves. As for those for whom General Samsonov had a new task, the mere fact that it took the form of a withdrawal from the right sector and transfer to the left (in readiness to support the onward march of 3rd Guards Tank Division) was better than staying where they were and being shot at by a skilled enemy they so rarely saw. Information from air and ground sources suggested that the Canadians were up to something, and, since they continued to stay put in Blickheim and Mendel, it seemed reasonable to suppose that they might actually be contemplating an attempt at regaining the crest line they had lost during the night. That would suit the Army Commander's plan to envelop their right as the breakthrough by 3rd Guards Tank Division developed, and it would also suit Samsonov who might be presented with the chance to win a defensive battle and, thereby, regain some of his lost prestige. So 1st Guards Tank Division, far from preparing for a renewed advance, allowed itself to be deluded into adopting a much more passive posture, ungeared to pursuing a retiring opponent at once.

Arrangements within Blickheim moved systematically and almost unimpeded towards the culminating moment for departure. Starting at 0915 hours, working as quietly as possible, with engine noise kept at a minimum and drowned out, when necessary, by short outbursts of artillery fire put down by Kendal, the M113s were assembled at the RV. Stealthily, too, the two Leopards and a pair of TOW detachments occupied the positions overlooking the sector from where they could give such support as was possible. And for neutralization as well as deception, the artillery, at the request of Major Brent, acting CO of 3 RCR Battle Group, began a bombardment at a sustained rate of fire, commencing at H−10 (H-Hour having been fixed at 1000 hours, the time at which abandonment of the position started).

By 0945 hours, all the infanteers less the rearguard, who continued to occupy perimeter trenches, had arrived – almost on tiptoe – at the M113s. By hand signals, with voices kept low, the men had been ordered out of their hiding-places and led to their vehicles, bringing with them weapons and as much ammunition as they could manage, some of them returning to fetch loads which could not be carried at the first attempt. Equipment and stores which could not be removed were either damaged on-site or prepared, where possible, for destruction by time-delayed explosive devices – although few of these were available and the time so short that total demolition was impossible. Similarly, no time or stores were available to set booby traps, much as some of the men would have liked to do as a parting gift to the enemy. Once more, the civilians had set a problem. The

THE THIRD DAY

evacuation of those who had stayed behind was rejected by Panton. At the same time, he was anxious they should not be permitted, should the idea occur to those of pro-Warsaw Pact leanings, to apprise the Red Army of what was impending. So those who remained were shut into the cellar of the ruined central hotel, placed under guard until H-hour and left in no doubt what would happen if they tried, prematurely, to communicate with the enemy.

At H-hour, precisely, all manner of things happened at once. Along the entire 4 CMBG front, the remaining knots of men in the most exposed positions began to vacate their positions. Simultaneously, concentrations of artillery fire descended upon the advanced enemy positions, and a few Leopards and Lynxes, here and there, made demonstrations by brief appearances and random shooting, with a view to hinting at the opening stages of an attack. The deception generally had the desired effect. Red Army artillery was persuaded to put down fire, not on the tender areas where the Canadian infantry was exposed in the open, away from their trenches, but instead on suspected (and unoccupied) assembly areas and FUPs in the rear. Mixed with the high explosive came smoke to screen Blickheim from enemy observation at the crucial moment of evacuation as the men at the perimeter clambered out of their weapon slits and the M113s began their dash across country. And helping to build up the screen and fill gaps where they threatened to appear, were the infantry's 60 mm mortars, along with the two Leopards lobbing over 105 mm rounds from behind the crest line above.

Panton stood, tense and anxious with his head out of the command M113. Inside, the Signals NCO was checking off the reporting and departure of each sub-unit as it drove by. Outside, the CSM was chasing up the scurrying men, upbraiding the slightest hesitation or sight of muddle as they clambered into the carriers. 3 Platoon was moving, 2 almost ready to go and the last members of 1 Platoon, so badly reduced in numbers, were coming into sight, stumbling up the street, flinching as a Canadian shell dropped short. The company 2IC was marshalling the M113s at the edge of the village, fixing Panton with a stare that pleaded for the signal to go; knowing that his OC was intent upon having them move all in a bunch if possible, rather than singly, in the hope of reducing to a minimum the time when targets were exposed to danger. Nose-to-tail they now stood as the gunfire to their front bubbled and the smoke wafted across the enemy lines. Miraculously, nothing was coming in their direction.

"Can't last much longer!" shouted the CSM to Panton, with a half-laugh. "Oscar Company luck!" called back Panton, and crossed his fingers for the second time. "For Christ's sake don't stall the engine!" prayed more than one Grunt as he squeezed into an M113 amid disordered piles of kit. And the universal cry went up: "OK! Let's go!"

The last platoon M113 was nosed up to the one ahead and Panton (as was his duty) was bringing up the rear of Company HQ when Captain Andrei Rusalski began to smell a rat. More widely informed in several ways, through gunner channels and by personal observation at the front, than the more narrowly circumscribed infantry and tankmen, he did not subscribe to the pessimistic opinion that the enemy was on the verge of attacking. Nothing to seriously suggest it had been presented to him, and the success apparently being won on the left flank made it more likely, in Rusalski's book, that the enemy would withdraw. The sight of an M113 (one of November Company's) driving backwards out of a thicket increased his suspicions. A rising cloud of exhaust smoke within Blickheim made him look all the harder to his front and piece together a pattern which made him certain the enemy was in retreat. His report,

Left: Waiting patiently for the order to mount.

sceptically received by his superiors, nevertheless carried enough conviction to prompt a speculative bombardment of Mendel, Blickheim and the enemy-held woods between Kuppenheim and Oos. But largely it was too late, for the birds had flown and it would be twenty minutes before ground reconnaissance elements could be alerted and then goaded into probing forward into what was now an unoccupied space. Meanwhile, a Hare helicopter, which rose steeply behind Favorite to spy out the land, saw nothing at first; and when it tried again, from closer to the front, had such a close shave from a Blowpipe belonging to the Vandoos that it coyly dived, nap of the earth, behind the crest line.

It was with a feeling of elation that Panton brought up the rear of Oscar Company and was then witness of the belated bombardment of Blickheim falling well short of his fast-retreating M113. Ahead he could see the rest of the combat team making what use of ground it could as protection from enemy fire, but concentrating chiefly on speed to seek safety in the desperate race for the crest line. Only the shell-fire which suddenly struck Mendel, across the line of retreat, bothered him, but the voice of his 2IC, clear as a bell over the radio, gave reassurance that all would be well. A simple, "All stations, this is 2 Bravo. Follow me to the left. Out!" was enough to prove that a way around the danger had been found and that hesitation at a critical moment had been averted.

Crossing the crest, without loss, and driving due west, Panton could see elements of Mike Company also on the move and a Leopard (Linkman's) standing watchfully in a well-concealed hull-down position dominating the slope to the east. Driving fast for Iffezheim (the company RV), he was fired on (and missed) from the left by what he assumed must be one of the T72s which had infiltrated northwards the previous night. Smoke grenades thrown out hurriedly got him clear, but from that moment he was careful to keep cover between himself and that threatening flank. As a precaution, he also sent a warning over the air to Linkman of the lurking menace to his own retreat. Ten minutes later he was skirting Iffezheim and halting to let all the other vehicles catch up at the RV, prior to making for the battle group check point at Hügelsheim.

At Iffezheim were to be seen all the familiar signs of destruction in the aftermath of a stiff fight, and here too, the remnants of Papa Company combat team standing to, ready to support the final evacuation of the crest line by Mike Company as it leap-frogged to

THE THIRD DAY

> **CONTROLLING FACTORS**
>
> ★ The vital necessity to make careful preparations in accordance with a well-established drill and to ensure that all ranks are aware of the plan.
>
> ★ The need to bear in mind the demoralizing effects of such an operation, and therefore to impose strong leadership at all times.
>
> ★ The vital necessity for security in breaking clean without being detected or interfered with.

the rear. Soon it would hand over to the covering force – the tanks and APCs of C Squadron RCD combat team which had already taken station in readiness for their next major task.

Action of the covering force – C Squadron Combat Team

A considerable and none too easily accomplished redeployment was required of the predominantly tank force in 4 CMBG after orders for a withdrawal were issued, and the burden of its execution fell squarely upon Lieutenant-Colonel Cowdray, whose task it would be to command and control the covering force astride the full breadth of the brigade group frontage. In accordance with the Commander's plan (which conformed, of course, with VII (US) Corp's orders), the RCD Battle Group would cover the withdrawal of 4 CMBG as it retired through the successive stages of battle group check points and battle group RVs. By stages, it would funnel onto the same two routes up which it had moved only 60 hours ago, crossing the brigade start point and going back to the next position where it would prepare for its next task – whatever that might be. Cowdray's mission encompassed prevention of enemy interference with the final stages of 4 CMBG's departure from its RVs. Within that came the imposition of delay on the enemy advance until 2000 hours – last light – at which time, hopefully, it would take shelter behind the next main line of resistance which had been set up some ten miles in rear.

Holding back a strong enemy to a rate of one mile an hour seemed, to Cowdray, a pretty tall order, bearing in mind the meagre forces at his disposal. It was not simply a matter of imposing a delay across the present front on ground which, intersected by streams and dotted by woods, villages and towns, offered numerous places in which to harass the enemy. Always hanging over his head was the threat of envelopment from the flanks, notably the right flank, where the enemy was, by pessimistic report, beginning to make dramatic

THE THIRD DAY

progress and liable at any moment to expand his incursion sideways. Cowdray had drawn out on the map one attractive line, based on a stream, where he might make a serious attempt to hold the enemy for a couple of hours or more. Between that intermediate position and his present line of resistance he had sketched in nodal localities upon which delay might, temporarily, be caused. He had dispatched his DCO in a Kiowa to reconnoitre the intermediate position, instructing him to radio a report and be ready, on site, to guide the withdrawing units of RCD battle group as they arrived.

So far as Major Lionel Groves was concerned, the operation described to him by Cowdray implied surrendering command of half his squadron. Appreciating that Groves could not command the entire combat team across what, in some places, was a frontage of

Below: Vital role – Kiowas seeking information about the enemy's principal axis of advance as the thinning-out continues.

THE THIRD DAY

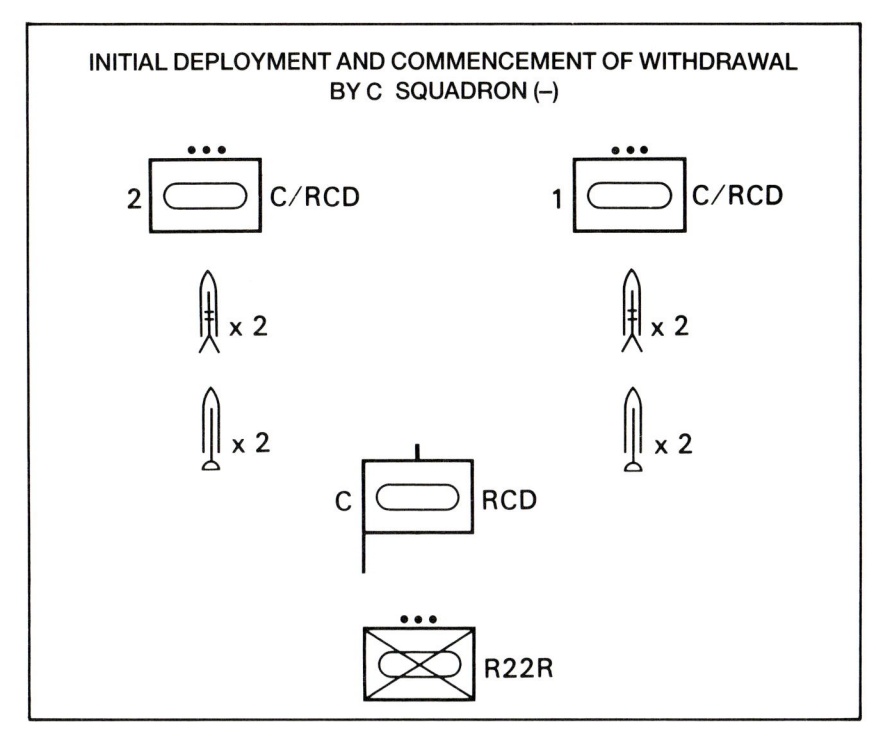

INITIAL DEPLOYMENT AND COMMENCEMENT OF WITHDRAWAL BY C SQUADRON (−)

11000 metres (much of it of a close nature), Cowdray decided to split C Squadron combat team into two and told Groves he would command the left sector (conforming to 3 RCR's original boundaries and taking the title of No. 6 combat team) and the right to the Squadron 2IC with the title of No. 7 combat team. Thus Groves would become responsible for about 5000 metres (too wide a frontage for him to be able to watch from a central axis) with a force consisting of only the following for its accomplishment:

- 2 x troops of tanks
- 1 x platoon of infantry (Vandoos)
- 4 x detachments of TOW
- 1 x platoon of mortars
- 4 x detachments of Blowpipe
- 1 x section field engineers
- 2 x Kiowa LOH
- 1 x battery 1 RCHA
- Squadron HQ (two tanks)
- 1 x ARV

THE THIRD DAY

For flank protection, he had at his disposal a single patrol of Lynx from D Squadron RCD, but this he did not contemplate employing as an integral part of his combat team, preferring that it should operate very much on its own initative in keeping him and Cowdray at battle group HQ informed of developments on the relatively secure left flank.

Redeployment of his combat team had posed problems caused by the existing close contact with the enemy of the leading infantry platoon and its accompanying troop of tanks in the woods between Iffezheim and Oos, and the close commitment of the rest of C Squadron combat team close by. By arrangement with the Vandoos on the right and Papa Company combat team in Iffezheim, he had to quietly extract the Vandoos platoon from the wood before 1000 hours and transfer 2 Troop to the left flank where it would take up an initial position in readiness for supporting Papa Company combat team in its withdrawal. Simultaneously, 3 and 4 Troops, along with the 2IC's tank from Squadron HQ, were drawn back and moved to the right flank, in readiness to cover the Vandoos as they departed. Finally, an arrangement was made with the TOW Platoon commander of 3 RCR for the transfer of command and change of deployment of his four detachments.

Uppermost in Groves' mind was the need to maintain firm control no matter what happened. The series of laid-down denial times stipulated by Cowdray in his orders provided the framework of the scheme. Groves emphasized to his subordinates that orders demanding that a line should be held until a certain time meant just that; but also, that, in the event of a breakdown of communications, abandonment of a line could take place. Groves was aware of the threat to morale which withdrawal implied and anxious that, at no time, should anybody in his combat team feel left in the lurch; it was vital that all should sense that their chances of survival were reasonably good providing orders were obeyed and the enemy made to pay a price in time and material for his territorial gains.

Essentially, Groves' mode of operation was founded upon the ambush. The selection of each delaying position was decided by its suitability to that technique – the manner in which defiles, extended fields of fire or locally unflankable ground could be adapted either to hitting the enemy from hiding at short range, or enabling him to be struck at long range as he drove across open country. Whatever the method, the intention was always to make the Red Army units

THE THIRD DAY

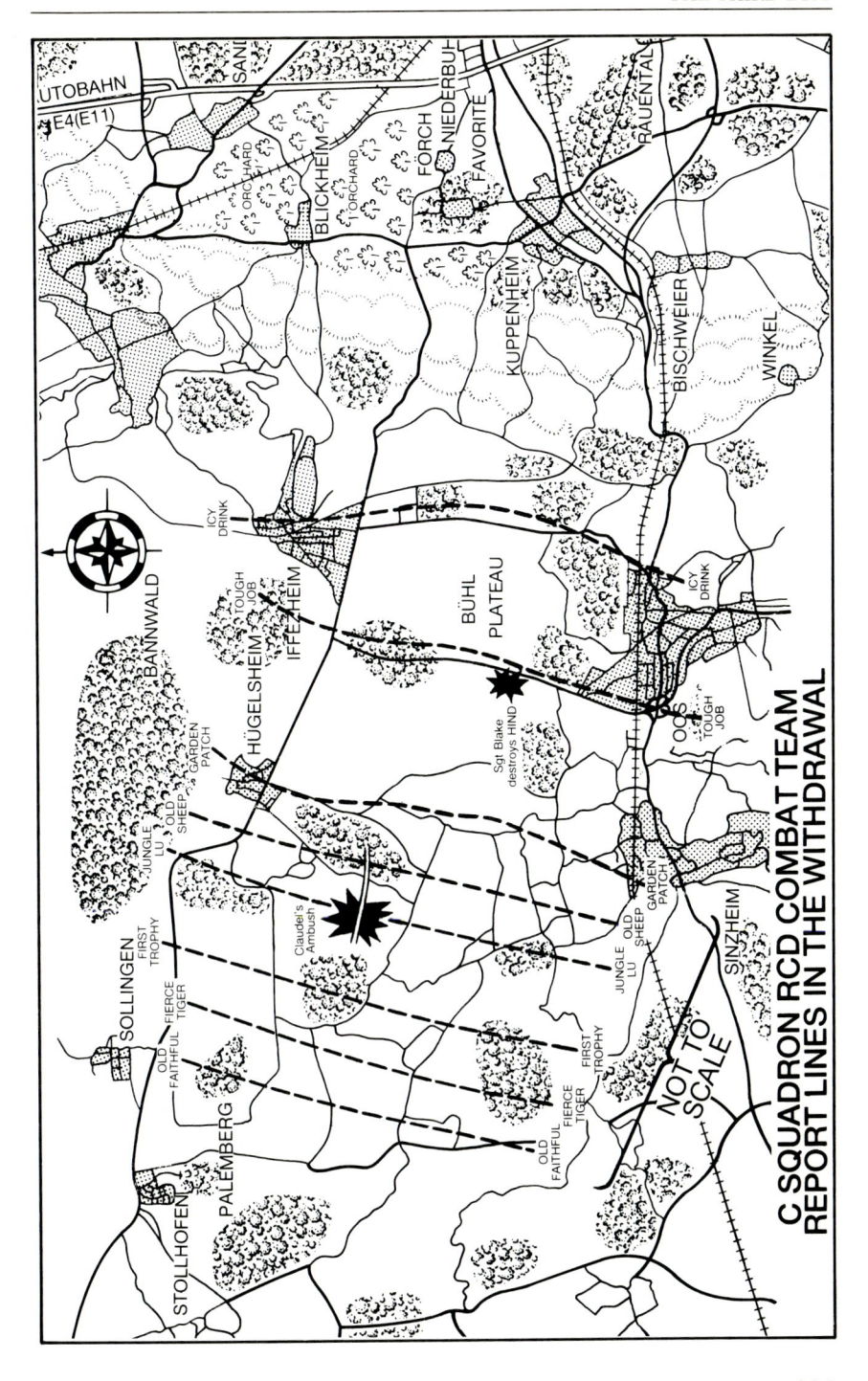

225

hesitate and, most desirably of all, waste time in cogitation, uncertainty and full-scale, time-consuming deployment from the line of march.

"Heaven knows, we aren't the biggest little army ever to try this sort of thing," Groves had said to his 2IC before they went their separate ways, "but we both play poker, and one of us at least knows how to bluff!" – a remark which drew a rueful grin from the 2IC who had been among the losers in a recent game played at Sinzheim while they assuaged the boredom of waiting in reserve.

Tanks were the instruments upon which Groves, of necessity, had chiefly to depend. Each troop, partnered with two TOW detachments and two detachments of Blowpipe, would be the pivot of his striking force – second, after the TOWs, to let fly at the longer ranges of engagement, and last to vacate each defensive line. C Battery of 1 RCHA with its 155 mm howitzers, nevertheless, occupied a prominent place in Groves' considerations. Already, the gunners had issued a new Continuous Fire Support Programme, the numbered crosses on the map covering the withdrawal route. Now he discussed tactics with the FOOs (one of whom was never far distant from the squadron HQ tanks) and gave them a clear indication of the system he would adopt. At least one tactical bound behind the tanks would usually be found the Vandoos platoon, he said, its principal task to protect the tanks in close country, to spring ambushes in defiles and provide a foundation on the main intermediate position when it was reached. Roving among his sub-units would be squadron HQ, either at the front to co-ordinate their offensive operations or save them from being overrun, or a tactical bound in rear while reconnoitering the next delaying line. Groves intended to use squadron HQ also as a fire base, ready in the last resort to help his subordinates out of trouble when the odds became too great or if the flanks were turned. Meanwhile, he had the A 1 Echelon top up each tank with ammunition and fuel; instructed each crew commander to have the mechanics rectify anything which could be fixed within the next two hours; and made sure the men had time for a meal – perhaps the last they would enjoy that day.

News of the redeployment of C Squadron RCD did come to the notice of 1st Guards Tank Division, but with insufficient impact to alter the general impression that the Canadians intended to stay put or even attack. Thus the first gratuitous successful bluff was achieved. Subsequently, the enemy would take more fooling,

THE THIRD DAY

although rarely did Samsonov put much influence on his right flank commanders to exert pressure, since for tactically astute reasons, he had no desire to frighten off the prey; premature departure of the Canadians might well rob him of a victim who if allowed to dally would fall to a flank envelopment. Not that 290th MRR, augmented by elements from 301st Tank Regiment, was going to be lax in its follow-up. Oblensky was as ambitious as the next Red Army Colonel, and delighted at the opportunity to demonstrate the superiority of mounted infantry in pursuit. In any case, there were scores to be settled.

Lieutenant Harry Owens had deftly changed his tanks' positions, when the alterations in plan had been announced, by leaving only one Leopard guarding the forward edge of the wood, pulling back the other two to the flanks and staying near the centre himself so he could easily withdraw along with the rest, when the time came. Because he was working, along with the TOWs and Blowpipes, unsupported (except on random occasions) by any other fire unit except the artillery, he had perforce to make his own, internal fire

Below: Once more, the BRDMs take the lead, as Canadian resistance is reduced.

THE THIRD DAY

and movement arrangements. Initially it was wise to send the TOWs back to their first supporting line, between Hügelsheim and Sinzheim, from where they could make best use of their long-range characteristic. In company went a pair of Blowpipe while the other pair stayed with the Leopards and the FOO. Shortly after 1000 hours, as the artillery fire supporting the withdrawal of the forward sub-units rose to its crescendo, and the fast-moving elements of November Company could be seen flitting among the trees away to the right, Owens warned his commanders to watch their fronts. Confidently, their replies came back, loud and clear – particularly from those occupying the two defiladed flank positions who were not in almost immediate confrontation with the enemy in the nearby wood. Yet it was a flanker who got in the first shot at a BRDM moving with astonishing carelessness towards Oos on the right flank, at about 750 metres range.

A single well-aimed round was enough, and again there was a pause while the Soviets seemed to stop to scratch their heads in bewilderment. Anyway, a Kiowa pilot, rising daringly to a hundred feet for a swift glance above the trees, reported nothing happening except a lot of dust rising over Blickheim to mix with the still-smouldering fires of the previous night's battle. But he was wrong. At 1050 hours, a mere ten minutes before Owens was due to withdraw, half a dozen artillery rounds fell amidst "his" wood and shots rang out from the enemy lines. Firing could be seen near Iffezheim, too, so presumably the enemy was making a concerted effort along the entire front. Owens was tempted to move at once rather than risk getting involved in a fire fight as he broke from contact. He compromised, sending away the Blowpipe detachment and telling his WO's tank, on the right, to pull back to the copse they had held in the penultimate stage of their advance earlier that morning. Anxiously he studied the front, and alternately glanced at his watch. Over the air, he heard a reminder from the FOO about a DF task that was planned to strike the threatening wood at the moment of abandonment. Reporting too, that the guns were ready. He gave the go-ahead and then:

"31 Alpha Bravo, this is 31. Move in figures one minute, over," and down the intercom, "OK, driver. Reverse out of here and let's go!" The leap-frogging had begun.

The five minutes of artillery fire caught the composite leading battalion group of 290th MRR as it was in the act of making ready to advance. The arrival of the shells did nothing to deter the leading tank platoon, but it did cause their commander to hesitate and seek a way round the shelled zone; experience at Förch the day before, having taught him the folly of risking BMPs against 155 mm projectiles. As a result, Call Sign 31 Bravo not only managed to slip away unhindered, but also took the opportunity to loose off a round of 105 mm HESH at the shape of a T72 its commander detected in the wood, before discharging a cluster of smoke grenades and backing off. Only Rusalski, again, managed to make a contribution on the Soviet behalf, but his 122 mm shell-fire merely frightened without damaging the mildly triumphant Owens as he drove rearwards, along with 31 Bravo and the FOO, and covered by 31 Alpha and 31 Charlie from their initial positions until he had taken up a new hull-down position based on Hügelsheim at the next tactical bound, 1500 metres distant. This, Owens reflected as he swung into shrubbery on a slight mound, was what the Leopard's speed was all about. And now, swinging round and making hell-for-leather for this next haven of safety, it was the turn of the team of 31 Alpha and 31 Charlie to move, watched over in their passage of the open ground by 31 and 31 Bravo and two TOWs, along with the Blowpipes.

Now began the battle of wits between the persistently advancing Soviet troops and the grudgingly retiring Canadians – the former striving with strength to accelerate the rate of advance, the latter endeavouring economically to buy time by use of the deterrence of action. Both were seeking to inflict the maximum harm at the minimum price in retribution; each, in the light of 48 hours' intensive battle experience, somewhat more professionally subtle and cautious in method than previously. For example, when Sergeant Oleg Nikolai sought ways of stealing round Oos, he was much more circumspect than in his approach to Förch at the outset of the campaign. He tended to spend more time examining the ground and possible danger spots ahead before sending forward somebody else in his patrol; and when he moved, it was gently to enable him, from a steadier platform, to take a closer look at the terrain. That way he hoped to discover trouble before trouble found him. Shulubin also took greater care, declining to throw caution to the winds by insisting upon a headlong advance into the unknown. He allowed the leading platoon of tanks to pick its way intelligently, and was diligent in ensuring that the point elements were carefully supported by those

THE THIRD DAY

in the second echelon. It might not look quite so dashing and it might take a little longer, but the price in men and machines was lower and the chances of doing the enemy harm when he disclosed himself that much greater. Anyway, Oblensky was not constantly goading him as before because Oblensky now valued the advantage of operating that way too, and was not, himself, being harried by Samsonov — whose attention was focused elsewhere on the left flank.

So, when the two point-tanks of Shulubin's Vanguard Company pushed their noses beyond the cover of the wood that 31 Alpha and 31 Charlie had recently vacated, they were not simultaneously joined by the other pair of T72s or the BMPs. These latter stood watch, ready to bring down fire and smoke instantly in the right direction. The opportunity came when a TOW successfully engaged the right-hand T72; and, twenty-five seconds later, Owens lased onto the left-hand T72 and got off a shot which missed because, already, smoke from Shulubin's support line was coming down to shield the threatened tanks and shots were throwing up eruptions of soil all around. Owens went backwards in high-speed reverse into a turret-down position and left it to the others to take up the shooting while he sought an alternative site. These would be the competing tactics of the day in this sort of fluid situation — acquire a target; take up fire position (watched over by at least one other friendly tank or TOW); shoot, scoot, try from somewhere else while somebody else took his turn in the shooting-gallery. Nearly always each troop group would move in unison within the combat team, ensuring mutual support.

The manoeuvring game began with Shulubin (the poorer by one T72) asking the reconnaissance experts like Sergeant Nikolai and the Hare LOH pilots to report safe ways round. Then directing the leading elements, supported by fire and covered by smoke as necessary, to infiltrate towards ground from which flank pressure and fire could be brought to bear to dislodge (if not destroy in location) the tenacious vehicles of Owen's team. Meanwhile, Owens would manoeuvre to maintain station until the designated time for departure, striving to pick off opponents or, at least, bring them under fire. Endeavouring to guess at the next counter-move in order not only to circumvent its intent but also, hopefully, to profit from it by a surprise move to a flank. It was cat-and-mouse stuff with the odds slightly in favour of the outnumbered defenders, but with the initiative firmly in possession of the attackers. In the preliminary bout, however, Groves' team held its own and managed to arrange

CONTROLLING FACTORS

★ The need to establish a coherent plan, known to all commanders and controlled by a predetermined time schedule, in order to impose strict control regardless of enemy action.

★ The need for reconnaissance of all routes and intermediate positions in advance of the operation.

★ The principle of making the enemy stop and deploy on as many occasions as possible without becoming heavily embroiled in close fighting.

★ The need to break clean from each delaying position.

★ The predominant importance of tanks and HAWs – with artillery as the last line of defence.

★ The likelihood that the enemy, once he has appraised the situation, will act with great speed and skill in overwhelming lightly defended positions.

★ The need to have anti-helicopter weapons well forward.

★ The need to be ready to counter electronic warfare through normal voice procedure drills.

★ The need, through recovery and demolition, to deny the enemy any abandoned equipment.

★ The need for casualties to be evacuated from the forefront of battle if possible.

its withdrawal on schedule. Its first serious setback did not occur until an instant before the next move back was due at 1115 hours from report line Tough Job to Garden Patch.

The electronic warfare problem

Jamming of 4 CMBG radio frequencies began. Without warning, the battle group and combat team nets were subjected to a roar of electronic interference which virtually blotted out every transmission, and ceased only momentarily when whoever controlled its source switched off in order to register the impact of his depredations. Groves, Owens and all the other leaders found themselves deprived of radio contact with their out-stations, most of which were also out of visual contact. The sensation was that of being unexpectedly rendered deaf and dumb, the result a sapping of confidence along with the threat of lost control. Lacking sufficient time to drive from one vehicle to another, they could only keep their fingers crossed and hope each commander would remember the

Above: A potent threat to unwary armour – a Hind helicopter armed with Sagger.

orders and abandon position on schedule. All, except one, did in fact do so, but 31 Bravo upset uniformity by starting back too soon, leaving Owens to retire on his own and in some peril. For the enemy's imposition of jamming coincided with a modification to his tactics – a noticeable attempt on the part of his foremost tanks and BMPs to "crowd" the Canadians, and the reintroduction of Hind helicopters to that corner of the battlefield, their crews on the lookout for stragglers which, out of range of ground-to-air missiles, might provide easy pickings.

Sergeant Eddie Blake regarded the appearance of the Hinds as a challenge to wipe out a few scores over his treatment during the defensive action near Blickheim. Denied many suitable targets for his Blowpipes, hammered for hours on end by every enemy weapon in the inventory, and forced to make two hair's breadth escapes from capture by Russian infantry, it was nothing short of a miracle to him and his detachments that they were still alive to tell the tale. A glance at his watch warned him that the time to leave report line Tough Job was nigh; and the roar of jamming in his headsets reminded him that orders were unlikely to come through. But there, hardly more than 3000 metres distant, was a big fat Hind, behaving in a manner suggesting that it might come within closer range. Dismounted and

THE THIRD DAY + 12 HRS ON

crouched behind a knoll, with the M113 20 metres farther back, he decided to take a chance and, if necessary, cut it fine in order to shoot this bird.

The Hind was at the hover, bobbing up and down behind a belt of trees. To his left he heard a Leopard – 31 Bravo – revving its motor and moving. A bit soon, he ruminated; anyway 31 was still around. The Hind had ducked behind the trees and now it had appeared again, sneaking through dead ground with only its rotors visible. Any moment it would be within range. More engine noise; 31 setting off. Dare he wait much longer? Now gun-fire to his right, replied to by 31. Smoke from grenades building up a tidy little screen in that direction. He looked over his shoulder and saw a member of his crew waving urgently from the M113. Let him wait! That Hind must rise soon. Yes, there it was and not looking his way either, with any luck, for it was pointing to a flank, probably at 31. Raise weapon, complete firing drills, press the button, feel the kick of the launch and collect the speeding missile as it rocketed away. Tracking it steadily with the thumb as so often in training, putting all other thoughts and fears aside, he concentrated hard on the target which had just launched a Sagger. That would not get far, for Blake's missile was perfectly on track and then exploding slap amidships, the Hind staggering out of the air to land with a crash, its Sagger grounding with a flash less than half-way on its journey. Blake sprang to his feet and began to run towards the M113, but something made him look right and flop down again. Not 20 metres off stood a BMP at the instant of firing its gun to hit the M113, to penetrate and detonate the cargo of Blowpipes, along with everything else, in one resonant bang. Five minutes later Blake found himself looking down the business end of a submachine-gun with its owner saying, what he assumed to be the equivalent, in Russian, of "For you the war is over!"

By the time Owens arrived back on report line Garden Patch, he was both furious and frightened. The premature withdrawal of 31 Bravo could well have thrown him and the rest of the troop into jeopardy. It irked him that 2 Troop, on the left, had been forced, with some handy shooting, to come to his rescue. Now, it seemed, Sergeant Blake, that fine gunner NCO with the Blowpipe, was missing, having very probably sacrificed himself on behalf of Owens by shooting down that Hind. Well, that was one for the record and a recommendation for gallantry – after the battle. "As of now!" he

233

snapped to his signaller corporal, "you re-establish communications. Failing that, comply with SOPs and switch to frequency Diana. See what you find there!"

Using all the tricks in the trade, the corporal was able, by repeated calling and "words twice" procedure, to make contact with nearby out-stations of the troop. This enabled Owens to put over his intention to stick to tactical plan and now, in accordance with SOPs, change frequency to Diana and hope to find it clear with combat team HQ already tuned. It worked – long enough, anyway, to hear Groves state in guarded terms that the difficulties in control and the enemy pressure made it necessary to accelerate the programme a little. Old Sheep would be abandoned fifteen minutes ahead of schedule and Jungle Lu would be left entirely to India 41 – assisted by a section of Sappers. The infantry of India 41 would be limited to a single section to actuate a small ambush, the value of which was dubious except as an irritant.

Ambush

Sergeant Pierre Claudel of 1 Platoon D Company, the Royal 22e Regiment, would have been at home among the old "coureurs de bois" of the past – a bold man of innate cunning allied with infinite determination in the search for prey. The business of setting an ambush with his section at the spot where a short bridge spanned a narrow stream running through soft ground was precisely in his line of business. Open terrain in the approaches to the defile, broken by scrubby trees close in along the banks on the home side, and enough ground and tree cover to offer a way of escape when the time came, suited his style. Discussing a plan with his platoon officer and the sergeant from 4 CER, it was decided to set a demolition charge on the bridge, to be fired by the sapper sergeant when the first enemy vehicle was within about 100 metres of the bridge, and bury concealed anti-tank mines at a couple of places of firmer going downstream where the enemy might also attempt a crossing. The platoon commander was in a hurry to drive on to the intermediate position at Old Faithful, and quite content to let Claudel do things his own way. Claudel decided to keep things simple, even to making allowance for a failure of the sapper to blow his charges in time.

A case of plastic explosive would be placed into a road culvert on the far side of the bridge, just to make sure. The bridge itself would be covered by a Carl Gustav and an M72, hidden in bushes in

THE THIRD DAY + 12 HRS ON

Above: Demolition – a sapper in his element, preparing to make a loud bang.

THE THIRD DAY + 12 HRS ON

the ditch at the roadside, some 50 metres beyond the west bank, and closely protected by a LAR. Two hundred metres further back, tucked in behind a crest, was the infantry's M113, in readiness to give support with 50 cal and a dismounted GPMG for the ambush party in its retreat. Sent right back, out of the danger zone, was the sapper M113 once it had disgorged its stores, the sergeant electing to travel with the infantry when the time to go arrived.

In considerable haste, the tanks and M113s of 1 Troop team crossed the bridge, Owens confirming to Claudel, as he passed, that he was the last. At once the demolition charges on the bridge were armed, and the ambush party settled into the hiding-places to await developments. These were not long coming. First in sight was a head and a pair of binoculars two hundred metres away, peering above a hedge at the corner in the road. Then a BRDM slinking round the corner, its place taken by another, probably a BRDM 2 (in fact the mount of Sergeant Nikolai, all of whose suspicions had been aroused by the blatant defencelessness of the little bridge now in sight).

Suddenly the Vandoo felt an impulse to do something spectacular, causing a heated discussion between Claudel and the sapper.

"Let the pig drive right on to the bridge before you press the button," he suggested. "No dice," replied the sapper. "Suppose the goddam thing doesn't go off? What then?"

"Suppose, it doesn't," responded Claudel, "there's nothing we can do about it. So, let the pig come on!"

"It's not a TV show here," complained the sapper, "I don't like waiting to the last second, but I'll blow it when you give the word."

But it did not work out that way. The BRDM, warned by Nikolai to take particular care, had pulled off the road into a farm-workers' lay-by. Two men jumped out and sprinted for cover in the ditch, starting to crawl towards the bridgehead with the idea of seeing if they could detect demolition charges and, perhaps, cut the wires. Claudel swore.

"OK, blow the damn thing now," he snapped, and the button was pushed with a most satisfactory bang which did all that was required of it to the bridge. "Get that scout car," shouted Claudel to the Carl Gustav man, "and the rest of you, 300 metres, man in vehicle at the corner of the road, rapid fire!"

Right: Ambush – the Carl Gustav operator awaits his moment.

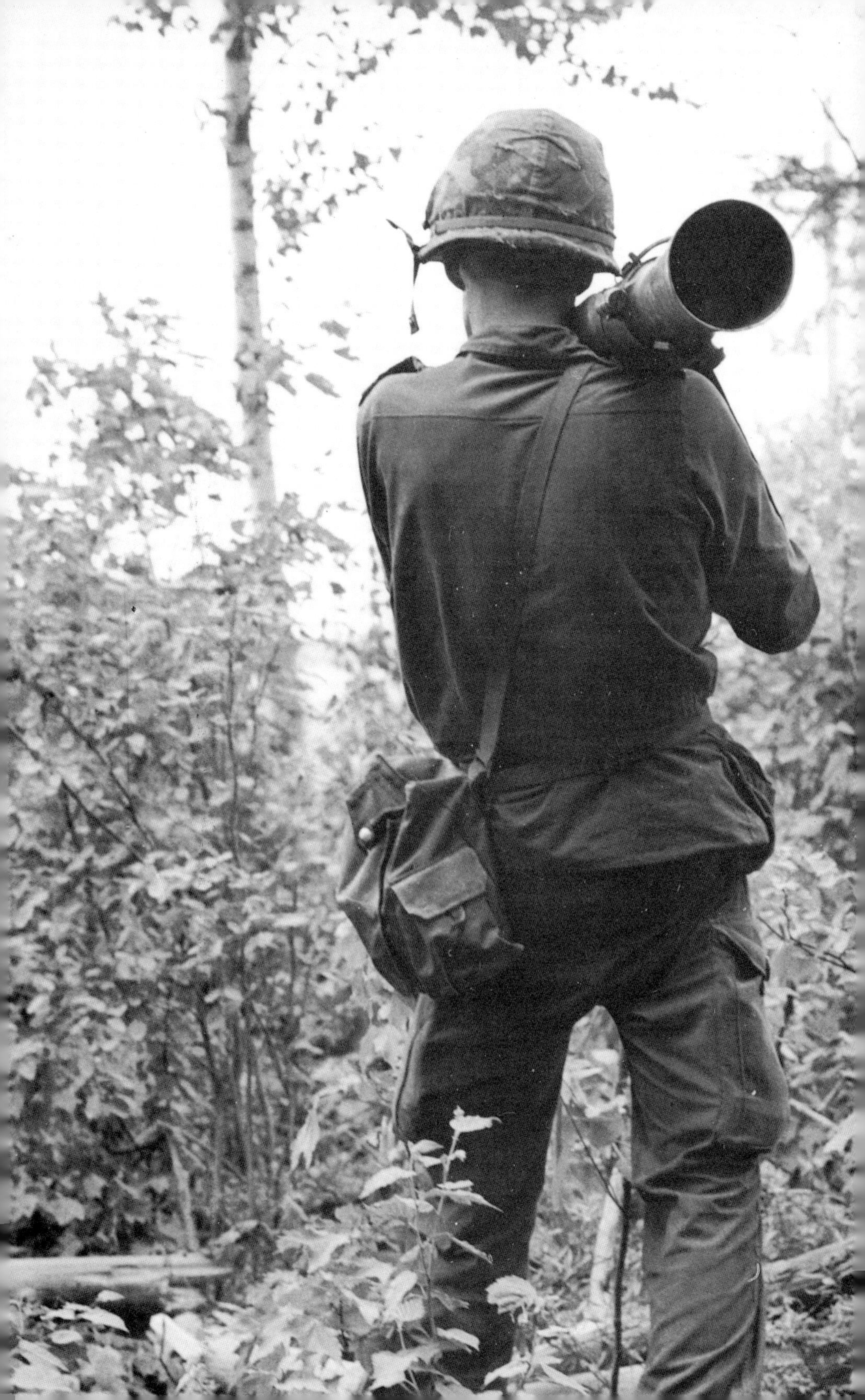

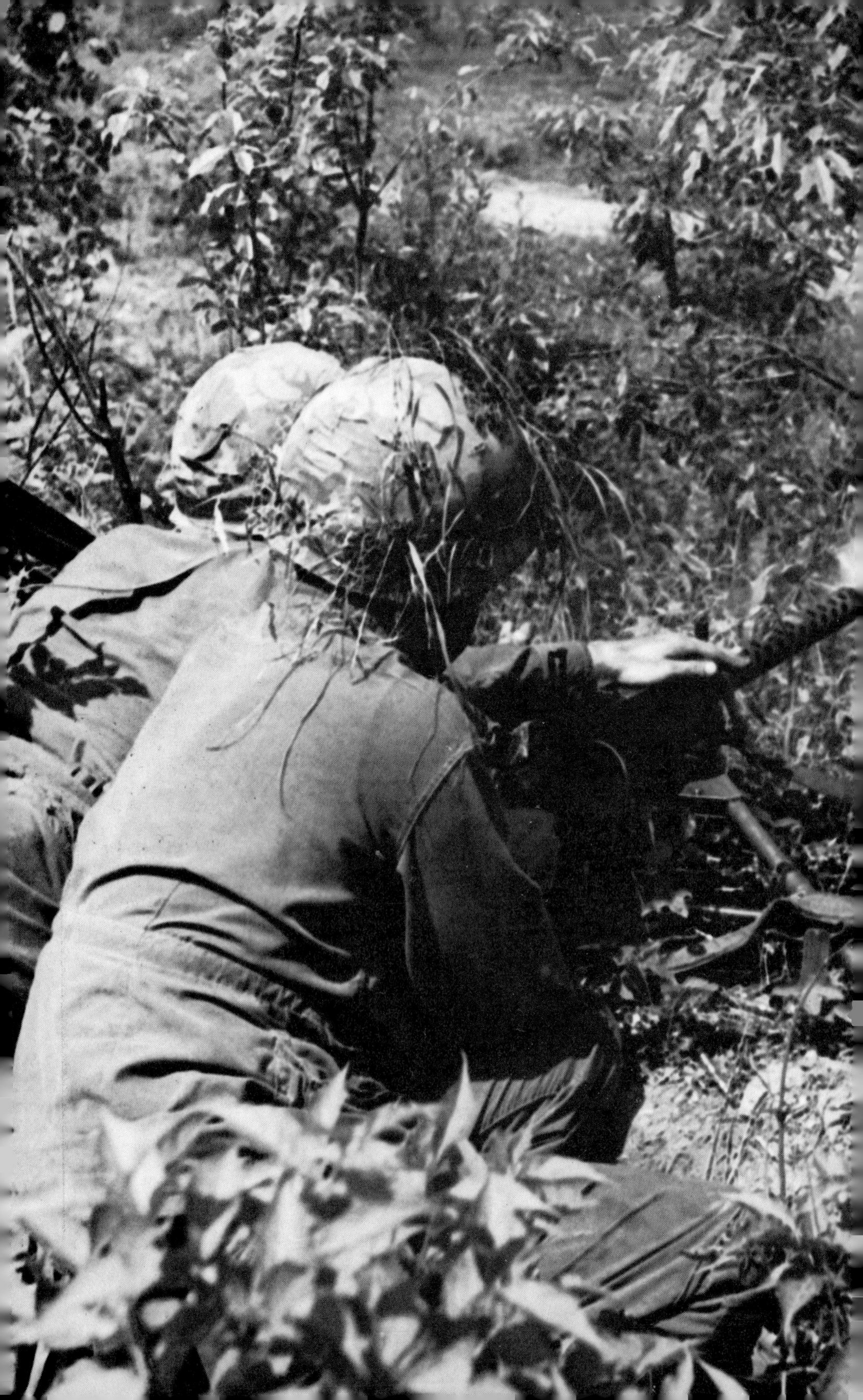

The springing of the ambush in no way astonished Nikolai, but the very accurate burst of 7.62 mm fire which wounded him in the shoulder was certainly something he had not expected, and a tribute to the LAR gunner who had taken a lot of care measuring the range when the others had been setting up the trap. The Carl Gustav man, on the other hand, was not so clever. He missed with the first shot and was compelled, under the lash of Claudel's tongue and a smattering of small arms fire, to reload and make a second attempt at a target which was fast reversing the way it had come. This time he was more lucky. The BRDM spouted flames and smoke and nobody got out.

"Time to go," said the sapper sergeant to Claudel.

"You go," said Claudel, "I'll wait around. See you back at the 113. I'll go get me a prisoner."

The sapper shrugged and decided not to argue. Back at the M113, peering through branches at the bridgehead, he watched Claudel crawl to the stream and out the other side. Saw him disappear from view and, five minutes later, heard a shot. Next moment, the Vandoo came into sight again, prodding with his SMG another man who crawled unwillingly through the long grass.

"What d'you know!" exclaimed the sapper to the 50-cal gunner beside him, "The man's mad, but he pulled it off." Then, practically, while scanning the far skyline where something fresh was looming into view: "Stand-by for squalls. That's a tank up there or I'm a Dutchman. Start up, get smoke grenades ready. Line up on that turret but don't fire unless I tell you."

Helplessly, they watched Claudel creep out of the stream, gather his party and begin the long crawl back to safety. For one dreadful moment, indeed, the sapper wondered if the Vandoo was going to attempt another exploit. But the short pause was only to look back over his shoulder; any extra-daring deed which had entered his mind had apparently been expelled. Claudel and his men were within 20 metres of the M113 before the enemy seemed to take notice and, even then, it was only a speculative burst of machine-gun fire which clattered overhead.

Left: 'Man at the corner! Rapid fire!'

"Hold it! Don't fire yet!" shouted the sapper, "I don't think he's seen us. Just get ready to go!"

With a rush, two minutes later, Claudel plus three private soldiers and one very crestfallen Russian were piling into the back of the M113, the engine of which was running. A moment later they were backing away, soon to be driving fast and unbothered for home, Claudel's only regret being an inability immediately to report this triumph since, once more, the jammers had found their frequency and blotted it out. As it was, by aggressive action, beyond the demands of his orders, he had prevented the enemy gaining early knowledge of the stream crossing and imposed extra delay. He had also, by capturing a prisoner, made it possible for the Intelligence people to discover that this enemy thrust by a mauled formation, was probably of subsidiary importance – and that was to be very valuable information indeed.

Intermediate position
The attitude and methods applied by Lieutenant-Colonel Brian Cowdray to the selection of the intermediate position on report line Old Faithful were very similar to those which had been adopted by the Brigade Commander and the two Infantry COs when planning the complex defensive position three days previously. The difference was mainly that of scale. Whereas extensive resources had been allocated for the previous operation that was intended to last for 48 hours, Cowdray possessed only minor facilities for an operation that, at best, would last two hours. Furthermore, Old Faithful Line lacked the same imposing topographical features of its predecessor: the crest line's features, such as they were, did not dominate the surrounding terrain, and the approaches provided useful cover for an attacker. Indubitably, the narrow stream which ran across the front for which Groves was responsible, supplied the spine, but hardly the rib-cage of an imposing obstacle. Nor were there anything like enough natural strong points, such as woods and villages, available on the main position: just a small copse on the right skyline and the village of Palemberg on the left, its church spire rearing above to mark its presence and provide a perch for some enterprising – and brave – FOO.

With but little time available for reconnaissance and consideration, Cowdray (in company with his DCO) had made a quick map appreciation of the ground and confirmed the DCO's conclusions with a plan based upon a rapid examination in person from a Kiowa. Leaving the DCO to control the occupation of the right, and less seriously threatened sector, Cowdray concentrated his attention upon the left in readiness for the arrival of Groves' fast-retreating combat team. First to put in an appearance was the Sapper Troop (less the party involved with the ambush on Report Line Jungle Lu). These he put to work laying surface mines quickly in the obvious routes of approach, the roads and tracks, in order to channel a fast-deploying enemy into specific killing zones. The presence of a few members of the German Wallmeisters supplemented the engineer effort by helping with the demolition of bridges and culverts. But nothing elaborate was possible in the short time available.

Next to drive up was the Vandoos platoon (less Sergeant Claudel's section). These Cowdray intended to employ as protection for the armour in conjunction with security of Palemberg and the copse – one section in the copse, the rest of the platoon (once Claudel returned) in the village. From close behind the crest line they might prevent enemy light vehicles and foot patrols infiltrating to close range of the tanks and M113s.

As a matter of principle, however, Cowdray wished to hit the enemy at maximum range and keep him at arm's length for as long as possible. The TOWs, in theory, would engage first, although again it was apparent that the normal European medium-class terrain would provide only limited opportunities to make full use of their maximum 3750 metres range and long time of flight. As usual, it would be the tanks with their high-velocity guns which would bear the brunt of the fighting from about 2000 metres inwards. So, as had been their role for generations, it was gunners and mortarmen whose power of hurting the enemy most, at all stages of action, would be heavily depended upon. Therefore the whole of 1 RCHA (all four batteries amounting now to 21 of the original 24 guns) plus the mortar platoons of 3 RCR and the Vandoos, had been deployed in support of the Old Faithful Line. Already the CO of 1 RCHA had made his reconnaissance, drawn up his fire plan (to include the part to be played by the infantry's mortars) and presented Cowdray with a preliminary target list which the Dragoon would not have had the time or heart to quarrel with, even if it had not been so obviously professionally comprehensive. In effect, the two-hour battle of the Old Faithful Line would be fought by artillery and mortars with the support of other arms.

THE THIRD DAY + 12 HRS ON

The other arms had prominent parts to play, for all that, and it had frustrated Major Groves that he could not be in two places at once to ensure that all would be right. One place was at the front controlling his withdrawing troops, the other planning the defence of the Old Faithful Line. But there was scant time to go to the latter, and Cowdray's instructions over the air, of great assistance though they were, had been fragmentary due to jamming. In the act, Cowdray met Groves as he drove into Palemberg, slightly more than one tactical bound ahead of his troops, and imposed his own plan upon the combat team commander, describing the existing deployment and letting him carry on from there. Additionally, however, Cowdray had to do more due to the semi-communications breakdown. Precise instructions could not reach the troops as they raced for safety. It was Cowdray in the Kiowa who performed the task of a sheepdog, searching out the moving tanks and dropping down to guide them straight to their allocated destinations behind the Palemberg crest line.

Twenty minutes before the enemy was expected to confront the line, most of the Blowpipe detachments had taken up position and the TOWs were driving in. Some 5000 metres distant the, by now, familiar signs of the closing enemy presence could be observed through tell-tale columns of rising smoke and dust. Overhead, the air war was warming up once more with helicopters skimming the horizon and fighter-bomber attacks strafing vehicles caught in the open. Here and there, civilians scurried in desperation before the advance; but in nothing like the milling crowds which had hampered the opening stages; presumably most had come to terms with their fate and decided to stay put. Intermingled with the traffic shifting westwards in the frontal zone were the advanced elements of the administrative sub-units and services – unit echelon vehicles close on hand to top up AFVs with ammunition; unit mechanics and 4 Service Battalion recovery teams jostling to repair or drag back failing or broken-down machinery to save it from the enemy's grasp; 4 Field Ambulances evacuation tentacles hanging on for last-moment deliveries of wounded from unit ambulance carriers which, as their role demanded, stayed as close as they dared to the fighting men they succoured; military police, grimed by dust from the passing vehicles, cajoling and hounding the traffic streams into order, untangling traffic blockages, rounding up or redirecting stragglers from all armies and keeping a sheriff's eye open for serious misdemeanours which might undermine the military effort. Every contribution to the prevention of wastage and the efficient direction of effort that was engineered in rear of the fighting line, enhanced the chances of the combat troops to win their battles. Every skirmish won bought time and eased the unhindered redeployment of 4 CMBG and the other NATO forces. Indeed, as the Old Faithful Line was about to greet the first hostile forces, the last of the disengaged combat elements of 4 CMBG were passing the original brigade start point of two days ago on the way to their next battle zone.

For the second time in 48 hours, Ivan Shulubin steered his vanguard company towards what, from the map, was recognizably a potentially well-defended enemy position. And once more, units of 4 CMBG prepared a reception worthy of the occasion. Already, a certain mutual respect had been generated between the adversaries, without in any way obliterating the distaste each held in mind for the other's presence. Warily, Shulubin directed his tanks in the direction of Palemberg copse; systematically the FOOs of 1 RCHA began to engage targets as they appeared, appreciating that the fire would not totally halt an opponent who was not prone to give up unless nearly annihilated. Remorselessly, the Soviet forces pursued the routine drill and rolled towards the slope, the sub-units at the front bearing their losses while those at the rear pressed on, sustaining the momentum.

Letting the TOWs make the best of their opportunities against armour from positions based on the village and the copse, and the Blowpipes, every now and then, to loose off at enemy helicopters which dared to fly too impudently, Major Groves concentrated upon the conservation of his tanks and selection of the most opportune moment for their intervention in the battle. This was geared to the acceptable rate of enemy advance in accordance with a picture of the map and a scheduled programme of stop lines imprinted on his mind – a schedule which was intended to impose delays which neither the Russian battalion commander nor his regimental commander could afford to permit.

As yet, of course, the Red Army men were not convinced that the Palemberg feature would be seriously defended. Shulubin, within the confines of his new-found caution, continued to press on. When the first sharp concentrations of artillery fire fell nearby, he regarded them as typical of enemy resistance during the past four or five hours. A few random shots from anti-tank guided missiles did nothing to alter that opinion. Not until a particularly heavy outburst of shelling

THE THIRD DAY + 12 HRS ON

rocked his own vehicle and persuaded the rest of his group to seek cover some 500 metres from the stream that crossed his front, did he concede that he might have more on his hands than at first seemed possible, even though nothing could be seen to the front. He bitterly regretted the loss of Sergeant Nikolai's patrol, for now the task of searching out opposition fell to his own less-expert followers. It was a good 15 minutes before a reticent infantry section commander came up on the air to report, in a diffident voice, that there were mines on the road leading to the bridge and that the bridge was demolished. Cursing somebody higher up for not having the

THE THIRD DAY + 12 HRS ON

helicopter people find that out already, Shulubin sought a way round to the left, taking the copse that showed on his map as a more promising objective than the village whose church spire was visible and which probably harboured an observer. Upon receipt of his report, however, Oblensky drew the conclusion that here was a place where the enemy intended to stand for longer than was permissible.

The effect of Oblensky's deduction was quickly made plain to Groves and all those under his command. As his own gunners began to intensify their attacks upon enemy troops closing in on the objective, a Soviet artillery bombardment of mounting ferocity began

Left: Palemberg in sight on the Old Faithful line.

245

THE THIRD DAY + 12 HRS ON

to engulf nodal points – chiefly the village and the copse – within his boundaries. Simultaneously, tanks and APCs began to advance on the stream and, to his annoyance, almost at once, with the loss of only one BMP, found a way through. The time to commit his armour had arrived too soon, for, according to the schedule, nothing must reach the crest for at least another 30 minutes – and here they were, just five minutes off!

Cross-fire from tanks of 2 Troop, jockeying from one position to another in the vicinity of Palemberg, was the first remedy – and not without effect. Densely-laid smoke was the immediate counter by Shulubin to screen the leading troops. This was combined with shooting by a platoon of tanks and a platoon of BMPs' Saggers. Inevitably, the shooting and persistence of 2 Troop declined; gradually those of the enemy who were over the obstacle began to build up their strength and ease ahead again. Inexorably, 1 Troop was warned to repel the enlarged threat to the copse. But sensibly, Owens side-stepped the main flurries of enemy shell-fire by driving wide to the right in order to come up (hopefully) outside his normal arcs of observation and occupy, to his own advantage, fire positions partially on the enemy flank. For two rounds-worth of rapid fire, the ploy of mobility succeeded. The leading Red Army battalion group was surprised and suffered several losses before finding cover again, and bringing lively direct and indirect fire to bear against 1 Troop.

To this clash of armour, the members of the Vandoos platoon, hidden away in their M113s within the copse and the village, were not even spectators, except for those on look-out reporting the movements of the enemy to their platoon commander. In these conditions of mobility, they remained mounted and prepared to fight. But towards the aim of attempting to hold the enemy at arm's length, they had virtually no role to play. Without an integral medium-range anti-tank weapon of its own, the platoon was compelled to rely to some extent on the TOWs, but mainly on the tanks, to keep the enemy at a distance. Once let the Soviets come to grips, and the chances of Carl Gustavs and 50 cals dealing for a prolonged period with the mobile enemy armour were remote. Although the M113 had demonstrated its ability to take more punishment than had been reckoned, its protection and fire-power were still low. Mobility was, therefore, at the heart of their salvation – and in this case likely to be enshrined in headlong retreat when the artillery and tanks could prevail no longer.

THE THIRD DAY + 12 HRS ON

Across the front, the artillery struggle hammered and roared; the atmosphere heavy with a smoke and dust cloud that assisted the attackers more than the defenders. Realizing that the TOW detachments were by now virtually neutralized by fire and obscuration, Groves (with Cowdray's approval) sent them back prematurely to the next bound from where they might help cover the extrication (in due time) of the remainder of his combat team. A similar function was not being forced, in the interest of prudence, upon the rest of the combat team and its neighbours. Wishing to avoid being ensnared in the exposed terrain behind the crest, without means of direct aid, Groves authorized each troop to pull back one Leopard to act as a fire base when the survivors were compelled to retreat. With every minute that passed, the chances of satisfying the terms of their orders, to hold on for two hours, came closer to realization. But each minute presented the enemy with more opportunities to close with and destroy the defenders in location. To leaders such as Cowdray and Groves, the courses open were becoming more pointedly what they had been less obviously throughout the entire withdrawal operation – a choice between satisfying the aim of the commander and hazarding the survival of their commands; or temporizing to the extent of rank disobedience, and saving what was left to fight another day. Cowdray was not the compromising sort of CO, but Groves was more inclined that way – and with 15 minutes to go before abandonment of the line was permitted (and the certainty that to delay that long would ensure disaster) gave the order to pull back from the copse. To nobody other than himself he said aloud:

"Goddam it, what's field rank for if it's not to take unpopular decisions! I'll argue the toss later. Let's go!"

Cowdray let it go too. In any case, he conceded, the copse was already almost undefended with only the infantry section present, the TOWs on their way back and 1 Troop fighting from a worthless flank. It could be held far better from a flank on the back slope. Moreover both 1 and 2 Troops had each lost a tank, and a Blowpipe detachment was declining to answer calls telling it to withdraw. The defence of the Old Faithful Line was coming to its predestined end, brought to a quickening conclusion by sheer weight of numbers on the ground and in conditions which favoured the attackers in most respects. Backing towards the next major defended position in rear, the most Cowdray and his combat teams could hope to achieve was a modicum of resistance behind a screen of artillery fire. As the last

THE THIRD DAY + 12 HRS ON

tanks of 2 Troop departed from Palemberg, supported from the next tactical bound by 1 Troop and the TOWs, it was behind a curtain of fire brought down by 1 RCHA together with a cloud of smoke to hide the rearguard Leopards driving flat-out for safety.

They got away with a feeling of being hustled and of not having achieved as much in terms of embarrassment and destruction of the enemy as they would have desired. Morale deteriorated to some extent. It would be for the leadership to explain that the aim of the High Command had been achieved at a price commensurate with the results. At the same time, the well-educated, of clearer insight, could read into the situation a portent that was both threatening and frightening. With every step backwards and at every reverse, a condition in which resort to nuclear weapons might be necessary, if not obligatory, came closer. In professional terms, therefore, it became all the more necessary to insist upon strict enforcement of quick refurbishment, prior to injection into the battle front once more – perhaps in defence, hopefully as an element in the highly desirable counter-stroke which would compensate for the set backs of the "FIRST CLASH" of war.

Below: Salvage. The recovery team races to save a broken down M113.